FROM IMMIGRANTS TO ETHNIC MINORITY

*For Wendell Trenton Wilberforce Johnson
and the late Doris Cope*

From Immigrants to Ethnic Minority

Making black community in Britain

LORNA CHESSUM

Aldershot • Burlington USA • Singapore • Sydney

Published by
Ashgate Publishing Ltd
Gower House
Croft Road
Aldershot
Hants GU11 3HR
England

Ashgate Publishing Company
131 Main Street
Burlington, VT 05401-5600 USA

Ashgate website: http://www.ashgate.com

British Library Cataloguing in Publication Data
Chessum, Lorna
    From immigrants to ethnic minority : making black community
    in Britain. - (Interdisciplinary research series in ethnic,
    gender and class relations)
    1. Blacks - England - Leicester - History - 20th century
    2. Immigrants - England - Leicester - History - 20th century
    3. West Indians - England - Leicester - Social conditions
    4. Leicester (England) - Race relations
    I. Title
    305.8'969729'042542

Library of Congress Control Number: 00-133523

ISBN 0 7546 1019 5

Printed in Great Britain by
Antony Rowe Ltd, Chippenham, Wiltshire.

Contents

List of Tables

List of Abbreviations

AIMS	Anti Immigration Society
ANL	Anti Nazi League
ARC	Anti Racist Committee
AUEW	Amalgamated Union of Engineering Workers
CARD	Campaign Against Racial Discrimination
CLS	Community Languages
CP	Communist Party
CRE	Commission for Racial Equality
DES	Department of Education and Science
EEC	European Economic Community
GIAs	General Improvement Areas
HAAs	Housing Action Areas
IRSC	Inter Racial Solidarity Campaign
JSG	Jamaica Service Group
LCCR	Leicester Council for Community Relations
LRO	Leicestershire Record Office
LUCA	Leicester United Caribbean Association
MSD	Migrant Services Division
NF	National Front
PRO	Public Record Office
RAF	Royal Air Force
SEN	State Enrolled Nurse
SRN	State Registered Nurse
TGWU	Transport and General Workers Union
UK	United Kingdom
USA	United States of America
VMA	Valerie Marett Archive

Series Editor's Preface

From Immigrants to Ethnic Minority is a peculiar story of people who descended from Africa but who live in societies structured in dominance. Other immigrants have since become citizens but people of African descent are condemned to the inferior status of ethnic minority on the basis of their gendered, class-specific racialisation. Although Dr Lorna Chessum focused on the African Caribbean Diaspora in Leicester and excluded African immigrants for the sake of her doctoral requirement to narrow the focus of her analysis, what she says about her subjects is applicable to the worldwide African Diaspora even in South and North America where hundreds of millions of people of African descent remain ethnic minorities while recent immigrants are already perceived as full citizens due to their Euro-Asian origins and relative affluence.

The author combines limited primary archival sources with abundant oral history and secondary sources to analyse public policy and national or local debates concerning the presence of large groups of black people in the East Midlands city of Leicester since the end of the Second World War – the largest such population outside London. The book demonstrates that just like all people of African descent in racist and sexist capitalist societies, the black people who were lured to Leicester with promises of abundant jobs arrived with immense skills and enthusiasm only to be marginalised into racialised and gendered menial jobs instead of being allowed equal opportunities. Although this could be said to be the experience of most immigrant groups, the persistence of racism, class-snubbery and sexism has meant that black men and black women have largely remained in their marginalised positions more than fifty years after the first generation was begged to come and serve the war-weakened 'mother country' while other richer or whiter groups of immigrants have fared better.

The book charts the amazing survival of black people in an incredibly hostile environment that has not stopped discriminating against them. In that sense, being regarded as ethnic minorities is a grudging acceptance that, as Linton Kwesi Johnson put it, 'No matter what they say, come what may, we are here to stay ina Ingland'. Compared to another group of racialised immigrants also regarded as part of the ethnic minority population of Leicester, the author found that the Asians (mostly middle class refugees from East Africa) were racialised on a higher hierarchy due to their relative access to economic and political power and their consequent access to the different classes of the British population whereas the African Caribbeans remain impoverished as working class and unemployed elements of the ethnic minority.

The major conclusion readers can draw from this book is that the marginalisation of the African Caribbean in Britain should be understood within the context of institutionalised racism-sexism-classism instead of being blamed on the attitudes of individuals alone. The book reveals that the national and the local governments were active in constructing the third-class status of the African Caribbean as an ethnic minority when policy attempts to restrict the growth of multicultural Britain was successfully resisted by the initial black immigrants and their descendants. Since the government played active roles in restricting the growth of the opportunities and numbers of African Caribbeans in Britain, the government should also be responsible for rehabilitating the descendants of the initial immigrants who were exploited and maltreated for so long in spite of their eagerness to help the 'mother country' back on its feet after the war.

Dr Biko Agozino
Associate Professor
Indiana University of Pennsylvania

Acknowledgements

I would like to thank Professor Panikos Panayi for his academic guidance, supervision and advice, as well as Professor David Thoms and Professor Pierre Lanfranchi for their good advice. Dr Ian Spencer drew my attention to a number of government documents for which I thank him and Professor Pat Kirkham helped me in clarifying my initial proposal for which I thank her also. The staff of the Institute of Race Relations were also helpful, particularly A. Sivanandan, Hazel Walters and Liz Fekete.

Other people who were very helpful were Terry Allcott, Gordon Baxter, Cynthia Brown of Leicester City Council's Living History Unit and Satish Kapur. I am particularly grateful to Paul Winstone, Ned Newitt and Dr Valerie Marett. I am especially thankful to my partner John Newsinger whose help and encouragement were invaluable.

People who have helped me with a great deal of technical assistance are Steve Gamble, John Macintosh, Marcia Ricketts, Viv Andrews and Judith Smith. I am very grateful to them.

Special thanks are also due to the many African Caribbean people in Leicester who have told me their stories and helped me in many ways with the research. Particular thanks are due to the late Doris Cope, Carlton Sweeney, Editha Drew and Oscar Frank whose assistance was invaluable to me as was that of Eric Hudson, Lee Morris and the late Clifton Robinson. I hope this work will be regarded as a positive contribution.

1   Researching Black History: Problems and Issues

Introduction

This book is about the place of black people in British society in the post war world. It focuses on the development of one community of African Caribbeans; that of Leicester, a medium size British city in the East Midlands.

The study links national and local government policy with respect to race and immigration, aspects of national identity as expressed in public debate by local people in Leicester, and the experiences of African Caribbean migrants in Leicester between 1945 and 1981. It outlines aspects of the development of the relationship between the position of African Caribbeans in the class structure and an evolving racialised identity constructed in public discourse. This study in historical sociology charts the way in which African Caribbeans made a life for themselves in a largely hostile environment. Policy decisions made at national and local level have influenced the composition and structure of the local population in the city of Leicester and have had far reaching implications for the lives of people. However, this is not to argue that the experiences of, and decisions made by, African Caribbeans are simply a reflection of state policies. Black people have actively constructed their lives but within the context of a pervasive racialised identity and practice.

African Caribbeans arrived in Leicester from the Second World War onwards bringing with them a wide range of skills, knowledge and experience. They were systematically prevented from exercising many aspects of this human capital in employment. Instead of slotting into the occupational structure in Leicester in a wide variety of industries, services and professions which needed workers, African Caribbeans were confined to a narrower range of jobs than white people. These jobs were those deemed suitable for them through racialised and gendered constructions of identity. Employment provides people with an important, defining feature of their identity. Over time African Caribbean people in Leicester became associated with particular industries and occupations, such as manual work in engineering for men and hosiery and nursing for women. The working

1

class profile of black people in Leicester has contributed to the development of an evolving racialised construction of what came, by the end of the period studied here, to be described as an African Caribbean ethnic group.

Sociological theorists have debated the relative importance of race, class and more latterly gender, in determining the nature of peoples' lives. It is argued that the historical approach adopted here reveals aspects of the way in which race and class interact in a complex dynamic relationship, a relationship that can only be exposed over time. Racialised groups exist in relation to each other. But whereas whiteness is usually covert; often unconscious and unacknowledged, for other groups, overt racialisation permeates every aspect of life. It is further argued here that it is only when different aspects of life are considered together and over time that the extent, nature and implications of racialisation become apparent.

Post war Caribbean migration to Britain has received attention from academics since it began and this interest has paralleled the migration itself. Early work included Kenneth Little's (1947) study of Cardiff, Richmond's (1954) work on Liverpool and Banton (1955) on Stepney. Less well known is Learie Constantine's work, *Colour Bar* (1954). In 1960 Ruth Glass (1960) looked at black immigrants and Sheila Patterson (1963) published *Dark Strangers* which was particularly influential. These were sociological studies. They provided a great deal of information about African Caribbeans and included interview material from black people in Britain. They tended to focus on race relations and usually adopted an 'immigrant-host' perspective. This sees the status of migrants as immigrants rather than as a racialised group as being the salient determinant of problems in relation to the native population. Patterson's study provided the best example of this approach and was important in influencing understandings of the position of black people in Britain. Concern focused on the everyday interaction of black and white people and her work was naive in its methodology, accepting at face value the claims made by white people that they were not 'colour prejudiced'. Accordingly it was thought that 'colour prejudice' would diminish as immigrants became assimilated into white society.

During the 1960s more attention was given to establishing evidence of racial discrimination and the studies of Rex and Moore (1967) and that led by Rose (Rose et al., 1969) were important. During the 1960s immigration became an increasingly important political issue and saw the development of studies of the causes of immigration, such as that of Davison (1962) and Peach (1968). During the 1970s the 'immigrant-host' model was challenged as more studies showed the extent of racial discrimination in British society and immigration legislation became more overtly racist (Smith, 1974). The 1962 Commonwealth Immigrants Act introduced by the Conservative government created a voucher system for potential immigrants from the 'New Commonwealth' and, while not overtly racist, was clearly intended to severely curtail the entry of black and Asian people to Britain. Racial discrimination was extended in the 1968 Act and subsequent legislation of 1971 and 1981 as black and Asian immigration continued to be an important issue in British politics throughout the period. But academic study continued to be located largely within the social sciences. However, more recently, historians have turned their attention to the study of black history.

James Walvin (1992) in an essay entitled 'The Emergence of British Black Historical Studies' wrote of the genesis of British Black Historiography over the past twenty years. He pointed to four important converging factors. These were first, the 'explosion' of African history. Second the flowering of African/American and Caribbean studies and third, the development of British Black social history. Walvin stated the importance of E P Thompson's (1963) *The Making of the English Working Class* as being both influential and path-breaking, creating respectability for diverse subjects of research. Walvin also mentioned as a fourth factor Eric William's (1964) revisionist thesis concerning the importance of slavery to the process of industrialisation in Britain which has continued to be of importance to historians of the Caribbean. Walter Rodney's (1964) book on '*How Europe Underdeveloped Africa*' also presents an economic analysis of slavery. While through the 1980s sociological studies continued to debate the relative importance of class and race (Castles and Kosack, 1973) in the by now established unequal position of black people in British society, historians have tended to concentrate on unearthing the hitherto forgotten black presence in Britain.

Important studies of blacks in Britain include Walvin's (1971) own work on slavery, Folarin Shyllon's (1974, 1977) study of black people in Britain, Sivanandan's (1982) essays on black resistance to oppression and Peter Fryer's (1984) *Staying Power*. Fryer's study has uncovered lost continuities of black communities. This project was founded on the need to challenge the construction of British history as the development of a racialised and culturally homogenous group. It is clear that in the battle over Britain's past, minority groups have been expunged from the record and in doing so a racialised national identity has been created (Cesarani, 1996). However, continuities can be artificially produced. The African

Caribbean communities which developed in Britain after the Second World War were not descendants of those earlier groups of slaves and former slaves from the eighteenth and nineteenth centuries although the cause of their presence can be seen, at least in part, as historically linked to slavery.

Historians are now turning their attention to uncovering the excluded and forgotten presence of minority groups in British history. Ron Ramdin's (1987) *The Making of the Black Working Class* also develops the continuities of black workers in their struggles against racism and exploitation at work. But black history is still in 'its infancy' (Casely-Hayford, 1990). Until recently it has been largely left to non-professional historians such as local community groups to publish small scale studies, often using oral history methods, recording the experiences of black people in Britain (*Forty Winters On*, 1988; Sewcharan, 1986; Sweeney, 1978; Murray, 1996; *Highfields Rangers*, 1993; *Highfields Remembered*, 1996).

The late Raphael Samuel (1995) pointed to some of the problems associated with the 'new wave' social history of the 1960s and 1970s and its 'history from below'. These included, he argued:

> the ambiguities attaching to the notion of 'ordinary people', a coinage of the 1930s, replacing older terms such as 'everyman' and 'the common people'.

He suggested that this focus may be 'less democratic than it sounds'. Certainly the tendency to turn their gaze downwards towards the poor and the powerless has often facilitated the approach of some social scientists who have seen the causes of poverty and powerlessness to lie within the cultures of those groups rather than in the relationships with the rich and the powerful. The problem with the 'great man' theory of history (Samuel, 1995) lies less with the object of study than with the perspective on the role of great men in society. The study of black people in Britain provides an example of a group of people whose disadvantaged position has often been attributed to the lifestyle or inborn characteristics of the people themselves. This study is an attempt to shed some light on the relationship between the nature of the lives of black people and the attitudes and behaviour of those with more power in the local community.

This is a study of black people of Caribbean origin who came to live in Leicester from 1945 onwards. It does not include black people of African origin nor does it include Asian people from the Caribbean or from the Indian sub continent. There are now many black people living in Leicester who were born in Leicester. Current estimates suggest that approximately 40% of blacks in Britain were born in this country; however, none were interviewed for this study.   The work is intended as a contribution to historical knowledge and understanding of the progress of a racialised group of people and their relationship to the local state and the wider society in a provincial city. It charts how people made a life for themselves in the context of a hostile environment. There have been few studies of modern black communities outside London and fewer that have taken an historical perspective. Leicester is the city with the highest proportion of what have come to be called ethnic minorities of any city outside London, yet there have been few studies of its population to date. Pearson (1981) studied West Indian organisations, Valerie Marett (1989) studied the arrival and settlement of Ugandan Asians who came as refugees to Leicester in 1972 and Margaret Byron (1994) has researched the small Nevisian community in Leicester. Nash and Reeder (1993) have at least considered the place of black and Asian people in what is a general history of Leicester in the twentieth century. This is the only study with an historical perspective. It is a central theme here that only by considering various areas of life such as housing, employment and education alongside each other, over time and in relation to the wider community can the nature of the experience of black people and the logic of response be understood.

Primary Sources

The lack of documentary evidence on the existence of black people in Leicester in the 1950s is remarkable. There is no written record of the arrival of people in the city by any body, official or unofficial, at local or national level. The lack of documentation reflects the lack of planning of central government during the 1950s which itself is a reflection of the desire by both Labour and Conservative governments to prevent the development of a multi-racial society and to exclude black immigrants. No planning was required because no provision was to be made for black immigrants. Any provision might encourage people to come. This lack of documentary evidence has been noted elsewhere.[1] Therefore, there are no reliable statistics on the characteristics of the people, for example, their age, sex, islands of origin or years of arrival.

The census, normally regarded as a reliable source of information, is inadequate in this case. The ten year cycle leaves too long a period in which a great deal of movement of people can take place, unrecorded. Certainly, in this case, oral evidence suggests that there was a great deal of movement of people both between the Caribbean and Leicester and between other cities within the United Kingdom (UK). Second, the figures are not comparable over time. The 1951 census records the birthplace of people living within the boundaries of the City of Leicester. There were 56 people born in British Guyana, Jamaica or Trinidad and Tobago.[2]   The 1961 census shows 1,347 people born in Jamaica or 'other Caribbean'.[3] The sample census of 1966 gave 10,087 people born in countries of the Commonwealth, except Canada, Australia and New Zealand.[4]   In 1971, there were, according to the census, 1,405 people born in Barbados, Guyana, Jamaica or Trinidad and Tobago[5] and in 1981, 2,551 born in the Caribbean.[6]   The census did ask about individual island of origin of migrants and that information will be available to researchers in the future, but it is not recorded in the published tables and is not available for public scrutiny at present. However, perhaps more important than the comparability and paucity of what is known, is the now widely acknowledged view that the census under-records the numbers of black people in Britain and, following, those in Leicester throughout the period (Lee). Peach compared information about immigration with the census and has estimated that the census underestimates the numbers of Caribbean born people by 20% in Britain as a whole (Peach, 1974). Oral evidence in this and other studies supports this view.[7]

There are several points to be made in relation to the lack of reliable information about the basic characteristics of the black people who moved to Leicester in the 1950s and 1960s. First the lack of documentation reflects government policy of the day and has negative significance. There was no planning by central or local government for the arrival of black immigrants to Britain and therefore no need to chart the migration. This lack of preparation was deliberate. Any provision, it was thought, may have encouraged migrants who were unwanted by the government. Second, history tends to privilege official documents as a source of information about the past and it could be argued that a lack of official records concerning black people in Britain contributes to the way in which minorities are 'written out' of historical accounts in the longer term: they become forgotten and ignored and the construction of a continuity of racialised white English history referred to above is thus facilitated. There are two sorts of evidence which establish that black people lived in Leicester in the 1950s. There are the oral testimonies of the people themselves which are very important. As Casely-Hayford (1995, p.59) has written:

The first generation of British Blacks are a vital source of information for present and future ages of local and general historians.

There are also the local newspapers which carried articles throughout the 1950s and 1960s about black people in Leicester, mostly showing Caribbean migrants in a very negative light, often as criminals in reports of court proceedings, or as highlighting the social problems of housing or health.

Third and perhaps most important, the question needs to be asked: how much does accurate charting of numbers contribute to our understanding? It has been argued that the obsession with numbers evident in public discussions of government immigration policy during the 1950s and 1960s was led by an assumption that there were too many black people coming into the country and this has led some to be wary of any discussion of numbers of immigrants. This is supported by the fact that public discussion has been only rarely informed by knowledge of numbers of immigrants per se, but rather assumed immigrants to mean black and Asian people. Indeed this continues to be the case: immigrant in popular discourse means black or Asian people with the term ethnic minority also being defined in a racialised way.

However, there are reasons for gathering basic statistical information about the characteristics of the people who came from the Caribbean to Leicester to live. In order to ensure that the testimonies gathered as oral evidence are not untypical it is important to try and make them reflect the composition of the African Caribbean population as much as possible. Without a 'sampling frame'; that is a profile of the characteristics of the people in terms of age, sex, island of origin and so on, it is not possible to reproduce the different kinds of people in the group selected from which to gather evidence. In the case of this study it was necessary to rely on a number of small scale surveys to provide such information. The first comprehensive attempt to survey the black and Asian populations of Leicester was not carried out by the City Council until 1983.[8] The people interviewed for this study are not representative, in a statistical sense, of the African Caribbean population of Leicester. However, they do come from a range of groups which reflect different kinds of people who make up the population: men and women, Antiguans, Jamaicans, Barbudans, Nevisians and other islanders, people who came from a spread of years from the 1940s to the late 1960s.

Numbers are also important in relationships between groups. The changing relationship between African Caribbeans, Asians and whites, as they are perceived as communities, in Leicester has been influenced by their relative size. Whereas African Caribbean migrants outnumbered Asians in the 1950s, by the end of the period, Asians were six times as numerous. This has had an effect on the relationships between the three groups and their relationships with the local state.

Numbers have also been important in personal relationships. A higher proportion of black people have personal relationships with whites, in a situation where it is still possible for only a few whites to have personal relationships with blacks. Indeed that has certainly been the case in Leicester, although the implications of this has not been addressed here.

Other primary documentary sources examined for this research included city corporation records such as minutes of Housing Committees, Education Committees and Medical Officer of Health reports. But it is only in the Medical Officer's reports that there was evidence of the existence of black people in Leicester during the 1950s. Other official documents examined included Chief Constables' Annual reports.[9] Despite the lack of concern of official bodies, the growing black community had a very high profile in the local Leicester press and this has been a very important source of information. The local newspapers were used as a source in two ways. First they provided information about events and people of the time. Newspapers can be extremely inaccurate and caution is needed. Wherever possible events and other facts recorded in the newspapers where checked against other sources. Second the newspapers provided a discourse on issues of race and immigration which can be seen as a powerful expression of views of the time.[10] In this way they are a primary source. The press was the only really comprehensive written source confirming the presence of black people in Leicester at all during the 1950s, where West Indians had a very high, and negative, profile.

By the 1960s references to black people, who were usually described as 'immigrants' or West Indians were appearing in the minutes of the records of the local authority, particularly in Education Committee minutes, Medical Officer of Health Reports and Chief Constables Annual Reports. During the 1970s representatives of the local authority gave evidence to the Parliamentary Select Committees on Race Relations and Immigration concerning the black and Asian communities in Leicester.[11] Other primary documentary sources examined included Minutes of the Leicester Council for Community Relations (LCCR) Trades Council minutes, annual reports and other documents of a variety private bodies.

Oral History

Of major importance was the oral testimony of Caribbean migrants interviewed for this study. Like the newspapers the oral testimonies provided evidence not only of what was happening (for which there was often no other source), but they also provided an understanding of the migrants own views of their experiences. Giving voice to the views of Caribbean migrants is an important aim of this work. There has been a tendency, not always articulated, to regard oral history methods as inferior to that of written records, particularly official documents. But something spoken is not necessarily inferior to written words in terms of quality of information. It could be that suspicion of oral evidence is based on a suspicion of ordinary peoples' ability to give accurate accounts of events, compared with the abilities of those in 'high places'. It is clearly important to distinguish between the subjective and partial perceptions of one individual compared with a considered account based on more objectively collected information. However, it should not be assumed that subjectivity is always a feature of the testimony of ordinary people and objectivity of members of the government or civil servants.

But oral history does create special problems. People's memories distort, select and rearrange events of the past. Particularly frustrating in this study was the common, if understandable, inability of people to remember the actual years when particular events occurred. Chronology was remembered, but not dates. Views were sometimes influenced by present circumstances. For example, disappointment at their achievements after living many years in Britain was felt by some. Particularly influential were the 'hard times' brought on by the recession that continued at the time of the interviews: the first half of the 1990s. Some had grown up children who were unemployed.

Documents are more likely to have been written contemporaneously. However, all information is subject to a framework of perception and of practical constraints, such as, for example, what to include in minutes, which has to be taken into account when considering the validly of that information. In this study the tone of the minutes of the Education Committee, for example, gave no hint of the emotional and acrimonious debate taking place in the local press at the time concerning the education of 'immigrant' children. But that debate clearly influenced the Committee. Indeed, as is the case with data gathered from newspapers and from individuals, it is sometimes the very perceptions which are of interest.

The information created in answer to questions asked for research purposes is necessarily different in kind from that created when information is provided for another purpose as is usually the case in written documents. Informants, usually, know the purposes of the research and can attempt to influence the researcher's perceptions. However, in both cases, the reason why the information is produced has to be considered and in this sense oral evidence is not different in kind from documents: documents are often intended to influence opinion too.

Paul Thompson (1988) wrote in the opening line of his book, *The Voice of the Past*: 'All history depends ultimately upon its social purpose' (Thompson, 1988, p.1). Thompson (1988, p.6) has written:

> Oral history ...makes a much fairer trial possible: witnesses can now also be called from the under-classes, the unprivileged and the defeated... It provides a more realistic and fair reconstruction of the past, a challenge to the established account.

By this means according to Thompson, history becomes more democratic (Thompson, 1988, p.21) and he continues:

> ...oral history offers a challenge to the accepted myths of history, to the authoritarian judgment inherent in its tradition. It provides a means for a radical transformation of the social meaning of history.

The lack of documentary evidence of black people in Leicester makes oral evidence in this case particularly important. However, to compliment this information searches were made in as wide a variety of primary sources as possible. Casely-Hayford (1990, p.59) has accurately described this process.

> The historian researching Black history has, therefore, to become a sort of rag-and-bone man, utilising materials from a wide range of sources to construct as clear a picture as possible.

Evidence collected for this study was scattered and fragmented and required considerable synthesising to create a coherent picture.

The Interviews

Interviews were carried out with twenty nine African Caribbean people who had lived in Leicester during the 1950s, 1960s and 1970s. People were chosen to reflect what is known about the composition of the population but were not a representative sample in a sociological sense. Of the twenty nine, eight were 'community leaders'. The interviews lasted between one and two and a half hours each. Most were recorded on tape and transcribed later. Some people were interviewed twice and one three times.[12] A number of other people were also interviewed or consulted. This group was mostly white but also included some African Caribbean people. There were in this group nine councillors or officials of Leicester City Council. Other people interviewed included the Director of the Race Equality Council, the Complaints Officer of the Commission for Racial Equality, East Midlands Region, a former member of Leicester Council for Community Relations (LCCR) a white employer and a former member of the Anti Nazi League. A number of academics working in this field were also helpful. Some African Caribbean community leaders were interviewed not for their testimonies of life in Leicester, but rather as 'gatekeepers' providing access to others and for information about organisations and who were important in providing credibility for the research. The interviews were carried out between 1993 and 1997.

Secondary Sources

The secondary literature in this field is extremely large. It cuts across the disciplines of history and social science. In addition, a social history of one group of people in one community in a specific time necessarily needs to relate to literature in more than one context. First, what happened in Leicester during the period needed to be put in the context of government policy of the day. Second, information gathered from sources was compared to existing knowledge gathered in sociological studies of other black communities in Britain. Third, the place of African Caribbeans in Leicester must to be located within the context of the wider local community of Leicester and the city's politics and social structure. A problem in studying a relatively small group of people in one city is that generalisations made to the wider group of African Caribbeans in Britain from the study are hard to sustain. This book is in effect a case study, not in the sense of a case study that is representative of all African Caribbeans in Britain, rather as a case study that stands in relation to current knowledge and theoretical positions and is intended to confirm or revise our current understandings. Wilson (1993, p.45), in a description which applies to this work precisely, argued that case studies have:

certain basic generic properties. First, they are particularistic, describing events in a specific situation. Second, they are holistic, exploring the multifaceted features of the situation through interrogation of a range of salient variables. Third, they are longitudinal and therefore dynamic; they trace developments over a length of time and chart their continuities and discontinuities. Finally they are based on qualitative rather than quantitative research.

Apart from the large body of literature referred to above and in the historiography, other secondary sources used for this study included thirty five unpublished MA dissertations, on African Caribbeans in Leicester produced in the Sociology department at Leicester University between 1959 and 1980. Also used were some small scale studies by non-professional local black people in Leicester. These were invaluable.

Objectivity

It was long held that objectivity and integrity demanded that researchers should not be influenced by being part of the group under study: researchers should be neutral. While the epitome of this position was reached in the functionalism school of American sociology, it was a view accepted by historians also. This position was associated with, mainly but not exclusively, quantitative research methodology. These methods were held to produce neutral and objective truth. Indeed objectivity and neutrality became almost synonymous. This positivism was attacked by ethnomethodologists and phenomonologists in the 1970s. Both anti-positivists and Marxists argued that it was possible to be truthful while also 'taking sides'. Neutrality was also challenged by feminists who established the legitimacy of qualitative research which studied social groups from the inside. In the case of the feminist critique, this was based on an exposé of the biased and distorted knowledge that was created as a result of the apparent objectivity of men who imposed their gendered understandings upon research findings. 'Neutrality' meant that the experiences and understandings of whole groups of people were excluded, ignored or marginalised. Not only were women and minorities excluded in this process but such research, far from producing work which was more accurate and truthful, distorted findings. The exclusion of women from studies of migration is an example which is discussed elsewhere in this thesis.[13]

This powerful critique has led to a new legitimisation of qualitative research which speaks from the experience of minority groups from the inside. The importance of qualitative research has also been argued in the context of the study of race. Barry Troyna (1993), for example, has questioned the validity of quantitative methodology in the study of racial harassment and the use of other traditional sociological methods in race research. He also argued (Troyna, 1995, p.31) that:

> qualitative researchers are interested in documenting and interpreting experiences as they are shaped by and within day-to-day experiences.

From this a new research orthodoxy has developed, in which such a stance is taken as the only legitimate way to study the disadvantaged. An important study carried out at the Birmingham Centre for Cultural studies began a debate in the academy with an argument that only black people can understand the black experience and only black people can legitimately research the black experience (Centre for Contemporary Cultural Studies, 1982). For example Natasha Sivanandan 'questioned the right of whites to talk about black experience' (Bornat, Burdell, Goom, Thompson, 1980, p.21). A parallel debate took place within feminism. Some took the view that only women were entitled to speak about their experiences.

This argument has developed in academic and in some areas of popular discourse with a number of different strands. The first concerns the way in which academic research by whites has lent support to racism (Moynihan, 1965). Black people have argued that academic research has often been used to justify inequalities in society and to pathologise the culture of blacks.

The second strand is an ethical one: that white researchers have exploited black people for their own ends, to make money or to build a career. Black people are frequently researched by white academics who turn their gaze downwards and continually put blacks in 'the looking glass'. This argument was forcefully put to the author in the course of this research. The author was requested to 'give something back' to the community in terms of work and help for various community projects. This proved to be a commitment which enhanced understanding. Much research, it was argued, has produced no advantages to black people and has lead to no improvements in the position of black people in society. Indeed the data collected has sometimes been used by the state against the interests of black people (Bourne, 1980, pp.331-352; Lawrence, 1982, pp.92-142). Natasha Sivanandan has argued that 'oral history could become yet another example of whites prying into the black community' (Bornat, Burdell, Goom, Thompson, 1980, p.22). Amrit Wilson has challenged the claim of oral history to give a central place to the experiences of black people. She has suggested that this 'smacked of the imperialism of anthropology and sociology in their concern with subject peoples' (Bornat, Burdell, Goom, Thompson, 1980, p.22). Black people should be able to control what was included in their history. It is hardly surprising that this position should be argued and has reached academic discussions much later in this country than in the USA. Ordinary people have often understood the falsity of academic claims to neutral commitments to unbiased truths.[14]   This position has provided a very powerful criticism of much of the academic work in the area of race and few have attempted to debate the points raised, at least in print. Barry Troyna (1993), as an exception, has argued that researchers should be committed not to any one group or another but to the values of 'social justice, equality and participatory democracy' (p.115). Those critical of whites who research issues of race have contended that white researchers can best make a contribution to anti racist struggle by focusing their attentions on white racism. A further ethical question which arose in this work involved the fact that long interviews recalling past experiences were sometimes painful for the interviewees. While some people enjoyed the opportunity to 'tell their story' others found the experience quite gruelling, despite their willingness to participate.

Throughout the late 1980s and 1990s the critique of positivism has continued and has been developed by some into a new orthodoxy. Highly theorised and often obscure and esoteric, postmodernism is in part, the descendent of the phenomenologism of the 1970s. Some feminist scholars have embraced this theory and become submerged within it. Postmodernism's child, postcolonial theory, purports to centralise the perspective of the subaltern; those who have been subjected to Imperialist domination in the past, has proved attractive to some scholars of race and ethnicity. The explosion of studies of ethnic and gendered identity can also be seen as having their origin in the critique of positivism. The perspective here is one which attempts to show a developing relationship between discourse and the material determinates of peoples' lives between 1945 and 1981. It is a gendered study which focuses on race and class. These salient dimensions of identity are socially constructed in complex formation which change and reform over time. Above all they are constructed through relationships between groups of people positioned through all three, along with other, dimensions of identity simultaneously.

Black women's critique of the essentialist and reductionist nature of some white feminist discussion of gender developed along with the second wave of feminism (hooks, 1982; Carby, 1982). The construction of 'blacks' as men and 'women' as white, which was so effectively critiqued by hooks (1982) and others produced a debate which resulted in a more sophisticated understanding of the ways in which the various permutations of class, race and gender can be constructed.

This study examines some of the most important aspects of African Caribbean Peoples' lives over the period such as home, work, education and politics. While gender, race and class are all relevant, the focus is predominantly of the evolving interrelationship between race and class.

The study is gendered where sources permit, but it is not primarily about gender. Social constructions of gender are always relevant but limitations imposed by sources, has at times made a proper consideration of gender impossible. The paucity of documentary evidence has been noted above. For example statistics of the local authority were often not gendered, or referred only to men.

African Caribbeans in Leicester

The pattern of post war immigration into Leicester of 'people of colour' has had a profound impact on the perceptions of the different communities formed. West Indians were the earliest arrivals. At end of the 1950s the African Caribbean population of Leicester was estimated to be twice as big as that of Asians. By 1970 it was one quarter the size of the Asian Community and by the end of the 1970s it was only one sixth. The arrival of Kenyan Asians in 1968 and Ugandan Asians in 1972 and the political furore which accompanied these events, locally and nationally (Marett, 1989) has tended to associate Leicester exclusively with these minority groups. A particular perspective developed in relation to this situation. African Caribbeans felt marginalised by the attention given to the needs and numerical superiority of, Asians. This marginalistion is reflected in academic work and there are a number of possible reasons for this apart from the numerical superiority mentioned above. One is that when researching 'immigrants' in Leicester Asians are easily identifiable in documents through names. African Caribbeans are rendered invisible because their names are indistinguishable from those of the majority white community. An example is provided in Pritchard's (1976) study of housing, in which the author acknowledged the fact that Asians were taken to represent 'immigrants' for precisely this reason. Once established, the tendency of academic study to draw on other studies exacerbates the problem. For example, David Nash and David Reeder's (1993) *History of Leicester in the Twentieth Century* described post war immigration patterns which match that of Asian groups but are inaccurate to describe African Caribbeans.

The binary division between racialised groups of majority whites and minority 'immigrants', defined in a racialised way, also leads to distinct groups of peoples with diverse origins and cultures being reduced to a simple unitary description of Asians. In addition, a political culture developed within the local authority which has made comparisons between two communities: African Caribbeans on the one hand and Asians on the other.

A final factor is the different social class profiles of African Caribbeans compared to Asian groups: Asians tend to have greater political and economic power and to be more evenly distributed through the class structure of British society. These various factors lend support to each other, so that, for example, the success of Asians in business means that they receive attention and this appears to suggest that African Caribbeans are less important. The cumulative effect of these factors is that African Caribbeans' place in the life of the city is overlooked and they have been compared unfavourably with Asians in the political culture of the city.

A major problem facing social historians and social scientists lies in choosing meaningful concepts with which to analyse ideas and actions. The choice of concepts is itself part of a battle over competing political ideologies. There is a long standing and continuing debate in social science about the idea of race. While there is widespread acceptance that race is a socially constructed concept, this idea still has to be defended against a common sense and minority academic view of race as biologically determined (Miles, 1994, p.191). The liberal position of the 1960s in popular discourse that race should not be relevant has been rightly challenged by social scientists in its failure to address social realities. But the dilemma remains. How is it possible to expose and understand the role of race in society without utilising as an analytical tool the issue which we wish to problematise? The use of race in parenthesis was a widely adopted approach. However, universal acceptance was not forthcoming and perhaps more important, this idea failed to dent the continuing 'everyday' understanding of race as a natural division of peoples. It is not possible or appropriate here to outline the evolution of the terminology about race and its relationship to social theory. The concept of 'racialisation' was first developed by Robert Miles (1994, p.75). He used the term racialisation:

to refer to those instances when social relations between people have been structured by the signification of human biological characteristics in such a way as to define and construct differential social collectivities.

In this definition racialisation does not necessarily imply negative evaluation. The concept of racialisation is widely used in the study of black and Asian minorities and does most commonly carry with it an assumption that the idea does include negative evaluation. Miles distinguishes between racialisation and racism. He reserves the latter to describe racialisation coupled with negative evaluation.

It has been recognised that the disadvantaged position of black people in society has not arisen solely as a result of the behaviour of racists as defined above. The concept of 'institutionalised racism' has been adopted to explain not only the persuasiveness of exclusionary practices, but the cluster of disadvantages experienced by racialised groups even though there may have been no overt intention to discriminate by decision makers:

> racism is embodied in exclusionary practices or in a formally non-racialised discourse - exclusionary practices that result in a disadvantage for racialised groups cannot be assumed to be determined wholly or in part by racism (Miles 1984, p.87).

A parallel, although different mixture of overt, covert discrimination and disadvantage produces inequalities between men and women.

However, the ideas of racialisation, racism and institutional racism remain contentious, and there is no consensus on the use of these terms. Small (1994, p.34) uses the term in a way which focuses attention on the racialistion of one group by another.

> When we examine the process of 'racialisation' we find that our beliefs about 'racism' and 'race relations' have more to do with the attitudes, actions, motivations and interests of powerful groups in society and less to do with the characteristics, attitudes and actions of those who are defined as belonging to inferior 'races'.

In public and academic discourse since the Second World War, immigrant has been defined in a racialised way. As Miles (1989, p.86) has argued:

> the language of 'immigration' and 'immigrant' therefore carried a set of implicit meanings or a subtext. As a result they were understood to refer specifically to 'coloured' immigrants (Miles, 1989, p.86).

This situation was quite clear in the documents of the Local Authority here. For example, in local Education Committee Minutes immigrants are defined in a racialised way. Immigrant children who came to Leicester in the post war period included groups with different skin colours, geographic origins, and ethnicities. There were white Europeans, black and Asian people of Caribbean origin, black and Asian people from Africa as well as Asians from the Indian subcontinent, but it is clear that 'immigrants' were defined as people with dark skins. The negative evaluation contained in this definition of immigration was also seen in the way in which immigrants were seen as a problem. White immigrant children were not seen like this. Additionally, the cause of these problems was seen to lie in the culture of black and Asian children, in the way Small described and quoted above. The situation was further complicated by the fact that black and Asian children in the 1950s and 1960s were lumped together as a group. It is clear that in education until the early 1970s attention was focused particularly on the culture of black children of Caribbean origin described at the time as 'West Indian'. The dominant discourse makes it hard for historians to establish the true nature of the composition of immigrant children in schools and, second, the true nature of the changes in schools produced as a result of this immigration.

Here the concept of racialisation is used in the same way as that of Miles. Racialisation is used as a way to describe aspects of the identity of both black and whites. However, while the racialisation of blacks has been negative, the racialisation of whites has been positive. The concept of racism is used here to describe racialisation in practice. But it also embodies a commitment to a critical, moral evaluation. It refers to the ability of dominant groups to impose negative definitions of racialisation on to less powerful groups and implies consequences which disadvantage these groups.

Definitions

Terminology here is problematic and contentious. There is no precise term to describe the group of people whose experiences and relationship with the wider community is charted. Neither 'Caribbean' nor 'West Indian' accurately describes the geographical origins of the group.[15] 'Black' can include migrants from Africa or the Caribbean and is also used as a political expression to describe those subjected to racism (UK: Fighting Our Fundamentalisms, 1995). The problem of terminology arises from the social construction of groups of people into racialised categories, and the plastic nature of these constructions which change and reform as part of an ideological battle over the position of groups of people in society.[16] African Caribbean, while problematic, has been adopted as a descriptor here, in line with the self classification of community members in the most recent research of opinion of the group in Leicester and which is also consistent with choice of the largest number of people in the 1991 census (African Caribbean People in Leicestershire, 1993). However, in this study, it includes people who regard themselves as black people originating from the Caribbean. It does not include people of Asian-Caribbean origin nor black people of African origin. Despite inaccuracies the terms 'black' and Caribbean migrant are used here interchangeably with African Caribbean. The term West Indian is used to describe British Colonial territories and migrants who came from these areas when it was used in sources or literature at a time when this was a common descriptor. While it is clearly inappropriate for black people born here, many African Caribbean people born in the Caribbean, are happy to call themselves West Indian. Terms like 'coloured' are adopted when they are used in sources or otherwise in parenthesis.

'Asian' is also used as a descriptor. This too is inaccurate to describe migrants in Leicester who arrived from India, East Africa and later Pakistan. However, this term has been retained as it is widely understood in Britain to mean immigrants whose antecedents originated from the Indian sub continent and it is also the description adopted by most of the people who themselves came from this area and who now live in Leicester.

This study is organised to show the evolving relationships between national and local government, policy towards immigration, the public discourse on race and the experiences of African Caribbeans in Leicester between 1945 and 1981. It is structured in a thematic way. The study examines a number of the most important areas of life: housing, employment, education, political organisations, leisure, cultural and religious life, but does so in a way that is consistent as far as possible with the chronological development of the policy, and decisions in relations to African Caribbeans.

Chapter Two discusses the causes of post war Caribbean immigration to Britain and shows the settlement of the African Caribbean population in Leicester in the context of the geographical distribution of African Caribbeans in Britain. It also outlines government policy on immigration through the period and thus the influence of this on the composition of the population of Leicester.

Chapter Three demonstrates that local government, in line with national policy, made no provision for the arrival of black people in Leicester in the period up to 1962 but shows that a racialised discourse concerning the arrival of black people was expressed in the local press. The first need of people after food is shelter and chapter four describes the experiences of African Caribbeans arriving in Leicester in relation to housing. Here again the local authority made no provision in this respect but policies had the effect of excluding African Caribbeans from public housing until the 1970s and allowed widespread discrimination in the private sector. Chapter Five discusses employment, an essential aspect of life for many people and at the heart of debates about black and Asian immigration. This chapter describes the 'colour bar' in Leicester which operated until 1981 and shows that this was not inevitable. The class composition of the African Caribbean community was forged as a result of exclusionary practices.

Chapter Six demonstrates the consistency between the remembered experiences of black people of their education in Leicester schools beginning in the early 1960s, and the policy of the Leicester Education Authority regarding the arrival of black and Asian children. Chapter Seven is concerned with the way in which African Caribbeans organised themselves politically and in relation to the local state. It also examines the growth of the far right in Leicester and the opposition to it. Chapter Eight shows how African Caribbeans were excluded from public places of entertainment and leisure facilities and how they developed a range of cultural organisations including religious institutions, as well as other organisations to protect their interests. These organisations developed a relationship with the local state through which an ethnic minority was formed.

In 1981, along with other cities in the UK, Leicester experienced what were considered street disorders by some and an uprising by others, involving black, Asian and white youths. These events can be seen as marking a turning point in the evolution of the construction of black and Asian people from immigrants to ethnic minorities. After 1981 the state, through local authorities, began to formalise this construction by fostering an ethnic identity through the funding of community projects. However, the continuity of a racialised element to the way in which black and Asian people were seen, remained. Both immigrant and ethnic minority are racialised concepts and in both popular and official discourse are defined in a racialised way.

Notes

1	House of Commons Sessional Papers 1975-76, Select Committee on Race Relations and Immigration, 'Memorandum Submitted by Leicester United Caribbean Association', 4 December 1975, HMSO, London, paragraph, 17; House of Commons Session 1980-81, Fifth Report from the Home Affairs Committee, Racial Disadvantage, 13 March 1981, HMSO, (Marett, 1989, p.1).

2	The 1951 Census, Leicester and Leicestershire, Table 20.

3	The 1961 Census, Leicester and Leicestershire, Table 10.

4	The 1966 Sample Census, Leicester and Leicestershire, Table 20.

5	1971 Census, County Report for Leicester Part 1, Table 14.

6	1981 Census, County Report for Leicester Part 1, Table 10.

7	See Chapter 2 for a fuller discussion of this issue.

8	*Survey of Leicester*, Leicester City Council, 1983.

9	See Bibliography for a complete list of sources.

10	See Chapter Three.

11	House of Commons, Sessional Papers 1972-73, Select Committee on Race Relations and Immigration, 'Memorandum Submitted by Leicester LEA', 24 May 1973, HMSO, London 1973; House of Commons Sessional Papers, 1975-76, Select Committee on Race Relations and Immigration, Memoranda Submitted by LUCA, 4 December 1975, HMSO, London 1976; House of Commons, Session 1980-81, Fifth Report from the Home Affairs Committee, Racial Disadvantage, Evidence was submitted from a number of representatives of Leicester City Council and Leicestershire County Council, 13 March 1981, HMSO, London 1981.

12	Where people were unwilling to be identified a pseudonym was used and this has been noted.

13	See Chapter Two.

14	In Philadelphia, for example, a group of black parents attempted too ban all intelligence testing in schools as a 'result of the way these have been used to keep black people down' (Comer, 1970, p.8).

15	For a discussion of the evolving history and problems associated with these terms see E.M. Thomas-Hope, *Perspectives on Caribbean Regional Identity*, Centre for Latin American Studies, University of Liverpool, Monograph Series 11.

16	In Leicester in the 1950s, African-American servicemen were also treated as part of a group which were then described as 'coloured'. This racialised category overrode their nationality. For example, the headline 'Coloured Man is Attacked' referred to an American. *Leicester Mercury*, 1 October 1958.

References

African Caribbean People in Leicestershire, January (1993), First Interim Report, Afrikan Caribbean Support Group Research Project, University of Leicester. See also Leicester City Council, derived from the 1991 census.

Banton, Michael (1955), *The Coloured Quarter: Negro Immigrants in an English City*, Jonathan Cape, London.

Bornat, Joanna; Burdell, Judith; Goom, Bridget and Thompson, Paul (1980), 'Oral History and Black History, Conference Report', *Oral History*, Vol 8, No 1.

Bourne, J (1980), 'Cheerleaders and Ombudsmen: The Sociology of Race Relations in Britain', *Race and Class*, Vol 21, pp. 331-352.

Byron, Margaret (1994), *Post-War Caribbean Migration to Britain: The Unfinished Cycle*, Avebury, Aldershot.

Carby, Hazel (1982), 'White Women Listen! In Centre In Contemporary Cultural Studies', *The Empire Strikes Back: Race and Racism in 70s Britain*, Hutchinson, London, pp.11.

Casely-Hayford, Augustus (May 1990), 'Black Oral History and Methodology: The Possibilities of Conducting Black Local History', *The Local Historian*, Vol 20, No 2, pp.59-64.

Centre for Contemporary Cultural Studies (1982), *The Empire Strikes Back: Race and Racism in 70s Britain*, Hutchinson, London.

Cesarani, David (1996), 'The Changing Character of Citizenship and Nationality in Britain', in David Cesarani and Mary Fulbrook (eds), *Citizenship, Nationality and Migration in Europe*, Routledge, London.

Cesarani, David and Fulbrook, Mary (eds) (1996), *Citizenship, Nationality and Migration in Europe*, Routledge, London.

Comer, J P (1970), 'Research and the Black Backlash', *American Journal of Ortho Psychiatry*, Vol 40, Part 1.

Constantine, Learie (1954), *Colour Bar*, Stanley Paul, London.

Davison, R B, 'West Indian Migration to Britain 1952-61', *The West Indian Economist*, 4, 1 April 1961.

Davison, R B (1962), *West Indian Migration: Social and Economic Facts of Migration from the West Indies*, Oxford University Press, London.

Forty Winters On: Memories of Britain's Post War Caribbean Migrants (1988), South London Press, London.

Fryer, Peter (1984), *Staying Power, Black People in Britain Since 1504*, Humanities Press, Atlantic Highlands, NJ.

Glass, Ruth (1960), *Newcomers*, Allen and Unwin, London.

Gundara, Jagdish S and Duffield, Ian (eds) (1992), *Essays on the History of Blacks in Britain: From Roman Times to the Mid Twentieth Century*, Avebury, Aldershot.

Highfields Rangers (1993), Leicester City Council, Leicester.

Highfields Remembered (1996), Leicester County Council, Leicester 1996.

hooks, bell (1982), *Ain't I a woman, Black Women and Feminism*, Pluto Press, London.

Lawrence, Errol (1982), 'In the Abundance of Water the Fool is Thirsty: Sociology and Black Pathology', in *Centre for Contemporary Cultural Studies.*

Lee, Trevor R (1977), *Race and Residence*, Clarendon Press, Oxford, p.9.

Little, Kenneth (1947), *Negroes in Britain*, Kegan Paul, London.

Marett, Valerie (1989), *Immigrants Settling in the City*, Leicester University Press, London.

Miles, Robert (1989), *Racism*, Routledge, London, p.86.

Miles, Robert (1994), 'Explaining Racism in Contemporary Europe', in Ali Rattansi and Sallie Westwood (eds), *Racism, Modernity and Identity*, Polity Press, Cambridge, p.191.

Moynihan, Daniel (1965), *The Negro Family: The Case for National Action*, Office of Planning and Research, US Department of Labour.

Murray, Robert (1996), *Lest We Forget, The Experiences of World War II, West Indian Ex-Service Personnel*, Nottingham West Indian Combined Ex-Service Association, Hansib, Nottingham.

Nash, David and Reeder, David (eds) (1993), *Leicester in the Twentieth Century*, Allan Sutton Publishers, Stroud.

Patterson, Sheila (1963), *Dark Strangers*, Tavistock Publications, London.

Peach, Ceri (1968), *West Indian Migration to Britain: A Social Geography*, Oxford University Press, London.

Peach, G C K (1974), 'Birthplace, Ethnicity and the Under-Enumeration of West Indian, Indians and Pakistanis in the Censuses of 1966 and 1971', *New Community*, Vol 3, part 4.

Pearson, David G. (1981), *Race, Class and Political Activism*, Gower, Aldershot.

Pritchard, R M (1976), *Housing and the Spatial Structure of the City*, Cambridge University Press, London.

Ramdin, Ron (1987), *The Making of the Black Working Class in Britian*, Gower, Aldershot.

Rex, J, and Moore, Robert (1967), *Race, Community and Conflict: A Study of Sparkbrook*, Oxford University Press , London.

Richmond, Anthony (1954), *Colour Prejudice in Britain: A Study of West Indian Workers in Liverpool, 1941-1951*, Routledge and Kegan Paul, London.

Rodway, Walter (1972), *How Europe Underdeveloped Africa*, Bogle-L'Ouverture, London.

Rose, E J B et al (1969), *Colour and Citizenship: A Report on British Race Relations*, Oxford University Press, London.

Samuel, Raphael (23 September 1995), 'The People with Stars in Their Eyes', *Guardian.*

Sewcharan, Radica (1986), *There's No Place Like 'Black Home'*, West Indian Senior Citizens Project, Leicester.

Shyllon's Black People in Britain 1555- 1833, Oxford University Press, London.

Shyllon, Folarin (1977), *Black Slaves in Britain*, Oxford University Press for the Institute of Race Relations, London.

Sivanandan, A (1982), *A Different Hunger, Writings on Black Resistance*, Pluto Press, London.

Small, Stephen (1994), *Racialised Barriers*, Routledge, London, p.34.

Smith, David (1974), *Racial Disadvantage in Employment*, Vol 15, Broadsheet, 544, London.

Thomas-Hope E M (1984), *Perspectives on Caribbean Regional Identity*, Centre for Latin American Studies, University of Liverpool, Monograph Series 11.

Thompson, E P (1963), *The Making of the English Working Class*, Penguin, Harmondsworth.

Thompson, Paul (1988), *The Voice of the Past* (2nd ed), Oxford University Press, Oxford, p.1.

Troyna, Barry (1993), *Racism and Education, Research Perspectives*, Open University Press, Buckingham.

Troyna, Barry (1995), 'Beyond Reasonably Doubt? Researching "Race" in Educational Settings', *Oxford Review of Education*, Vol 21, No 4.

'UK: Fighting our Fundamentalisms: An Interview with A. Sivanandan by CARF', *Race and Class*, Vol 36, No 3, 1995.

Walvin, James (1992), 'From the Fringes: The Emergence of British Black Historical Studies', in Jagdish S Gundara and Ian Duffield (eds), *Essays on the History of Blacks in Britain: From Roman Times to the Mid Twentieth Century*, Avebury, Aldershot.

Walvin, James (1971), *The Black Presence: A Documentary History of the Negro in England, 1555-1860*, Orbach and Chambers, London.

Williams, Eric (1964), *Capitalism and Slavery*, Andre Deutsch, London.

Wilson, S (1993), 'Explorations of the Usefulness of Case Study Evaluations', *Evaluation Quarterly*, 3.

2 The Background to African Caribbean Settlement in Leicester

Introduction

This chapter brings together four different, but related, aspects of the wider context which contributes to an understanding of the origins of the Leicester African Caribbean community. First the chapter explores the existing literature on the causes of immigration from the Caribbean to Great Britain after 1945. Second a critique of the ungendered nature of much of the literature is discussed and this is linked to the experiences of African Caribbean women migrants to Leicester. Third the origins of the Leicester community are discussed in the context of what is known about the pattern of settlement in Britain as a whole. It is argued that the specific causes for the development of the community in Leicester are unclear, but possible contributory factors are suggested. Finally the chapter outlines British Government policies regarding immigration between 1945 and 1981. Governments are in a powerful position to foster or discourage, to allow or prevent, immigration and it is argued that the composition of the City of Leicester as it developed during the period can be seen to be closely related to that policy.

Causes of Migration

Migration has been the subject of intense investigation and debate since the late nineteenth century. Migrants are usually divided into two groups: refugees from political, racial or religious persecution and economic migrants.[1] The underlying causes of the migration which forms the focus of this study, are economic and cultural. Immigration has been a highly contentious issue in political debate, world wide, since 1945 and this has spawned a rich literature, examining the causes of and issues surrounding migration of particular groups of peoples in specific historical periods. While the search for general causes, applicable to all situations, is thought to be important, few have attempted such a task. Colin Holmes while focusing on one receiving society, the British Isles, has produced an overview of migration of diverse groups of people over a relatively long period. This work is one of only four 'general histories of immigrants in Britain over any length of time' (Panayi, 1994, p.1).[2] Holmes' study suggested both general factors as well as specific conditions contributing to particular episodes of movement of particular groups of people over the period. But as Panayi (1994, p.24) has argued, Holmes' study stops short of a comprehensive theory of migration. This chapter reviews current literature on the causes of West Indian migration to Great Britain, post World War Two, in the light of Holmes' generalisations.

In addition to economic conditions in the sending and receiving societies, Holmes included the mechanism by which movement is achieved, the perceptions of people about migration as a possible course of action, psycho-social influences and the historical relationship between countries. These factors interact in complex ways so that, for example, improved methods of transport and communication not only make actual physical movement easier, but also facilitates the spread of information from recent to potential migrants. This encourages more movement and itself stimulates the development of transport provision. Patterson (1963), Peach (1968) and Rose (1969) have all referred to the ways in which the transfer of information from West Indians in Britain to people 'back home' encouraged more people to follow them. Indeed, the flow of information was crucial to Peach's thesis and of central importance in Philpott's (1973) study of migration from Montserrat.

The Caribbean has, what John Holt (1992, p.376) described in relation to Jamaica as, a 'centuries of tradition of out-migration' (Thomas-Hope, 1977, pp.13-71). According to Thomas-Hope (1977, p.14), freedom of movement came to assume an importance for most Caribbeans far beyond the search for mere economic advantage. Immediately after emancipation people moved from one Caribbean island to another. Movement was permanent, long stay and seasonal (Thomas-Hope, 1977, p.16).

By the mid 1850s the overall emigration rate from Jamaica was regarded as being so extensive that it was compared by the island press to the 'Irish Exodus' (Thomas-Hope, 1977, p.18).

In the late nineteenth century Caribbeans went to Panama to work on the Canal and to other areas of central America. Migration within and beyond the Caribbean was continuous until the 1930s (Thomas-Hope, 1977, p.15). Movement accelerated during the Second World War. West Indians migrated to the United States of America and to Britain, while maintaining the traditional pattern of inter-island movement. Britain became a favoured destination after the Walter-McCarran Act of 1952 which restricted entry into the USA and when migration to Britain was restricted in 1962, movement to Canada was increased. This was facilitated by the removal of restrictions to black immigration into Canada just four months before the passing of the 1962 act in Britain (Thomas-Hope, 1977, pp.48-49). In 1965 the United States abolished the quotas for Caribbean migrants there and immigration to this destination resumed. Many people who came to Britain first then moved on to Canada and the United States. According to Thomas-Hope (1977, p.68):

> Rather than accept the work relationships of their pre-migration status many people would emigrate again, even repeatedly, and ultimately stay permanently abroad.

Repeated migration is a feature of Caribbean society not always acknowledged in the British literature. Most of the people interviewed for this study had networks of relatives and/or friends living in Canada and the United States. Some spoke of moving to these destinations at some time in the future.

The post war migration from the former British colonies to Great Britain has been subject to examination in a number of studies beginning soon after the movement itself began (Little, 1947; Banton, 1952; Roberts and Mills 1958; Davison, 1961 and 1962). The docking of the *Empire Windrush* in June 1948 with 492 Jamaicans on board achieved publicity in the press and on cinema newsreels and has come to symbolise the beginning of the migration movement. It was not, however, the first passenger ship to bring West Indian migrants. The *Ormonde* arrived in early 1947 with 110 Jamaican workers, including ten stowaways, on board (Harris, 1993).

A long-standing debate centres on the relative importance of economic conditions in the country of origin compared to those in the receiving society as factors leading to migration: push and pull factors. Those studies which have emphasised push factors in this case include Glass, (1960) Patterson (1963) and Foner (1979). These three studies were concerned primarily with the experience of West Indians in Britain. Work which emphasises pull factors has been most often, but not exclusively, located within the Marxist reserve army of labour theory and consequently includes an international perspective. This theory examined the way in which the capitalist economies of Western Europe drew in workers to meet labour shortages. The most influential study is that of Castles and Kosack (1973) but more recent studies include that of Akgunduz (1993) and Harris (1993). However, probably the most influential advocate of pull factors is Ceri Peach (1968) who, while not arguing from a Marxist perspective does regard the demand for labour in Britain as the salient factor in West Indian migration. Writers in the first group have all emphasised poverty as important in the cause of migration. Foner mentioned the importance of both push and pull factors but her detailed discussion concentrates on conditions in the West Indies. However, while it may appear obvious that poverty and migration are linked, the exact nature of the relationship is sometimes not considered. Poverty is neither a necessary nor sufficient condition to produce migration.

The concept of poverty has been subjected to scrutiny and how poverty is defined is itself subject to intense debate (Townsend, 1979). The debate concerns the characterisation of poverty as an absolute or relative state. This is important in the context of migration. Lynn Hollen Lees in her well argued discussion of Irish migration to Britain in the nineteenth century wrote that poverty alone was insufficient as an explanation. It was not the poorest people who were the most likely to leave their home (Hollen Lees, 1974, p.24). Indeed extreme poverty can be an obstacle to emigration. In 1864 Sir William Wilde described those left behind [from emigration from Ireland in the 1840s] as including:

> the poor, the weak, the old, the sick, the blind, lame, the dumb and the imbecile and insane (Wilde, 1864, pp.40-41).

The increase in numbers leaving Ireland during the 1840s has led to the famine being regarded as a major cause of Irish emigration. Hollen Lees (1974) argues that this emigration had been in progress for centuries before the famine and Irish emigration was part of the general movement of people from rural to urban environments which accompanied the industrial revolution.

Returning to the West Indies, Ceri Peach regarded poverty as a 'permissive' rather than a push factor. Elizabeth Thomas-Hope in a complex analysis centred on the Caribbean as a sending society, rather than immigration to any one destination, also argued that:

Below a certain threshold of income (which in absolute terms would vary within specific conditions at any one place and time), emigration is hindered rather than stimulated (Thomas-Hope, 1977, p.24).

Overpopulation like poverty is often cited as a factor in emigration and again like the concept of poverty has been used imprecisely. It is sometimes not clear whether a territory is regarded as overpopulated in relation to physical density, or to available food, or to opportunities for employment. While there can be a relationship between these three aspects of 'overpopulation' they are often conflated. Foner has a detailed discussion of population and links population size to other factors in Jamaica.

The extremely limited job opportunities were, and still are, aggravated by the Island's very high population size. By the end of 1962 the island had a population density of 377 per square mile, 'higher than that of India'...Jamaica has a density of 1,050 persons per square mile of agricultural land and nearly twice that figure per square mile of agricultural land excluding permanent grassland. Moreover, the crude birth rate of Jamaica was more than forty (per 1000) in 1962, and the rate of natural increase exceeded 3% (Foner, 1979, p.8).

While it may seem obvious that these facts must be cause enough for people to migrate, Peach (1968), Thomas-Hope (1977) and Davison (1961, 1962) argued that there is no correlation between population density and migration. Peach (1965, p.32) also criticised Glass for citing population growth as a factor in West Indian migration.

The population of the former West Indies increased at a very high rate; 2.29 % per annum between 1946 and 1960 yet those territories which had the highest rate of increase did not experience the greatest degree of emigration. British Guyana and Trinidad and Tobago had in fact the lowest rate of emigration and the highest inter censal increases, while emigration from Montserrat was so large that its population declined from 1946-1960.

A similar discussion of the relative importance of population growth exists among scholars of nineteenth century European emigration (Baines, 1985). Panayi argued in relation to immigration into Britain between 1815 and 1945, that population growth made emigration more likely rather than being a cause in itself during the nineteenth century (Panayi, 1994, p.26).

Despite the difficulty in structuring the role of various push factors in relation to migration, economic conditions in the West Indies have been invariably included as part of an understanding. Fryer (1984), for example, pointed to a doubling in the cost of living in the West Indies during the Second World War. There were no state benefits to help the unemployed. Glass drew attention to the high level of unemployment and underemployment after the war and the 1946 Report on Jamaica shows how difficult it was for ex-servicemen to find work.[3] Peach argued that there was an inverse relationship between gross domestic product per head of population and degree of migration in islands of the area except for Jamaica. But 60% of migrants to Great Britain in the 1950s and 1960s came from Jamaica and as Peach asserted this has made it an important exception. He therefore concluded that there is no correlation between economic conditions and migration (Peach, 1968).

While some writers emphasise push factors there has been a general consensus in the literature that both push and pull factors must be considered in migration. As Holmes (1988, p.278) has argued:

Few would wish to argue now that the motivation for movement was ever monocausal or homogeneous.

The relative importance of pull factors is contentious and is particularly important in the discussion of West Indian migration to Great Britain. Watson (1977, p.38) for example wrote:

The difficulty with this approach [that emphasises pull factors] is that it obscures the inherent complexity of population movements, and as some critics have pointed out ... often treats the subjects as if they were automatons reacting to forces beyond their control.

But this is to confuse explanation at the level of individual behaviour with that of sociological or historical change or perhaps the how with the why.

As Morokvasic (1983, p.28) argued:

To an individual migrant, her or his decision to emigrate may appear as her/his own or influenced by another individual. Emigration appears as an individualised act in answer the inevitable question of the interviewer: why did you leave? But whatever the migrant may answer to that question, the individual motives for emigration are of poor explanatory value in relation to the migration process as a whole.

The relative attention paid to various factors relates to wider theoretical approaches to immigration and race. The assimilationist perspective on race relations adopted by Patterson (1963) is accompanied by a view of migration which emphasises conditions in the West Indies. Those who emphasise the pull of the British labour market include Peach and Holmes. Peach (1968) has a carefully structured argument in which he demonstrated that the number of emigrants to Britain fluctuated in accordance with demand for labour in Britain in the period 1956-1960. He rejected the emphasis on push factors arguing that emigration did not take place during periods of economic depression in the Caribbean. Those who examined migration within the reserve army of labour theory tended to place West Indian migration into Britain in the context of a wider movement of peoples who were sucked into the capitalist economies of Europe to alleviate labour shortages in the immediate post war period. Castles and Kosack (1973, p.27) argued that immigration has become a structural necessity for the economies of the receiving countries.

> Every period of economic expansion since the war has led to labour shortages which have been alleviated through the recruitment of migrant workers.

Unemployment, poverty and underdevelopment have been seen as permissive factors. Labour migration according to Castles and Kosack (1973, p.27) was a kind of aid given by poor countries to rich. In his study of Turkish immigration to West Germany, Akgunduz (1993, p.156) argued that:

> After the Second World War most Western European countries enlarged their labour force with so-called repatriates, a bi-product of the process of decolonisation. The Netherlands for example observed the arrival of an estimated 250,000 to 300,000 repatriates from Indonesia between 1946 and 1962, and 125,000 Moluccans in 1951. By the beginning of January 1983 the Netherlands had received from its scarcely populated colonies of Surinam (which became independent in 1975) 140,000 people and from the Dutch Antilles 42,000.

He went on to discuss migration into Western Europe from other European countries as well as from colonies and ex-colonies and in doing so he put the economic needs of the receiving societies at the centre of an explanation for migration. Clive Harris who also discusses Caribbean migration to Great Britain in the context of the reserve army thesis, has argued that recruitment of workers from outside the natural boundaries of Britain had become an economic necessity. But in a development of the theory he argued that economic conditions in the Caribbean were part of a world-wide economic system which links demand in capitalist economies with underdevelopment. In this analysis push and pull factors are part of a whole (Harris, 1993).

Some attention is paid in the literature to the way in which some large employers such as London Transport, the National Health Service and The British Hotels and Restaurants Association recruited workers directly from the West Indies. London Transport executive established an arrangement with the authorities in Barbados through the Immigration Liaison Service, whereby emigrants were lent their fare to England which was then repaid through their wage packets (Sutton and Makeisky, 1975, p.120, Thomas-Hope, 1977, p.64). The significance of this direct recruitment has been somewhat contentious. The numbers of people involved were small in relation to the migratory movement as a whole. Peach regarded sponsored migration as an important but minority element in the flow which was essentially fuelled by a 'free movement of labour' (Peach, 1991, p.4).[4] However it has become important politically in the debate concerning the treatment of black people in Britain. It does demonstrate that the increasingly acknowledged position of the British governments of the 1940s and 1950s of attempting to prevent the settlement of black people in Britain, was not a consistent one. While, arguably, the development of a multiracial society was resisted at all levels of society, some government departments and some employers wanted the labour of black people.

The mechanism by which movement is achieved is Holmes' second general factor to consider in migratory movements. In the case of Caribbean migration there is little doubt that it was not only the availability of sea transportation which facilitated movement but migration which stimulated the development of transport. Harris (1993, p.128) referred to a response in the House of Commons in 1946 by the Minister of Labour, George Isaacs, to a question about the importation of West Indian labour. 'The problem of shipping' was held to be a reason why this solution to labour shortage was dismissed. Holmes (1988) refers to the 'ratchet-effect' which was produced by the expansion of transport opportunities and the large profit of steamship companies. Glass (1960) describes travel agencies springing up in many islands with their headquarters in Kingston. These agencies conducted an advertising campaign which encouraged people with easy payment plans. Philpott (1973, p.32) wrote that in 1952 only six Montserratians applied for passports to go to Britain. But in 1953 an Italian shipping line began calling at the island on return from South America. In 1955, 1,145 Montserratians applied for passports. In 1956 an airstrip was constructed. Between 1955 and 1961, 3,835 Montserratians came to Britain from a population of 12,000 (Philpott, 1973, p.37).

But transport and communication were also important in spreading information from recent to potential migrants. Some of the passengers on the *Ormonde,* and two thirds of those on the *Windrush* were drawn from Caribbean soldiers, airmen and munitions workers stationed in Britain during the war.[5] The information they and others who followed them provided for people back home, was crucial in encouraging others. The flow of accurate information about the state of the labour market in Britain was crucial to Peach's thesis and detailed studies such as that of Philpott's provide the evidence. By close attention to individual cases Philpott was able to demonstrate the validity of his case in a way which has not often been available to historians. He describes one person who came to England on the first boat which stopped on Montserrat in September 1954. By sending money home he was joined by ten people, all close relatives. Over a twelve year period twenty two people came to England following him. Philpott (1977, p.107) described how:

> Returned male migrants frequently recount stories of their experiences abroad at rum shops and other places where men gather, such exploits ranking with sexual adventures in the building of reputation, and obviously relish the prestige which accrues to those who have been abroad.

Foner (1979, pp.10-11) quoted one man who said:

> friend was here and said would I like to come to England... I knew they were looking for men in England. I'd been thinking of coming for a couple of years. It was sort of half and half. Half what I was leaving (not making much money) and half that I knew there were good jobs in England. There were plenty of people in my town who'd gone, and I was sent to stay with a friend of my father's.

Byron (Byron, undated, p.33) too in her study of Nevisians in Leicester wrote that the significance of the island / village/ kinship based network in the accommodation search for the arriving Nevisians cannot be overemphasised. Many of the interviewees in this study also initially stayed with friends or relatives when they arrived in Leicester.[6] The role of information in the migratory process was extensively explored by Thomas-

Hope (1977, pp.30-31) in her thesis. Her evidence questions the accuracy of migrants' stories sent home. She wrote that the greatest hardships were rarely reported by the migrants themselves to their friends and families at home.

> Then as now it was essential for the migrants to minimise all aspects of failure in the eyes of the community back home, and to dispel the conclusion that the value of migration was not as great as assumed.

Holmes' (1988) third consideration is that of people's perception of migration as a possible course of action. This is something more easily examined where oral history methods are possible. It has already been argued that poverty is a relative condition and that people's expectations of an improved standard of living must be an important part of the decision to migrate. Foner (1979, p.10):

> Whatever the absolute level of living most were and considered themselves to be poor and deprived relative to the middle and upper classes in the island.

The idea of emigration as a possible course of action must too, be facilitated in societies where there is a tradition of emigration. Elizabeth Thomas-Hope (1977) makes the perception of emigration in relation to a view of the world as central to an understanding of Caribbean migration. She argues that Caribbean peoples were:

> oriented towards emigration whether or not the opportunities arose which permitted the actual move. Some West Indians leave their native islands permanently, others return after a number of years, while others for a brief sojourn once in a life-time and still others move back and forth continually...the population of small islands has been heavily depleted at times when permanent or long-stay emigration predominated over brief departures (Thomas-Hope, 1977, p.4).

She continued that:

> emigration is shown to have been a deeply entrenched component of West Indian behavioural pattern.

She argued that economic advantage was insufficient as an explanation for migration, which was 'an intrinsic part of the quest for a new identity' (Thomas-Hope, 1977, p.14). However, the importance of such cultural factors, independent of material facts in the causation of migration is hard to judge.

Holmes' final general cause of migration is the historical relationship between sending and receiving societies. Foner (1979) is one of the few writers, other than Marxists, who related the economic conditions in the West Indies to colonial rule, described the underdeveloped state of Jamaica's economy as the legacy of British colonialism. Since Jamaica's independence in 1962 there has been a continued dependence on neo-colonial power and multi-national corporations. Plantations historically have not only occupied most of the island's land but also the best quality land. In 1954 farms of under five acres represented 70% of all farms but occupied only 14% of farm acreage. Foreign corporations owned factory capacity which processed plantation crops and large numbers of Jamaicans did not have enough land to farm. Mechanisation on estates since 1945 reduced the number of jobs available and 15,000 jobs were lost in the post war period (Foner, 1977, p.7). Work as cane cutters on the sugar estates were low status jobs associated with slavery. The continued underdevelopment of Jamaica meant that while the work force in agriculture fell from 70% in the 1880s to 38% in 1960, there was no corresponding expansion in other areas of work. The historical legacy has also been linked to population growth. During the colonial period, the British and white planter elite encouraged population growth to supply cheap labour for the plantations. However, the under development of British colonies in the West Indies was replicated in many other areas of the British Empire, from which no migration occurred.

Migrants were British subjects ruled from London and as such were entitled in law to come to Britain. No documentary evidence of British nationality was required for people from the colonies, at least, in theory, until 1962.[7] 'Britishness' was fostered by the West Indian education system. People were:

> taught in English-speaking schools by teachers with English middle-class values...In their schools West Indian children were taught from English text books about the history of the 'Mother Country' and learned as loyal subjects of the Crown to sing 'Rule Britannia' and 'God Save the King' (Foner, 1979, p.7).

Despite the problems of the assimilationist perspective of Patterson, Glass and Foner, these studies have all provided moving evidence from the testimony of West Indians of the shock experienced by migrants when they met the reality of Britain compared to the image maintained in the

Colonies.

> We didn't feel strangers to England. We had been taught all about British history, the Queen, and that we belonged. When I got here it was a shock. A shock to discover people knew nothing about us. I discovered we weren't part of things. My loyalty at age fifteen was to England. The shock was to find I was a stranger[8] (Foner, 1979, p.9).

Holmes referred to Britain and its carefully cultivated image of a society characterised by fair play justice and liberty. Given that Caribbeans in the twentieth century have also migrated to the United States and to Canada, the role of the political link with Britain in the migration process could have been overemphasised.

Finally there are a number of specific conditions which are applicable to the West Indian situation. Most important of these is the Walter McCarran Act of 1952 which virtually ended immigration to the United States. This had been an important destination up until this date. Sutton and Makiesky (1975, p.120) in a study of Barbadian emigration wrote that:

> The economic situation and immigration policies of the North Atlantic industrialised countries were the primary determinants of the direction that the post-war outflow from the West Indies took...In the United States a sharp drop in agricultural recruitment programmes and the passing of restrictive legislation in 1952 curtailed West Indian immigration. At the same time labour shortages in Britain and an open immigration policy attracted increased numbers of West Indians to that country particularly from 1952-1962.

In the case of Montserrat, Philpott (1973, p.109) argued that there were specific conditions which account for the 'staggering scale of Montserratian migration to Britain'. These were a unique combination of economic and political events in the early 1950s. Some authors point to the 1951 Jamaican hurricane as a contributing factor to economic hardship. It is, however, hard to establish exactly the role played by such events. It is easy to add natural disasters to a list of causes because of a temporal coincidence of events.

Men and Women

The literature on migration has been criticised for being ungendered. Gender is one of the fundamental organising principles of behaviour in any society. While there may be many similarities in the attitudes and behaviour of men and women with respect to migration, the behaviour of women cannot be subsumed within a description of that of men or ignored without an impoverishment of the analysis. Nor can the position of women, for example of dependency upon men, be assumed. Mirjana Morokvasic (1983, p.13) wrote:

There is, of course, a literature in which migrant women are totally absent; in the general theories of migration, migrants are usually sex-less units; if they are constructed into sociological objects then they are male and a considerable number of studies have used exclusively male samples (Phizacklea, 1983, p.101, Potts, 1990, p.215).

She continued:

This has happened not only in contexts where the sex ratio in the migratory movements was in favour of males - as in most countries in Europe particularly in the sixties - but also in other contexts where women outnumbered men (Morokvasic, 1988, p.14).

Morokvasic (1988, p.15) described a second kind of literature which mentions women as 'an accessory of a process they are not really taking part in'. In this group of studies women were seen as dependants; the migrant being a male breadwinner and the dependent woman part of the migrant's family. Characterising female migrants in this way has contributed to the invisibility of women and has stereotyped migrant women as:

followers, dependants, unproductive persons, isolated, illiterate, sociologically, migrant women are only visible within the framework of the family (Morakvasic, 1980, p.16).

Although as she herself stated:

It is sometimes difficult to draw a clear line between the literature which excludes women completely and that in which they are mentioned only as an accessory of a process they are not really taking part in (Morakvasic, 1988, p.15).

Morakvasic's characterisation concerning the literature on migration can be demonstrated in studies of post war Caribbean migration to Great Britain and in the sociological studies of settlement which have appeared concurrently with the movement itself. An example of a study which excludes women completely is Lawrence's (1974) entitled *Black Migrants: White Natives*. This is described as a study of 'race relations in Nottingham' and was based on a social survey among immigrants and the native white population. However, the survey included only males in the two groups. Lawrence seemed unaware of the significance of his exclusion. He did not seek to justify or even comment upon it. Other studies mention, but pay scant attention to women, acknowledging their existence only, as it were, in passing. Pryce's (1979) study of West Indian life-styles in Bristol was such a study. Pryce (1979, p.300) unlike Lawrence, comments on his exclusion of women thus:

> A further problem arises out of the built-in limitations of the participant observation technique is that as a male researcher I had only limited access to the women in the West Indian community for research purposes.

He went on to suggest that a female West Indian researcher could look at the women's point of view. His study contained a section concerning 'Women on the Receiving End' in which he described how the:

> 'love them and leave them' attitude of the men in his study takes a heavy toll in the lives of individual women in the hustler's own West Indian Group (Pryce, 1979, p.92).

However, while there was sympathy, there was no empathy and little explanation for their position and Pryce appears to identify with the attitudes of his male informants. The central theme of the work - the characterisation of six 'life-styles' within the West Indian community in Bristol, was developed in relation to men only and in doing so women's life-styles were not considered in the analysis presented. Banton's work on Stepney in London is also a study which included women largely in relation to one area of life, that on inter-marriage between black men and white women. Banton (1955, p.13) wrote that:

> Conventional British attitudes towards coloured people are such that few women will associate with them; those who do are mostly women who have failed to find a satisfying role in English society and their unstable temperament lies at the root of the unhappiness in many mixed marriages.

In this Banton was not only expressing the popular view of the 1950s that white women who develop relationships with black men were 'not respectable' but he also presented 'coloured people' and 'women' as mutually exclusive groups. The assumption that people are men unless otherwise stated, is of course, embedded in most if not all the literature on migration as it is in most sociological and other academic work before the feminist critique developed in the late 1960s. Pryce (1979, p.37) expressed this in his discussion of a club when he writes that 'apart from women, white people are not allowed in'. In some studies the effect of excluding women from aspects of analysis is hard to evaluate. Pritchard (1976) in his study of housing in Leicester, for example, defines multi-occupation as 'properties where there were more than two adult males with different surnames'.

One of the most influential writers on the causes of migration is Ceri Peach. His thesis is that the most important factor in the migratory process has been labour demand in Britain. Push factors have been seen as permissive. In Peach's (1966) writing women were included selectively. The correlation between labour demand in Britain and the annual rise and fall of migrant numbers was argued using ungendered statistics. But he developed his argument further using the changing pattern of male and female migration.

If it is argued that the total of West Indian migration is sensitive to the employment situation in this country, then it should follow that the section of the migrant group namely the men, which is most dependent upon the demand for labour should be most sensitive of all (Peach, 1966, p.153).

He continued:

The 'solid core' of migrants were dependent women and children joining an already established man. A survey of Jamaican emigrants in 1961 showed that 39% of male migrants had their trips financed from sources in the United Kingdom compared with 72 % of the women (Peach, 1966, p.153).

This assumption of female dependency is inadequate. The economic dependency of West Indian women has been explored very little and even recent studies have assumed that 'primary' migrants were male (Spencer, 1997, pp.60 & 68). However, such evidence as exists suggests that economic dependency upon men is true for only a proportion of West Indian women. It has been suggested that women have had to 'help produce the means of subsistence' because of the 'forced and migrant labour of men' (Potts, 1990, p.215). Field-work for this study included women who came on their own to Great Britain to join friends or female relatives as well as women who came before their husbands or partners. The survey conducted by Davison in 1961 and referred to by Peach as evidence of the dependency of women found that 18% of the 72% of women who had their trip financed from the United kingdom received loans rather than gifts which does not suggest dependency. Davison also wrote that in *most* (my emphasis) of the remaining 54% this money came from husbands now established in Britain. But 15% of the men also had their passage paid for by gifts from the United Kingdom (Davison, 1961, p.32). That less than half of West Indian women had their passage paid for by husbands could be interpreted as evidence of the economic self sufficiency of West Indian women. In Phippott's (1977, p.134) study of Montserrat, siblings were the most frequent source of passage money, followed by parents. Spouses and intended spouses were no more significant than parents, siblings or cousins. The dependency of women is not crucial to Peach's analysis. A more comprehensive approach to gender difference in the migratory process may prove to strengthen a thesis based on labour demand.

Studies of black women in Britain have shown a high level of workforce participation compared to that of white women. It has been suggested that women have had to 'help produce the means of subsistence' because of the 'forced labour of men' (Brown, 1984; Phizacklea, 1982; Bryan, Dadzie and Scafe, 1985, pp.17-57; Walby, 1986, pp.47-49; Bruegel, 1994, pp.178-196). Black women are more likely to be in paid employment and more likely to be employed full time rather than part time compared to white women (Potts, 1990, p.215). Differences in employment patterns between black men and women are referred to in Peach's (1991, pp.26-28) later work. In addition, what is known about the structure of black families suggests that a relatively high proportion of West Indian women are less dependent on men than women in white English families. The high proportion of women to men in Caribbean migration compared to other post war migrations into Europe is an interesting feature and hard to ignore. Cinema newsreels of people arriving on steam ships in Britain in the 1950s and 1960s clearly show women and children arriving alongside men.[9] Mary Chamberlain in her study referred to the gender of Barbadian migration to Britain, a feature 'often obscured by more conventional approaches to the subject' (1994, p.132). There has been little attempt to explore the significance of what appeared to be a divergence from the expected pattern of migration. Davison (1961, pp.15-16) wrote:

In the Jamaican survey, it was found that both the sexes were almost equally represented - there were 185 men and 179 women. This was a surprising result for it was expected that men would predominate by a considerable margin over women; it was the result obtained by Roberts and Mills in their study of migration from Jamaica in the years 1953-55. The impression gained in the 1961 survey was that the migration had changed its character - the men had gone first, now the women were following them.

Davison presented no evidence that women were following men. One survey of 1961 found that, not only was the number of female migrants equal to the number of men but, three quarters of the women were single (Bryan, Dadzie and Scaffe, 1985, p.25). Ruth Glass too in her study assumed that the high proportion of women and children who arrived in 1958 and 1959 constituted the dependent families of men already here (Glass, 1960, p.5). Sheila Patterson (1963) in her influential study included much more detailed information about women and gender differences than most studies. However, this knowledge did not inform her understanding and she too assumed 'maleness'. Philpott's (1973) very detailed study which charted individuals was of necessity obliged to consider women and children notwithstanding his reference to migrants as 'he'. This study provides a great deal of empirical evidence of the importance of women as economically independent human beings in Caribbean households and in the migratory process. His study is necessarily gendered. From Montserrat the number of female migrants is only slightly less than that of males (Philpott, 1973, p.185). This understanding is confirmed in this book.

Settlement in Leicester

It has now been established that there has been a continuous presence of black people in Britain since Roman times. Elizabeth I ordered the rounding up and deportation of 'Blackamores' and at the beginning of the nineteenth century there were estimated to be 14-15,000 black slaves and former slaves living in London (Fryer, 1984; Shyllon, 1977; Grant, 1996). Little is known about black people who may have lived in Leicester and Leicestershire in the past (Afrikan Caribbean Support Group Research Project, 1993, p.21). It is known that there were at least individuals in Leicester before the Second World War. But there has been no published research on Leicestershire which parallels the work of Walvin (1973), Fryer (1973), Shyllon (1977) and others at a national level or that of Bush in

Northamptonshire. The existence of a Leicester City centre public house called the 'Black Boy' suggests that research would be fruitful.[10]

The origin of the modern movement of people from the West Indies to Great Britain lies in the Second World War. Ten thousand West Indians served in the Royal Air Force during the war of whom 2,000 remained in Britain afterwards,[11] despite attempts by the Air Ministry to ensure that they should not be discharged in the UK (Sherwood, 1984, p.40). There were 1,200 British Honduran forestry workers in Scotland of whom only 700 accepted repatriation. The rest settled in Scotland and the north of England. One thousand West Indian technicians were recruited for service in war factories on Merseyside and in Lancashire. There were 'thousands' more in the Merchant navy (Hyam, 1992, p.29). As has already been noted above some of the passengers on the *Ormonde* which arrived in 1947 and two thirds on the *Empire Windrush* which arrived on 21 June 1948 were former servicemen who had spent all or part of their war time service in Britain. Of the 7,000 Jamaicans who served with the British forces, about one third stayed on after VE day (*Forty Winters on: Memoirs of Britain's Post War Caribbean Migrants*, 1988, p.48).

Black people are known to have come to the East Midlands during the war as members of the armed forces. West Indians in the Royal Air Force were stationed at Church Langford near Rugby in Lincolnshire[12] and at other East Midlands locations. A group of women in the Auxiliary Territorial Service (ATS) from the West Indies spent some time in the army camp at South Wigston, just outside Leicester. Lousie Osbourne was one of those who joined the ATS in St Lucia in 1944. Her job was to train new recruits. She stayed on after the war but returned to St Lucia in 1947 (Bousquet and Douglas, 1991, p.122). Bruntingthorpe and Chelverston in Leicestershire were bases for American airmen, both white and black throughout the 1950s. There were 'coloured' nurses working at Leicester general Hospital from 1945 onwards through a scheme sponsored by the Colonial Office.[13] There were students at Leicester University College from Africa, Asia and the West Indies.[14]

Among the earliest of West Indian settlers who came to Leicester after the war, were a small group of former Royal Air Force (RAF) men, mostly from Jamaica who had spent part of the war years in central and east England. This group included people such as Clifton Robinson, Mervyn Ishmail, Eric Hudson, Frank Henry, Ronald Rochester and others. Some of their experiences are described here. By 1951 Leicester had a small and stable community of West Indians who operated an informal support network and it was this group which later developed in to the Sports and

Social Club which was established in 1957. It is clear that this group was important in beginning a chain from which others followed.

Accurately charting the pattern of Caribbean migration to Britain over the following thirty years has proved to be a problem to social scientists, historians and others. The issue of numbers has also assumed great significance in post war British political debate where migration and race have been conflated fuelling ignorance and racism among the general public. Solomos (1989, p.50) argued:

> The racialisation of the migration issue was in other words done through coded language. 'Commonwealth immigrants' were seen as a 'problem', but race itself was not always mentioned as the central issue. The politicisation of such terms was later to lead to a situation where despite the continuing scale of white immigration popular common sense perceived all migrants to be black and immigration became a coded term for talking about racial questions.

The problem of acquiring accurate figures on Caribbean migration has been extensively discussed in the literature (Davison, 1962, Peach, 1968, Patterson, 1963). Before 1962 no accurate official statistics were collected by the British Government. The only count made before 1955 came from those arriving or leaving on long sea voyages (Peach, 1968, p.31). This excluded those arriving via other European ports. Many West Indians came on Italian or Spanish ships through this route. It also excluded those arriving by air, although before 1955 this may have been a very small number. An unknown number of people arrived as 'stowaways' on ships from the West Indies. A Cabinet meeting on 19 June 1950 discussed this problem and minutes refer to a ship arriving 'at Bristol on the following day which had at least fourteen coloured stowaways on board'.[15] This compares with a later parliamentary answer given in the Commons in November 1960 by a government spokesman who estimated that 16,000 people arrived in 1951, 1,000 in 1952, 2,000 in 1953 and 10,000 in 1954 (Davison, 1962, p.6). Little is known about destination within the UK or about island of origin for arrivals before 1955, although it is usually accepted that Jamaicans constituted the majority of early settlers (Davison, 1962, p.5).

After 1955 the Home Office kept a count of arrivals from the West Indies through a check on passports. This number however included people who were not migrants. The other source of information was the Migrant Services Division of the West Indian High Commission in London (MSD). Every territory in the British West Indies notified the MSD when a ship or plane of migrants left for the UK. This therefore excluded people travelling from other parts of the world or travelling as individuals. The Home Office figures are therefore likely to be overestimates and the MSD figures underestimates.

Table 2.1   Arrivals in the UK from the British Caribbean Territories 1955-1961

Year	WI MSD (London)	British Home Office
1955	24473	27600
1956	26441	29800
1957	22473	23000
1958	16511	15000
1959	20397	16400
1960	52655	49700
1961	52849	57700

Source: Davison (1962, p.5)

The pattern of arrivals was used by Peach (1968) to demonstrate his thesis that Caribbean migration can be explained by demand for labour in the UK. The fall in numbers arriving in 1957 and 1958 is explained by economic recession. The marked surge in numbers in 1960 and 1961 was a result of the knowledge that the British Government was likely to introduce legislation to curb entry and people attempted to 'beat the ban' (Davison, 1962, pp.7-8). The 1962 Commonwealth Immigrants Act was the first overtly official action by the British Government to restrict entry of black and brown people but was by no means the first attempt at limiting numbers of such people coming to Britain (Thomas-Hope, 1977, p.50).

Attempts to measure the size of the Caribbean born and those considering themselves part of the African Caribbean population of the UK at the end of the period would need to take into account births, deaths and remigration to a new destination as well as return migration. Elizabeth Thomas Hope (1977) has shown how people who first came to Britain then moved on the United States or Canada. Return migration began early, in 1957 more than 2,000 West Indians returned home (Thomas-Hope, 1977, p.59).

Before the war an estimated 15,000 black people lived in Great Britain, although how many of these were Caribbean born is unclear (Sherwood, 1984, p.3). By 1951, the development of the post war Caribbean community is obvious. Intercensal changes between 1951 and 1961 shows the changing size of the Caribbean population of the UK.

Table 2.2   Birthplace of Caribbean Population of UK 1951 and 1961

	Caribbean Born (est)	UK Children of West Indian Born (est)	Best Caribbean Ethnic Population
1951	17218	1	18000
1961	173659	2600	200000

Source: Peach (1991, p.2)

How is the geographical distribution of African Caribbeans in Britain to be explained? Peach's (1963, p.163) thesis concerning labour demand was developed in his study of settlement patterns in Great Britain. He has argued that West Indians have gone to 'the decreasing urban cores of expanding industrial areas'. This is because, according to Peach, where labour demand was high but where this demand could be met by white workers, they were the preferred workers. So that 'coloured' migrants moved to areas which are characterised by both high labour demand and low white immigration or net outward white migration.

Regions where coloured labour settles in proportionately largest numbers are those with permissive conditions that have failed to attract enough white population (Peach, 1963, p.158).

These were the largest towns which were the least attractive to the white population, who have tended to move to smaller towns. Thus the 'coloured' population was seen as a replacement one. Peach tended to assume the free movement of labour and presented the process of settlement as if it were a kind of natural phenomenon unhindered by decisions influenced by the ideology of racism, whether it be on the part of employers or indeed the British State. He regarded the sponsorship of workers from Barbados as insignificant in terms of explanation. Harris and James (1993) argued that labour demand existed at all levels of the occupational structure and yet it was only white workers who obtained jobs at the middle or the top. Black workers got, by and large, only 'semi and unskilled jobs in specific branches of production'.[16] The case of Leicester is consistent with a theory which emphasises shortage of labour combined with an outward movement of white people to the suburbs of Leicester and indeed to other countries. These issues are discussed in Chapters Three, Four and Five.

A comprehensive explanation of the distribution of black immigrants would need to include the operation of the colour bar and beliefs about jobs considered suitable for black men and women. An assumption about economically rational decisions made in a free labour market is inadequate. Recent research has also revealed more about the role of governments - both the Labour government of 1945-51 and the Conservative Government which followed it - in intervening in Commonwealth immigration. The view that governments' positions were characterised by a 'laissez-faire' approach (Patterson, 1974, Chapter Two) through the 1950s has been progressively modified as evidence has accumulated. The assimilationist perspective of early sociological studies of post war migration has meant that the evidence of official intervention to disperse black immigrants has been seen as an attempt to promote harmonious race relations rather than as part of a government policy designed to prevent black people forming large groupings and becoming a 'problem'. For example Banton (1952, p.47) reported that:

> The various labour districts of the country co-operated in an attempt to start dispersing immigrants by moving them in teams to other parts of the country.

Sheila Patterson described how through the 1950s the managers of the Brixton employment exchange were:

> virtually qualifying as sponsors in their persistent efforts to persuade employers all over London to try coloured labour and to persevere with it, and in the endeavours to direct a stream[17] of hand-picked coloured 'pioneers' out of the South London area into undermanned industries as far afield as Ipswich, Aldershot, Nottingham, Coventry and even Yorkshire (Patterson, 1963, p.421).

Discussions took place in the Cabinet on 18 May 1950. A memorandum by Mr Griffiths, Secretary of State for Colonies, described action which was decided by an inter-departmental meeting including a decision:

> to set up a working party of representatives of the government Departments concerned to tackle the problem of those colonials already here by dispersal, by finding employment and accommodation and by arranging for voluntary

repatriation of the misfits[18]

Further evidence of attempts to disperse black people in Britain is provided by Mark Duffield (1988, p.5), in his study of Indian Foundry workers in the West Midlands. He wrote of:

the collaboration of government agencies, trades unions and the majority of employers to restrict and disperse those blacks coming into the regions.

The lack of reliable information on the pattern of migration from the Caribbean to Great Britain from 1945-62 has already been noted. A similar paucity of data exists on the distribution of migrants once inside the country. The MSD met all large parties and collected information on intended destination of migrants. Patterson (1963, p.421) used this information and local estimates of the Caribbean population of the major West Indian settlements in Britain to produce a detailed table showing numbers in forty-two towns and cities in addition to London. Selected information from that table is reproduced here.

Table 2.3   **Major West Indian Settlements in Britain (Estimates)**

	Mid 55	End 56	End 57	End 58	End 59	Mid 60	Mid 62
London	15000	28000	41000	40000	51000	60000	135000
Birmingham	8000	23000	27000	27000	27000	36000	67000
Manchester	2000	3500	5000	4000	4500	5500	7000
Nottingham	200	3500	4000	4000	4300	5900	9500
Derby	1000	2500	1000	1000	1000	1500	3000
Sheffield	1000	2000	3000	2000	2300	4000	5700
Liverpool	1000	2000	2000	2500	2500	2500	4000
Bristol	200	1000	1500	2000	2000	35000	48000
Leicester	1	800	1000	1500	1000	2000	3700

Source: Patterson (1963, p.421)

Patterson argued that the lack of a figure does not indicate the lack of a settlement but rather that the settlement may have been small. There were towns or cities which had estimated numbers of 500 in 1955 such as Glasgow Cardiff, or Stafford ie numbers larger than Leicester, but by 1962, apart from those shown in the table above, only Huddersfield, Bedford and West Bromwich had larger estimated communities than Leicester.

Davison's (1962, p.24) survey of 439 Jamaican migrants conducted at the end of the period in the Spring of 1961, also asked about destination. Leicester was mentioned by two people in this survey. However, this cannot be taken to indicate the size of the Leicester population at that time. A survey of black elderly residents of Leicester conducted in 1986 shows that only 48% of those interviewed came straight to Leicester on arrival in the UK, 19% went to London first, 13% to Birmingham and another 11% to other places in the South of England (Black Elders in Leicester, 1986, p11). In Pearson's (1981) survey of Leicester, 63% came directly to Leicester.

The size and composition of the black population of Leicester in the late 1940s is extremely difficult to estimate. The 1951 census gives the following information about people born in the Caribbean in Leicester and Leicestershire.

Table 2.4   Caribbean Born Residents of Leicester 1951

	Men	Women	Total
British Guyana	5	1	6
Jamaica	14	7	21
Trinidad & Tobago	1	1	2
Other Caribbean	17	10	27
Total	37	19	56

Table 2.5   Caribbean Born Residents of Leicestershire 1951

	Men	Women	Total
British Guyana	12	4	16
Jamaica	27	19	46
Trinidad & Tobago	5	1	6
Other Caribbean	23	22	45
Total	67	46	113

Source: 1951 census [19]

In 1951 the population of Leicester was 285,000 and of Leicestershire 632,000. The equivalent figures for 1961 were as follows:

Table 2.6   Caribbean Born Residents of Leicester 1961

	Men	Women	Total
Jamaica	183	173	356
Other Territories in Caribbean	534	457	991
Total	717	630	1347

Table 2.7   Caribbean Born Residents of Leicestershire 1961

	Men	Women	Total
Jamaica	208	197	405
Other Territories in Caribbean	571	492	1063
Total	779	689	1468

Source: 1961 census [20]

In 1961 the population of Leicester was 282,000, and of Leicestershire as a whole, 682,568. The census is generally regarded as a very accurate source of information on the characteristics of the population. However there are reasons to think that the census underestimated the Caribbean born population of the city and the county. Peach (1963, p.155) has argued that the recorded net inward movement of people from the Caribbean between 1951 and 1961, allowing for a death rate of two per 1000 per annum, would produce an expected total of Caribbean born residents nationally of 205,918. In fact the 1961 census records 171,796 people. This is an underestimate of 20%. It could be assumed that this underestimate is equally distributed throughout the country. An additional 20% added to the 1961 figure for Leicester city would give a total for Caribbean born residents of 2,694.

People born in the Caribbean may have been excluded from the census either because they were not aware of their legal obligations or because they chose not to be included. Many migrants joined the existing households of family or friends on arrival and moved about especially in the early stages of becoming settled. A person interviewed for Radica Sewchararn's (1986, p.3; Byron, 1994) small study of Leicester's black elders said:

> It was a big house, all the rooms had different people, you don't even know who is living there and who don't.

The accurate recording of all occupants may be more difficult in multi-occupied houses with a changing composition. In addition, people may have had good reason to avoid being included. Although legally entitled to enter the UK there were considerable efforts made by the state, through a variety of agencies to dissuade people from coming. Hill (1963, p.82 and pp.81-85) wrote of:

> The widespread fear in the immigrant community of giving any information to the authorities. This is particularly so when such information may lead to an enquiry into their housing conditions and other allied matters. There can be no doubt that the same fears and misunderstandings were acute amongst the migrants when the 1961 population census was taken.

The discussion which took place in the Cabinet on the arrival of the Windrush has already been noted. Passengers on the Windrush listened to the radio as they approached Southampton and were aware of feelings in Britain (*Forty Winters On: Memoirs of Britain's Post War Caribbean Migrants*, p.8).

The MSD also recorded the individual West Indian territories from which the migrants came. While this gives an indication of island of origin, it is not an accurate measure as this was a record of the start of a journey. Elizabeth Thomas-Hope (1977, pp.42-51) has shown how inter-island movements in the British West Indian territories were common during the war and that return and second phase movement of people in the Caribbean was common after 1945.[21] Davison (1962, p.6) reports that a ship from Antigua with seventy passengers contained only twenty eight native Antiguans.

Table 2.8   **Emigration to the UK from the West Indian Federation 1958-1960**

	1958	1959	1960	%
Antigua	422	353	741	2
Barbados	1147	1514	4340	8
Dominica	577	1116	1946	4
Grenada	680	594	1809	4
Jamaica	10137	12573	31447	66
Montserrat	323	455	620	2
St Kitts/Nevis Anguilla	928	779	1508	4
St Lucia	541	970	1308	3
St Vincent	304	310	838	2
Trinidad & Tobago	939	937	1892	5
Totals	15998	19637	46449	100

Source: Davison (1962, p.7)

Caribbean migrants may well have been wary or even fearful of responding to questions emanating from official sources. The widespread operation of the colour bar in jobs and housing, racist abuse and attack would have added to insecurity as residents of the UK. In addition, some West Indians may have had problems filling in forms.[22]

If the census is unreliable, what other evidence exists on the size of the African Caribbean community in Leicester as it has changed over time since 1945? Personal perceptions are unreliable and indeed interviewees for this study varied in their estimates of numbers of Caribbean born people in the city in the early 1950s, from around twenty to 200. One person said that black people were so few in 1950 that if you saw another black face in the town you stopped and talked.[23]   Other estimates have also varied widely. The Institute of Race Relations estimated that the 1960 population was 400,[24] whereas a *Leicester Mercury* editorial of 1963 typically reported the local African Caribbean population to be 10,000.[25]   A police estimate for 1961 was 4,000.[26]

If evidence on the number of black people in Leicester up to 1962 has been hard to find, so too is information on other characteristics of West Indian settlers in Leicester. The composition of the population in terms of islands of origin, age and sex is difficult to establish. As has already been noted, 60% of migrants to the UK are Jamaican. Information about island of origin is important for the debate about the causes of migration, particularly for those seeking to examine a variety of push factors such as population density and growth and economic conditions. It has also been important in charting the development of communities in Britain, where patterns of chain migration have led to particular towns and cities in Britain having clusters of people from particular islands. However it can be seen that official and other documentary evidence is sparse concerning island of origin and much of our knowledge comes from oral evidence provided by settlers in Britain and their descendants.

Island differences have been important to West Indians. Not only are the islands spread over a large geographical area but there are important differences in history, social structure and culture between islands (Peach, 1965, p.33). People born on the smaller islands of the region have resented being assumed to be Jamaican when they came to Britain. While some early pioneers of the Leicester community did come from Jamaica, there were also people from other islands from the early 1950s. In Leicester as elsewhere, family and friends followed in a classic 'chain migration' pattern. A number of small surveys have confirmed that the single largest group of Leicester African Caribbean residents in terms of island of origin is Antigua and the second largest is Jamaica.

Table 2.9   **Island of Origin of Leicester's Caribbean Migrants (Leicestershire County Council)**

	%
Antigua	32.1
Jamaica	27.5
Nevis	9.2
St Kitts	5.5
Barbados	8.3
Montserrat	5.5
Dominica	3.7
St Vincent	2.8
Grenada	1.8
Trinidad & Tobago	.9
St Lucia	.9
Other	1.8

Source: Black Elders in Leicester (p.9)

Table 2.10   Island of Origin of Leicester's Caribbean Migrants (Pearson)

	%
Antigua	25
Jamaica	19
Barbados	14
Nevis	10
St Kitts	7
Montserrat	7
Barbuda	6

Source: Pearson (1981, p.38)[27]

In a detailed study of Nevisians in Leicester, Margaret Byron (1994, p.146) has charted the development of the community from the first arrival who,

> found a bed in a boarding house off Westcotes Drive in Westcotes ward. He was directed to this location by a member of staff at the railway station. Within two months he moved to a boarding house in the inner city ward of Wycliffe. As most of the 1955 arrivals depended on John to receive them his Wycliffe ward location of 4-6 Evington Road became a focal point for Nevisians during their very early months in the city.

Byron (1994, p.149) showed the migration network of Leicester Nevisians in the following way:

> The significance of the island/village/kinship based network in the accommodation search for the arriving Nevisians cannot be over emphasised. The network diagram reveals that few Nevisian migrants to Leicester were not recruited by a relation or a friend in the city. The person who received the new arrival   for initial access in the room he/she then occupied door in another room, rented in advance for the expected arrival.   One man described the occasion when he   moved to better quality lodgings but   rented his former room by paying full rent for it for a close friend who was due to arrive from Nevis within two months.   The considerable expenses incurred due to the uncertainty about his friend's arrival date was dismissed as 'what anyone should do for their people...'   This attitude was widespread and it played a part in sustaining Nevisians during their early months in Britain.

This remarkable pattern of assistance was nearly always informal and uncoordinated. There was, however, at least some more formally organised help which cut across island communities in the form of the Anglo-Overseas League. This was set up by the Anglo-Overseas Association in the 1950s. The League helped migrants with problems of all kinds but particularly accommodation. Unfortunately, little is known about the organisation.[28]

The Role of Government

Recent scholarship has led to a revision of understanding of the role of government policy in matters of emigration and immigration in the post war period. While the period before the 1962 Act had been regarded as one of 'laissez-faire' in terms of government policy, there has been increasing recognition of the racialised nature of attempts by the British government to manage population matters. Ian Spencer (1997), building on the work of Carter and others (Carter, Harris and Joshi, 1993, pp.55-71; Carter, Green and Halpern, 1996, pp.135-157; Kushner and Lunn, 1990; Joshi and Carter, 1984, pp.69-70), has now established that the British Government adopted a consistent policy of attempting to keep black and Asian migrants out of Britain. This was achieved in the century before the 1962 Immigration Act through administrative measures, but the failure of this obstruction to prevent black and Asian immigration in the seventeen years from 1945 led, after a decade of Cabinet discussion, to the passing of the 1962 Act. Government documents now show that legislation was discussed on various occasions through the 1950s. It was largely the economic and political links with the Colonies and Commonwealth countries which prevented the Government from acting sooner. While Spencer clearly establishes the policy with respect to keeping out blacks and Asians, it is Kathleen Paul who has shown the other side of British policy. She shows how 'keeping out blacks' was complimented by a policy of encouraging both white emigration into Britain and white emigration to other parts of the Colonies and Commonwealth in order to entrench British interests in the world. Kathleen Paul (1995, p.249) has written:

> Members of both Labour and Tory political elites subscribed to a racialised understanding of the Empire's population.

Government policy was somewhat contradictory, reflecting a range of pressures. According to Paul the appointment of the Coalition Government's Royal Commission on Population in 1944 was due to 'popular and widespread fears that the 'British Race' was declining (Paul, 1995, p.255). The Commission reported in 1947 and confirmed that the population was reproducing itself at 6% below replacement level and the Commission concluded that:

> the need to increase the working population is not temporary; it is a permanent feature of our national life (Paul, 1995, p.256).

However these pressures which would have encouraged policies fostering immigration were countered by the perceived necessity to maintain the British Empire and its racialised characteristics. Attlee, as war time Dominion Secretary, argued in October 1942, the need for:

> larger populations in the dominions if the British Empire is to exercise a strong influence in the post war world (Paul, 1995, p.255).

The need to strengthen the Dominions by encouraging white British people to settle in them was, argued Paul, accepted by the post war Labour government which supported imperial migration. A variety of schemes were established including the Southern Rhodesia, the state sponsored 'British Stock' immigration to South Africa and the Free and Assisted Passage Schemes for 'British Stock' veterans and civilians to New Zealand. A 1950 Cabinet memo prepared by the Minister of Labour and Commonwealth Office argued that:

> not to encourage emigration and thereby to permit the percentage of 'British Stock' population in the Dominions to diminish, could affect Britain's 'future strength, influence and safety in ways that cannot be forecast' (Paul, 1995, p.263).

It is interesting that little academic attention has been addressed to the reasons for British emigration during the post war period.

Concern about the loss of labour to the British economy was expressed within government but not publicly. The extent of the racialisation of matters of immigration and emigration can be seen in the policy of recruiting European aliens into Britain to staff essential industries in preference to black labour from British colonies. British white workers lost by emigration to the British Dominions were replaced by foreigners displaced in Europe by the war. In addition, agreements were made with governments in the Dominions that white Europeans would be eligible for emigration to the Dominions whereas black and Asian former servicemen would not. Paul (1995) reports that debates in the House of Commons show a belief in the ability of Britain to turn European aliens into British subjects whereas black and Asian migrants might threaten the 'racial character' of the Dominions.

While Paul's work is the most thorough exploration of the extent of racialisation of British Government policy, in relation to emigration as well as immigration in the immediate post war period, others have also pointed to the racialised nature of British policy. David Cesarani (1992, pp.83-133), for example, has shown how former Balt and Ukranian members of the Nazi SS were favoured as immigrants to Britain over the Jewish victims of Nazism.[29] The contradictory and racialised nature of policy with regard to immigration and emigration has increasingly been recognised with respect to the immigration of Caribbeans.

Evidence of the attitude of the British government towards Caribbean migrants is provided in various memoranda to cabinets in the late 1940s and 1950s. For example a memorandum by Creech Jones, Secretary of State for the Colonies to the Cabinet concerning the arrival of the Empire Windrush makes clear that the passengers were unwelcome:

> every possible step has been taken by the Colonial Office and the Jamaican Government to discourage these influxes.

The memorandum goes on to describe 'possibilities of employment overseas':

> The doors of Cuba and Panama are now closed and employment in the United States of America is very restricted. These men[30] want work in England. We shall try to open out possibilities in British Guiana and British Honduras. There have been psychological difficulties about employment in Africa and I am informed that it is doubtful if the men have the skills that are wanted there from time to time. But that problem will be explored further though my present enquiries are not encouraging.[31]

In a memorandum on 'Coloured People from the British Colonial Territories', written by Mr Griffiths, on 18 May 1950, West Indians brought to Britain for war service were discussed. All were eligible for repatriation but:

though persistent efforts were made to induce as many of them as possible to return home a good many preferred to remain in this country.

The document goes on to describe action taken so far:

Colonial governments have made it their practice to warn potential migrants of conditions in the UK and to refuse passports in proper cases. My predecessor sent a despatch to the governors of the Colonies suggesting ways and means of preventing stowing away in colonial ports.[32]

Attempts would be made to exclude 'national status' from British travel certificates so that immigration officers in the UK would no longer be obliged to admit people carrying such certificates. On 19 September 1949, the Home Office had issued revised instructions to immigration officers so that they could refuse leave to land to persons unable to prove their status as British Subjects or protected persons. This document also discussed ways of extending repatriation from the 'destitute or incapacitated' and to include colonial seamen employed by ship owners from colonial ports.[33]

Black people were not welcomed by the British Government, but the labour shortage produced great pressure to accept them as workers. The government discussed ways of excluding black immigrants throughout the 1950s (Spencer, 1997, p.50), but nevertheless they were encouraged by some government departments and welcomed by many employers. Jim Prior (1986, p.52) in his memoirs recalled how colleagues were annoyed over Enoch Powell's 'rivers of blood' speech made in April 1968 because:

They remembered all too clearly how as Minister of Health he had stubbornly refused to improve a two and a half per cent pay increase for nurses in 1962. Selwyn Lloyd, the Chancellor, and John Hare as Minister of Labour were begging him to make a better offer. But I was told that he had been adamant that, if nurses didn't wish to accept his pay award, he could recruit plenty of women from the West Indies and other places; so much for immigration policy.

The 1962 Immigration Act was clearly intended to limit black and Asian immigration while allowing white people from the colonies and the Commonwealth to enter for settlement. Potential migrants were required to have a job voucher before entry. There were three kinds of vouchers. The first were for those who had a job arranged. The second were for those who possessed special skills or skills which were in short supply. The third were for all others. The Act excluded from its provisions those who were born in the UK or who held UK passports issued by the British Government. This was intended to protect white people. Ian Spencer has argued that the Act was significant in influencing the subsequent composition of the black and Asian population of Great Britain. First the threat of entry produced a 'beat the ban' rush in the two years before the Act came into force. Second it encouraged those who had intended to stay only three to five years to settle more permanently in order to secure future choices. Third, the Act allowed for family reunion, a factor more important in Asian than Caribbean migration. Fourth it controlled, but nevertheless allowed, black and Asian migration (Spencer, 1997, pp.129-134).

In 1965 the Government ended the third category of immigration altogether and reduced the numbers of 'A' and 'B' vouchers; those with a job to go to or who had special skills. Other changes further restricted the entry of dependants (Spencer, 1997, p.135). The immigration Acts of 1968 and 1971 can be seen to have formalised a policy that had been racialised since the turn of the century and earlier.[34] The formalisation of the racialisation of policy in relation to black and Asian immigration through legislation which began in 1962 coincided with a new initiative in relation to the immigration of white people. The first application by Britain to join the EEC was made in August 1961 (Spencer, 1995, p.127) and Britain joined on 1 January 1973, the same day that the 1971 Immigration Act came into force (Spencer, 1995, p.144). This enabled any member of an EEC country, a group of people who were nearly all white, to enter and settle in Britain.

The development of the composition of the population of the City of Leicester between 1945 and 1981 can be seen to reflect government policies on immigration through the period. There were 285,000 people living in Leicester in 1951.[35] By 1981 the number had fallen to 276,000.[36] Leicester was described as one of several cities where outward movement has been 'noticeably large' (Britain: An Official Handbook, undated).

Migrants from the West Indies, wanted by employers for their labour, but regarded as a problem and rejected by racialised policies, joined Polish, Ukrainian and Italian people who came to Leicester as a result of the Second World War.[37] The number of aliens living in Leicester rose steadily from about 1,000 at the end of the war to around 3,000 in 1954.[38] The largest single group, about one third, were of Polish origin but there were also people from twelve other European states.[39] The numbers of aliens continued to rise to about 4,000 until 1961 when the counts were no longer made in the same way. These white immigrants received no attention in the press or in public debate at all. The different ethnicities of white people have not been considered worthy of much attention. These immigrant groups joined older Irish and Jewish communities. Indeed Leicester's prosperity had meant that it had long been an attraction to migrants. People from the north of England had moved to Leicester in the 1930s (Pritchard, 1976, p.78). While Asians also came to Leicester from 1945 onwards, they were initially fewer in number than those from the Caribbean. At the end of the 1950s the African Caribbean population was estimated to be twice as big as that of Asians. However, in the late 1960s, Asians from Kenya came to Leicester and this, in turn, produced a chain of migration which led to Leicester being a favoured destination for Asians expelled from Uganda in 1972. By the end of the 1960s the Asian community was four times as big as the Caribbean population and at the end of the 1970s, it was six times as big, creating Leicester's 'East African' connection. The first survey of the composition of the population of the City of Leicester was not carried out until 1983. By this time the population of Leicester had come to be seen as divided into three groups now referred to as ethnic groups; white, Asian and black. This superseded the binary division of white and 'immigrant'. This was in part a response to the acknowledgement of the increasing proportion of black and Asian people born in Britain. Immigrant was clearly wrong as a description for them. Now new identities based on ethnicity prevailed, but the salience of racialisation continued.

Table 2.11   Place of Birth of Leicester Residents 1983

Place Of Birth	Number	%	Total From 1981 Census	
			Number	%
England, Scotland, Wales	226600	79.2	222388	80.5
Northern Ireland	1600	0.6	1299	0.5
Irish Republic	3000	1.0	3886	1.4
Other European Country	3023	1.1	3582	1.3
West Indies/Guyana	2530	0.9	2551	0.9
India	20706	7.2	18235	6.6
Pakistan	1086	0.4	911	0.4
Bangladesh	616	0.2	394	0.1
Kenya	9810	3.4	8052	2.9
Uganda	6678	2.3	5604	2.0
Malawi	2649	0.9	2323	0.8
Tanzania	2730	1.0	2224	0.8
Zambia	610	0.2	419	0.2
Other Africa	860	0.3	463	0.2
Other	3283	1.2	3914	1.4
Not Stated	239	0.1		
TOTAL	286020	100	276245	100

Source: Survey of Leicester, Leicester City Council[40]

The racialised nature of divisions between people is significant in this survey. 'Other European country' includes white migrants to Leicester. In the same survey a larger number of people described as 'West Indian' who were born in Leicester than the number of 'West Indians' whose birth place was in the Caribbean.

Table 2.12   Ethnic Origin by Place of Birth of Leicester Residents

Place of Birth	Ethnic Origin									
	White		Asian		West Indian		Other		Total	
	Nos	%	Nos	%	Nos	%	Nos	%	Nos	%
England, Scotland & Wales	204345	95.3	17901	28.3	2610	51.4	1744	51.4	226600	79.2
Northern Ireland	1462	0.7	138	0.2					1600	0.6
TOTAL	205807	96.0	18039	28.5	2610	51.4	1744	51.4	228200	79.8
Irish Republic	2912	1.4	25		13	0.3	50	1.5	3000	1.0
Other European Country	2805	1.3	31		19	0.3	168	4.9	3023	1.1
TOTAL	3717	2.7	56	0.1	32	0.6	218	6.4	6023	2.1
West Indies, Guyana	113	0.1	132	0.2	2253	44.3	32	0.9	2530	0.9
India	389	0.2	20166	31.9			151	4.5	20706	7.2
Pakistan	44		1023	1.6			18	0.5	1086	0.4
Bangladesh			603	1.0			13	0.4	616	0.2
TOTAL	433	0.2	21.792	34.5			182	5.4	22414	7.8
Kenya	176	0.1	9509	15.0			125	3.7	9810	3.4
Uganda	25		6622	10.5			31	0.9	6678	2.3
Malawi	50		2567	4.1	13	0.3	19	0.6	2649	0.9
Tanzania	25		2705	4.3					2730	1.0
Zambia	19		559	0.9	19	0.3	13	0.4	610	0.2
TOTAL	295	0.1	21962	34.8	32	0.6	188	5.5	22477	7.8
Other Africa	132	0.1	527	0.8	44	0.9	157	4.6	860	0.3
Other	1820	0.8	490	0.8	113	2.2	860	25.4	3283	1.2
TOTAL	1952	0.9	1017	1.6	157	3.1	1017	30.0	4143	1.5
Not Stated	38		188	0.3			12	0.4	239	0.1
TOTAL	214355	100	63186	100	5084	100	3395	100	286020	100

Source: Survey of Leicester, Leicester City Council[41]

Conclusion

It is not possible to provide comprehensive reasons for the development of an African Caribbean community in Leicester since 1945. However, a likely contributory factor was a shortage of workers, including those in occupations which have traditionally employed women. Marett (1989, p.31) suggests that opportunities for women were influential in drawing people form other towns and cities such as Coventry and Birmingham. White people were moving out of the city centre creating vacancies in accommodation: cheap housing was available. Other possible factors include Leicester's geographical location in the centre of England and good communications with other towns and cities. The small number of former servicemen who had been stationed in the area during the war may have led the migration movement. This group included Jamaicans and Antiguans and was probably responsible for these islands providing the majority of Leicester Caribbean settlers.

Finally the composition of the population of Leicester, a medium sized Midlands city, can be seen as a reflection of contradictory government policies. Government policy is not just significant for the racialised nature of decisions about who or who should not enter the country. The desire to discourage black and Asian immigration in the 1950s while promoting Britain's influence by fostering both emigration and immigration of white people was also reflected in policies towards black and Asian people who had arrived. No provision was made to help settle immigrants, to facilitate housing, employment and later, the integration of black and Asian children into schools. This is despite the fact that the government was monitoring the 'coloured population' of Britain from the Second World War. No attempt was made to counter the prejudices and ignorance of the local population. Indeed it is clear that government policy, in part, reflected those same prejudices that were held by members of the government as individuals. The public discourse on immigration involved a racialised perspective which the government at national and local level largely ignored. It is the nature of the public debate as it took place in the Leicester Local press through the 1950s which is the subject of Chapter Three.

Notes

1   The validity of this distinction may be questionable in some cases. The European Economic Community (EEC) has introduced progressively

greater restrictions on immigration into the EEC from peoples outside it. One mechanism which governments have used to restrict entry is to define 'refugee' ever more narrowly. As part of the ideological battle over immigration, refugees are seen as legitimate and 'economic migrants' are not. This division of migrants into 'goodies' and 'baddies' is a characterisation somewhat analogous to the distinction made between the 'deserving' and 'undeserving' poor. The Ugandan Asians who arrived in Britain in 1972 were refugees but are usually described as part of the post war migration of people of Indian origin to Britain.

2   Panayi names the three others as: (Cunningham, 1969), (Walvin, 1984); (Holmes, 1988). See also (Potts, 1990).

3   1946 *Report on Jamaica*, Colonial Office, HMSO, London 1947.

4   Barbados was the only island where such an arrangement existed.

5   CAB/129/28 CP 948 154, 18 6 1948 'Arrival in the United Kingdom of Jamaican Unemployed': Cabinet Memorandum by Mr Creech Jones, cited in Ronald Hyam (ed), *The Labour Government and the End of Empire 1945-1951*, HMSO, London 1992, page 27.

6   See Chapter Four for some examples of this.

7   The administrative procedures used to obstruct immigration into Britain in the years before the 1962 act are discussed in Moore and Wallace (1975), (Spencer, 1997).

8   Similar feelings were expressed by interviewees in this study. See Chapter Eight.

9   'Racism or Reaction, A History of Immigration', extracts from BBC Timewatch, in *A History of Racism*, (Video) Association for Curriculum Development, 1986.

10   Between 1541 and the mid nineteenth century there were sixty one taverns called the Black Boy recorded in London and many more in the Provinces. They suggest the presence of black slave boys (Fryer, 1984).

11   CAB 129/40 CP (50) 113 18th May 1950 'Coloured Peoples from British Colonial Territories', Cabinet Memorandum by Mr Griffiths, cited in Hyam, (1992), p.29.

12   Interview with C E B Robinson, 6 February 1995.

13   *Illustrated Leicester Chronicle*, 5 March 1955. Nothing is known about this scheme.

14   Eldridge, J, 'Race Relations in Leicester University', MA Thesis, University of Leicester, Department of Sociology, 1959, page 22. There were forty-eight students from these continents from a total of 918 in 1958.

15   CAB 128/17 CM 37 (50) 19 June 1950, 'Coloured People from British Colonial Territories: Cabinet Conclusions', cited in Hyam, op cit, page

34. The stowaways were West African.

16   Harris and James (1993, p.4) criticise the Marxist industrial reserve army thesis and Peach for ignoring ideological considerations such as race in the way that the labour market operates. This can be seen to parallel the feminist critiques for the way in which the labour market is structured by considerations of gender.

17   CAB 129/28 40 CP (50) 113, 'Coloured people from British colonial Territories': Cabinet Memorandum by Mr Griffiths, Hyam, op cit, page 31.

18   CAB 129/28 40 CP (50) Hyam, op cit, page 31.

19   1951 Census, Leicester and Leicestershire, Table 20, page 46.

20   1961 Census, Leicester and Leicestershire, Table 10, page 15.

21   Thomas Hope, (1977) pages 42-51. Respondents interviewed for this study told of periods of work in various Caribbean islands including a woman born in Jamaica who had worked for seven years in Trinidad prior to coming to Leicester. There was also confirmation that people embarked from places which were not their homes.

22   Interview with C E B Robinson, 6 February 1995.

23   Interview with Eric Hudson, 28 April 1994.

24   Quoted in 'General Survey of West Indian Children in the Primary Schools of Leicester', C E B Robinson, Dip. Ed. Special Study, University of Leicester 1964.

25   *Leicester Mercury*, 5 July 1963.

26   *Illustrated Leicester Chronicle*, 24 August 1962.

27   Pearson (1981) surveyed 100 residents and noted that there were also people from St Lucia, St Vincent, Dominica and Trinidad.

28   See Chapter Seven.

29   David Cesarani, *Justice Delayed*, Heinemann, London 1992, pages 83-133.

30   There were also women on the *Windrush*.

31   CAB 129/28 CP (48) 154, 'Arrival in the United Kingdom of Jamaican Unemployed': Cabinet Memorandum by Mr Creech Jones, cited in Hyam, op cit, page 27.

32   CAB 129/40, CP (50), 113, 'Coloured people from Bitish Colonial Territories': Cabinet Memorandum by Mr Griffiths, cited in Hyam, op cit, page 31.

33   Ibid.

34   The first legislation to control immigration was passed in 1905 and was intended to limit the entry of Jewish migrants from eastern Europe. (Spencer, 1997, p.10).

35   The 1951 Census, Leicester and Leicestershire, Table 20 page 46. Numbers to nearest 1,000.

36   The 1981 Census County Report for Leicestershire Part I, Table 10, page 21, numbers to nearest 1000.

37   There was an Italian Prisoner of War camp at Syston, a village to the north-west of Leicester during the Second World War.

38   LRO, L352.2, Chief Constable's Annual Reports 1945-1954.

39   LRO L352.2, Chief Constable's Annual Report 1954.

40   *Survey of Leicester*, Leicester City Council, 1983, Table 2.

41   Ibid, Table 3.

References

Akgunduz, Ahmet, 'Labour Migration from Turkey to Western Europe (1960-74)', *Capital and Class*, Vol 51.

Baines, Dudley (1985), *Migration in a Mature Economy: Emigration and Internal Migration in England and Wales, 1861-1900*, Cambridge University Press, Cambridge.

Banton, Michael (1952), 'The Economic and Social Position of Negro Immigrants in Britain', *Sociological Review*, New Series, 1,2.

Banton, Michael (1955), *The Coloured Quarter: Negro Immigrants in an English City*, Jonathan Cape, London.

Bousquet, Ben, and Douglas, Colin (1991), *West Indian Women at War: Racism in World War II*, Lawrence and Wishart, London.

Britain: An Official Handbook, Central Office of Information, undated.

Brown, Colin (1984), *White and Black in Britain*, Policy Studies Institute, London.

Bruegel, Irene, 'Sex and Race in the Labour Market', in Mary Evans, op cit.

Bryan, Beverly; Dadzie, Stella and Scafe, Suzanne (1985), *The Heart of the Race: Black Women's Lives in Britain*, Virago, London.

Bush, Julia (August 1993), 'Moving On and Looking Back', *History Workshop*, 36.

Byron, Margaret, *The Housing Question: Caribbean Migration and the British Housing Market*, Research Paper 49, School of Geography, University of Oxford, Oxford undated.

Byron, M (1994), *Post-War Caribbean Migration to Britain: The Unfinished Cycle*, Avebury, Aldershot.

Carter, Bob; Green, Marie and Halpern, Rich (1996), 'Immigration Policy and the Racialisation of Migrant Labour: The Construction of National Identities in the USA and Britain', *Ethnic and Racial Studies*, Vol 19, No 1.

Carter, Bob; Harris, Clive and Joshi, Shirley (1993), 'The Conservative Government and the Racialisation of Black Immigration', in James and Harris.

Castles, Steven and Kosack, Godula (1973), *Immigrant Workers and the Class Structure in Western Europe*, Oxford University Press, London.

Cesarani, David (1992), *Justice Delayed*, Heinemann, London.

Chamberlain, Mary (1994), 'Family and Identity: Barbadian Migration to Britain', *International Yearbook of Oral History and Life Stories*, Vol 3, Oxford University Press, Oxford.

Cunningham, W (1969), *Alien Immigrants to England*, (2nd ed), Frank Cass, London.

Davison, R B (1961), 'West Indian Migration to Britain 1952-62', *The West Indian Economist*, Vol 4, No1.

Davison, R B (1962), *West Indian Migration: Social and Economic Facts of Migration From the West Indies*, Oxford University Press, Oxford.

Duffield, Mark (1988), *Black Radicalism and the Politics of De-industrialisation - The Hidden History of Indian Foundry Workers*, Avebury, Aldershot.

First Interim Report: Caribbean People in Leicestershire, Afrikan Caribbean Support Group Research Project, Centre for Public Order, University of Leicester, January 1993.

Fitzpatrick, D (1980-81), 'Irish Emigration in the Later Nineteenth Century', *Irish Historical Studies*, Vol 22.

Foner, Nancy (1979), *Jamaica Farewell: Jamaican Migrants in London*, Routledge and Kegan Paul, London.

Forty Winters On: Memories of Britain's Post War Caribbean Migrants, (1988) South London Press, London.

Fryer, Peter (1984), *Staying Power, The History of Black People in Britain*, Humanities Press, Atlantic Highlands.

Glass, Ruth (1960), *Newcomers*, Allen and Unwin, London.

Harris, Clive (1993), 'Post-War Migration and the Industrial Reserve Army', in Winston James and Clive Harris (eds), *Inside Babylon: The Caribbean Diaspora in Britain*, Verso, London.

Harris, N (1995), *The New Untouchables*, Penguin, London.

Hill, Clifford S (1963), *West Indies Migrants and the London Churches*, Institute of Race Relations, Oxford University Press, London.

Holmes, C (1988), *John Bull's Island: Immigration and British Society, 1871-1971*, Macmillan, Basingstoke.

Holt, Thomas C (1992), *The Problem of Freedom*, Johns Hopkins University Press, Baltimore.

James, Winston and Harris, Clive (eds), *Inside Babylon: The Caribbean Diaspora in Britain*, Verso, London.

Joshi, S and Carter, B (1984), 'The Role Of Labour In The Creation Of A Racist Britain', *Race and Class*, Vol 15, No 3.

Lawrence, Daniel (1974), *Black Migrants: White Natives*, Cambridge University Press, London.

Leicestershire County Council Social Services Department, *Black Elders in Leicester*, November 1986.

Little, Kenneth (1947), *Negroes in Britain*, Kegan Paul, London.

Lunn, Kenneth (1990), 'The British State and Immigration, 1945-51: New Light on the Empire Windrush', in Tony Kushner and Kenneth Lunn (eds), *The Politics of Marginality*, Frank Cass, London.

Marett, Valerie (1989), *Immigrants Settling in the City*, Leicester University Press, London.

Moore, Robert and Wallace, Tina (1975), *Slamming the Door: The Administration of Immigration Control*, Martin Robertson, London.

Morokvasic, Mirjana (1983), 'Women in Migration: Beyond the Reductionist Outlook', in A Phizacklea (ed), *One Way Ticket: Migration and Female Labour*, Routledge and Kegan Paul, London.

Panayi, P (1994), *Immigration, Ethnicity and Racism in Britain 1815-1945*, Manchester University Press, Manchester.

Patterson, S (1963), *Dark Strangers*, Tavistock Publications, London.

Patterson, Sheila (1969), *Immigration and Race Relations in Britain, 1960-67*, Oxford University Press, London.

Paul, Kathleen (1995), 'British Subjects and British Stock: Labour's Post-War Imperialism', *Journal of British Studies*, Vol 34, No 2.

Peach, Ceri (1965), 'West Indian Migration to Britain: The Economic Factors', *Race*, Vol 7.

Peach, Ceri (1966), 'Factors Affecting the Distribution of West Indians in Great Britain', *Transactions of the Institute of British Geographers*, Vol 38.

Peach, C (1968), *West Indian Migration to Britain: A Social Geography*, Oxford University Press, London.

Peach, Ceri (1991), *The Caribbean in Europe: Contrasting Patterns of Migration and Settlement in Britain, France and the Netherlands*, Paper in Ethnic Relations, Number 15, Centre for Research in Ethnic Relations, University of Warwick.

Pearson, David (1981), *Race, Class and Political Activism: A Study of West Indians in Britain*, Gower, Aldershot.

Philpott, S (1973), *West Indian Migration: The Montserrat Case*, University of London, Athlone Press, London.

Phizacklea, Annie (1982), 'Migrant Women and Wage Labour: The Case of West Indian Women in Britain', in Jackie West (ed), *Work, Women and the Labour Market*, Routledge and Kegan Paul, London.

Potts, L. (1990), *The World Labour Market, A History of Migration*, Zed books, London.

Prior, Jim (1986), *A Balance of Power*, Hamish Hamilton, London.

Pritchard, R M (1976), *Housing and the Spatial Structure of the City*, Cambridge University Press, London.

Pryce, Ken (1979), *Bristol Endless Pressure: A Study of West Indian Life-styles in*

Bristol, Classical Press, Bristol.

Ravenstein, E G (1885), 'The Laws of Migration', *Journal of the Royal Statistical Society*, Vol 48, June 1885.

Roberts, G W and Mills, D O (1958), 'Study of External Migration Affecting Jamaica 1953-55', *Social and Economic Studies*, Vol 3, No 2.

Rose, E J B et al (1969), *Colour and Citizenship*, Oxford University Press, London.

Sewcharan, Radica (1986), *There's No Place Like Back Home? West Indian Senior Citizens Project*, Leicester.

Shyllon, Folarini (1977), *Black Slaves in Britain*, Oxford University Press, in the Institution of Race Relations, London.

Shyllon, Folarini (1974), *Black People in Britain 1555-1833*, Oxford University Press, London.

Solomos, John (1989), *Race and Racism in Contemporary Britain*, Macmillan, London.

Spencer, Ian R G (1997), *British Immigration Policy since 1939*, Routledge, London.

Thomas-Hope, Elizabeth (1977), 'Population Mobility in the West Indies: The Role of Perceptual and Environmental Differentials', PhD Thesis, University of Oxford.

Townsend, Peter (1979), *Poverty in the United Kingdom*, Penguin, Harmondsworth.

Walby, Sylvia (1986), *Patriarchy at Work*, Polity Press, Cambridge.

Walvin, James (1973), *Black and White, The Negro and English Society 1555-1945*, Allen Lane, Penguin Press.

Walvin, J (1984), *Passage to Britain: Immigration in British History and Politics*, Penguin, Harmondsworth.

Watson, J L (ed) (1977), *Between Two Cultures: Migrants and Minorities in Britain*, Blackwell, Oxford.

West, Jackie (ed), *Work, Women and the Labour Market*, Routledge and Kegan Paul, London.

Wilde, Sir William (1864), *Ireland Past and Present, The Land and the People*, Dublin.

3 Race and Immigration in the Leicester Local Press, 1945-1962

Introduction

When African Caribbeans arrived and settled in Leicester from 1945 onwards no provision was made by national or local government. Both Labour and Conservative governments had contradictory policies. On the one hand successive governments were concerned with trying to find ways of preventing black and Asian people settling here, but on the other, were welcoming their labour to meet widespread shortages. There was some attempt to disperse black and Asian people throughout the country. At local government level the arrival of black people in Leicester was ignored through the 1950s. By the 1960s policy decisions were unavoidable in some areas, for example in education which is discussed in Chapter Six.

This lack of policy, however, did not imply a lack of concern in public debate about the changing nature of British society. This chapter explores the nature of that debate as it took place in the local Leicester press. It is argued in this chapter that this debate illustrates a racialised identity among white people in Leicester. Later chapters show how a racialised consciousness informed policy and practice in areas of public life between 1945 and 1981.

The discussion here is not intended as a comprehensive study of racism in the local press in Leicester during the 1950s. The racist nature of the content of national and local newspapers has been explored by others (Hartmann and Husband, 1974; Husband 1975; Gordon and Rosenberg, 1989; Van Dijk, 1991; Troyna, 1981). Nor is it intended as an engagement with the debate about the relationship between public attitudes, behaviour and media influence (Katz and Lazarsfeld, 1955; Cohen and Young, 1972; Eysenck and Nias, 1980; Morley, 1980; Herbert and Reuss, 1986). It is not argued here that the views expressed in the *Leicester Mercury* and the *Illustrated Leicester Chronicle* are representative in a simplistic way of the views of the people of Leicester, rather as Hartmann (Hartmann and

Husband, 1974, p.128) has written:

> Newspapers make people aware of certain things and suggest the degree of importance that different events and issues have by the amount and prominence of coverage that they give to them.

Regardless of the extent to which the local press helped to form public opinion, it is important as one expression of the views of the time. The papers also give voice to opinion expressed by local people about West Indian migration in articles and letters. These views are organised by the newspapers in an interpretative framework, that is to say that it is possible to identify a consistent construction that the newspapers put on the events they reported. Apart from a racist ideology demonstrated in studies such as those by Hartmann and Husband (1974), Troyna (1981), Van Dijk (1991) and others, national and international events, government policy and the opinion of politicians also contributed to that framework. It is suggested here that certain features of the developing racist discourse in the two papers reflect and illustrate some important concerns of English society about its changing nature and its position in the world in the period after the Second World War and up to the passing of the Immigration Act of 1962.

Local newspapers link local and national events and issues in a particular way. The general concerns of the wider society are expressed through the prism of local events and issues. The focus here is on racialised identities and on views about how the relationship between racialised groups should be organised (Gilroy, 1987). The ideological context within which events and issues were presented helped to construct white identity in relation to black. Responses to West Indian migration to Leicester from 1945 onwards rendered this context more visible. The local papers gave voice to opinions expressed by local white people and others about West Indian migration and about black and white people in articles and letters. These were organised within an interpretative framework which presented a contrasting view of black and white people as mutually exclusive groups with particular characteristics. These identities were forged in relation to each other.

In 1945 there were three local newspapers on sale in Leicester. The most important of these was the daily *Leicester Mercury* founded in 1874 and having a sale in 1945 of approximately 100,000. It was on sale at 4.45pm along with the *Leicester Evening Mail*, which had a much smaller circulation and both papers were targeted at people returning home from work. The third paper was the weekly *Illustrated Leicester Chronicle*. This paper contained more pictorial features of general interest; a 'Picture Post' type publication. It had been started in 1810. In 1945 all three newspapers were controlled by the Hewitt family through their company, News Holdings Ltd. In 1954 ownership passed to Associated Newspaper Ltd. The editors through this period were, of the *Mail*, Ken Clapham, of the *Mercury*, H W Bourne until 1948 when he was followed by E J Fortune who had moved from the *Chronicle*. The editorship of the *Illustrated Leicester Chronicle* then passed to Douglas Goodhead until the paper ceased publication in August 1979.[1]

The *Leicester Mercury* is considered to have a particularly important place in the life of Leicester. Its readership penetration is high compared to other local papers. The circulation of the *Mercury* rose from 100,000 at the beginning of the period to 180,000 in 1963. While during the 1950s it was customary for the greater majority of households in Leicester to take a morning national paper as well as a local evening paper, rising prices led to the proportion doing so falling to 60% by the beginning of the 1960s. This is in line with national trends, although at national levels the decline in newspaper readership was even more marked. The circulation of the *Chronicle* rose over the period from 10,000 in 1945 to around 30,000 in the early 1960s. After that circulation began to fall. The *Leicester Mercury* became even more important as a source of information after 1960 and content was changed to include more national and international news.[2] However the *Mercury* has always contained a mixture of local, national and international news. It has a reputation for introducing local connections, however tenuous, to national and international stories, for parochialism and for its support for the Conservatives. During the 1950s this support was expressed with restraint and moderation in editorials with no overt calls for readers to vote Conservative.[3] For an example, an editorial on 7 October 1959 concerning the General Election of that month, described 'innate British conservatism' and continued:

> Signs are propitious for another conservative return to office. They have not unduly blotted their copy book, have a formidable list of success on the credit side and a Prime Minister who has inhaled the nectar of power and shown that the heady scent made a larger man of him not a lesser.[4]

White Emigrants and Black Immigrants

The first feature of the racist discourse in Leicester local papers to be discussed here is the contrasting way in which stories about migration out of Britain is presented compared to those about black migration into Britain. 'Keeping them out' has been identified as the main issue in relation to black and Asian migration in studies of racism in the press (Hartmann and Husband, 1974, pp.127-28). While migration control for black people was an important theme in the pages of the *Mercury* and the *Chronicle* of the 1950s, attention was also paid to another kind of immigration. Throughout the 1950s there was a great many accounts of white emigrants, usually from Leicester, moving to other parts of the world, particularly the white Dominions of Canada, New Zealand, Australia and to the white dominated Dominion of South Africa. Migration in these stories is treated positively, emphasising the pioneering spirit of brave people seeking a better life. Throughout the decade the *Mercury*, and to a lesser extent, the *Chronicle*, was peppered with these stories. They were often accompanied by photographs of white people, both men and women, with smiling faces. The stories reflect the government policy in encouraging emigration of British whites to the Dominions and colonies which has been raised in Chapter Two.

The first half of the year 1959 can be used to illustrate the way in which these stories appeared regularly in the *Leicester Mercury*. The issue of 17 February 1959 contained a full page of letters from emigrants originally from Leicester, writing home from Australia. They reported how good life was 'down under'.[5] Similar letters follow on 19 February 1959 including one stating 'We will always be English and proud, but we are proud to be immigrants too'.[6] The issue on 19 March 1959 carried a story about emigrants to New Zealand.[7] Alongside these stories were accounts of emigration of local people to African colonies and accounts of visits by local people to exotic climes. On 6 April 1959 a *Mercury* headline read 'Expedition to Pygmy Land' and continued:

> former Wygeston school pupil flies to Africa in June to set up a laboratory in the Belgian Congo. He is to carry out zoological and botanical research in the area where pygmies live.[8]

A report on 10 April 1959 told us of 'Colourful life in the heart of Africa ... Leicester business man to return to Tanganyika'.[9] 1 May 1959 carried a story with the headline 'Emigrants in search of the sun at 70'.[10]

On 26 May 1959 we were told 'Family set out for South Africa with only two or three pounds'.[11] Arriving in a strange country with very little money was seen as a brave and positive act if carried out by white people. 2 June 1959 contained a story of 'Missionaries home from Rhodesia' and continued, 'Leicester couple return after fifty years of missionary work in an area inhabited by primitive tribes'.[12] The issue of 17 June 1959 offers a piece under the headline 'Back in Leicester after 38 years in New Zealand', accompanied by photographs as these items often were.[13] On 20 June 1959 we were told 'Canadian back in Leicester, his old home town'.[14] Although these stories were now often about men than women, a view of white migrants as families often prevailed.

These tales of emigration and homecoming emphasised the links between Leicester whites and Commonwealth whites in other parts of the world. The use of the word immigrant interchangeably with emigrant emphasises an identification with the society (or more accurately the dominant group in that society) to which people were moving: the white Dominions and colonial societies of the former British Empire. Emigrant or immigrant; if you are white it is the same thing; you are one of 'us'.

It has been argued that consciousness of Empire among the British dissolved in Britain after the Second World War and that the immigration of people from the colonies and Commonwealth during the 1950s was seen as separate and unrelated to England's imperial past. For example Stuart Hall (1978, p.25) has argued:

> The development of an indigenous British racism in the post-war period begins with the profound historical forgetfulness - what I want to call the loss of historical memory, a kind of historical amnesia, a decisive mental repression which has overtaken the British people about race and empire since the 1950s.

Errol Lawrence agreed and cited the Social Survey Unit investigation of 1951 which found that 59% of the population could not name a single British colony. However others have argued that this indifference to Imperialism was not confined to the post war period but was a continuous feature of British domestic politics 'apart from a brief aberrant (and indeed disputed) burst of jingoism in the last quarter of the nineteenth century' (Mackenzie, 1984). To agree that knowledge of even basic information about the Empire was lacking among ordinary British people is not to suggest that a consciousness of Britain as an imperial power was not an important feature of British national cultural identity. It is rather that the notion of Britain as an imperial power was represented in particular aspects of British culture. John MacKenzie (1984) has shown the importance of Empire in creating for the British a world view which was central to their perceptions of themselves. This consciousness of Empire seeped into many areas of life and in some of these continued into the 1950s and beyond. In film, in children's literature and of course in school text books and extra curricula activities, tales and ideas of Empire were present. For example, as late as 1950, school text books were asking pupils to 'discuss the importance to the homeland of the colonial territories in Africa' (Mackenzie, 1984). Imperial themes were proclaimed in the packaging of products and in advertisements. MacKenzie argued that these 'Imperial themes' prolonged their shelf life until the 1950s. He concluded that 'the values and beliefs of the imperial world view settled like a sediment in the consciousness of the British people' (Mackenzie, 1984, p.258).

The way in which stories of white emigrants from Leicester were presented in the press formed a small but recognisable aspect of the continuing consciousness of Empire in the minds of British people. This identification of the Dominions as an extension of Britain could be seen most clearly on 27 August 1958 in the headline accompanying a letter prompted by the Notting Dale and Nottingham 'riots'. It read 'Don't let Australia go Foreign'.[15] On 20 January 1960 a report commented on the possibility of a Commonwealth Festival for Leicester:

> Many Leicester people have emigrated to Commonwealth countries and historical records of connections between the city and these countries would make an interesting display.[16]

Whereas whites in these stories were 'us', 'coloured' immigrants who were residents of Leicester were very much 'them'. The comparison with black immigrants arriving in Leicester from the West Indies and also South Asia was never made explicit. Indeed the use of the word immigrant in these two contrasting contexts carries completely different connotations. In one context the word was used positively suggesting bravery, adventure, courage and enterprise, the other negatively associated with problems, disorder, crime, disease and social decay. Indeed the existence of these white emigrant stories alongside the 'keeping them out' theme of black immigration to Britain, with never a reference made to each other, illustrates the depth of British lack of awareness of the importance of a racialised component of what it meant to be British. Yet the message was clear and unequivocal: whites in South Africa, Canada, Australia and New Zealand were seen as part of Britain, as 'ours'. While these stories were usually short, they appeared very regularly throughout the decade and into the 1960s and because they were about real, ordinary people they can be seen as a powerful source of meaning. They bridged the divide between text and reader: these were 'true' stories of readers' relatives, neighbours and friends and other members of the community. White migrants included women as family members whereas black migrants were usually configured, with the exception of nurses as single males.

Black British citizens as 'them' can be illustrated by the writings of Cyril Osborne, Member of Parliament for Louth. Osborne (to become Sir Cyril in 1961) had an important role in the local papers in Leicester. He lived in Rothley, a village in Leicestershire. He was a Leicester Magistrate and Chair of Leicester's Welfare Council, as well as being a member of Leicester's Chamber of Commerce. He was described as a 'Leicester Stockbroker' and had a high profile in the *Mercury* from 1955 onwards. It was during this year that Osborne introduced a private member's bill in the House of Commons seeking to restrict immigration. He was an important figure nationally as an early and prominent campaigner for 'coloured' immigration control (Layton-Henry, 1984; Solomos, 1989; Holmes, 1989; Hiro, 1992; Carter, Harris and Joshi, 1993; Foot, 1965, pp.128-138). Osborne's views on 'coloured' immigration and his racist characterisations of black people could not provide a greater contrast with the benign descriptions of white emigration/immigration as unproblematic adventure stories.

Under the headline 'Stop the Jamaicans demands Cyril Osborne MP' the front page of the *Chronicle* of 8 January 1955 is almost completely occupied by Osborne's views. Extracts from this piece are quoted here.

Last year 10,000 Jamaicans immigrated to this country. This year there will be even more unless it is stopped. I want it stopping. This is a white man's country and I want it to remain so ... If the flood of coloured immigration is not controlled we shall have as bad a colour problem as they have in the United States of America. That to my mind would be a tragedy. Jamaicans are attracted here because to them this is a land flowing with milk and honey. They can live better here without work than they could in their own land doing a full days work. Their island is small, poverty stricken and over populated. Jobs are difficult to get even at their low wages. There are about one and half million of them. Nearly all would like to live here. ... When they come whether they work or not we shall have to keep them. If too many come it will inevitably mean a lowering of the standard of living for British people ... They could be a source of cheap labour. Our Trades Unions would have a big problem - a problem which has plagued the Trades Unions of America and South Africa for many years passed.

But it is not only the Jamaicans we have to fear. Everyone born in the Commonwealth is entitled to come and live in England. As the law stands they are British citizens and cannot be stopped from coming here. If the Jamaican is followed by the West Africans, Maltese, Cypriots and by all our coloured peoples we shall be compelled to put a stop to it.

India for example has a population of about 450 million. Our average income is ten times greater than theirs ... How they would like to get our social service payments. India could loose fifty million people and scarcely miss them. They could swamp us.

No Dumping Ground
In Australia, New Zealand and Canada, all emigrants must have a job to go to and someone responsible for keeping them and they must be prepared to pay their passage back if things prove unsatisfactory ... Why should England be the dumping ground for the Commonwealth?

A West African was recently sentenced to 10 years imprisonment for raping an eighteen year old Norwegian girl. Two of his fellow countrymen in turn assaulted the poor girl... At a London Court another West African was sentenced to prison for living on the earnings of prostitution... The police officer said there were hundreds of thousands of coloured men living on prostitution. DO THESE MEN MERIT A WELCOME HERE?

We Must Act Now!
A short time ago a Jamaican was taken to a London Court for molesting an English maiden lady. She had lived in the same flat since 1914. She lived alone. He came here in 1948 with £2 but has since bought the house she lived in and wanted to compel her to give up part of her flat to a coloured man.[17]

This contrasts quite dramatically with the favourable and sympathetic story of white emigrants to South Africa who arrived with just £2 quoted above.

The country that was 'owned by white men' included the white women who lived here. The danger to white women from black men was a common theme in popular and, at times, academic discourse of the 1950s and 1960s: the ownership of sexual rights to white women, who were often constructed as sexually innocent, were threatened by the presence of black men. White women who did develop personal relationships with black men were presented as having 'loose morals' or even as prostitutes. These themes descend from the time of slavery, and seek allegience of white women to this racist and sexist discourse through fear of violation or reputation. In contrast white migrants, both men and women, were seen as happy family members. Black women were almost invisible.

The issue of 15 January 1955 contained a full page of letters in response to Osborne's piece, one of which supported him and five which opposed.[18] On 29 January 1955 Osborne was again given space for his views at length.[19]

The racist nature of press treatment of immigration in post war Britain and the importance of the issue in British politics in general has been widely discussed. Just one month later the *Chronicle* followed up Osborne's piece with one on 5 February 1955:

Hello West Indies
The *Illustrated Leicester Chronicle* has put the spotlight on Jamaica with the controversy concerning the influx of Jamaicans to this country. Here Sam Hepper tells you about the island they leave to seek a living with us ...

But if in Jamaica man and his work leave much to be desired, nature by contrast is gorgeous and abundant ...

The article goes on to describe 'native women' and continued:

Could you imagine primitive Zulus working as conductors on Leicester Corporation buses? No? Neither could members of the Leicester Parliamentary Debating Society when they were in session at Leicester's Guildhall on Friday ... they were worried about the trickle of Jamaicans now entering Britain might develop into an overwhelming flood of Indians, Burmese and African savages unless restrictions were imposed on colonial immigration.

Nine members turned up to debate the red-hot political problem that is becoming the Midlands number one talking point. Speaker Mr Edwin Bettles 'Prime Minister' put forward the motion 'that coloured immigration should be controlled'.

Mr P J Murphy said 'I realise there is a colour bar in Britain ... and up to a point I support it. It is wrong for us to have to live cheek by jowl with coloured immigrants'. The resolution was carried.[20]

Osborne was also given a chance to state his views on other occasions. The *Leicester Mercury* of 11 October 1958 carried a story with the headline 'Mr Cyril Osborne made the Lions Roar' and continued:

Mr Cyril Osborne, Leicester Stockbroker and MP for Louth was given rough treatment in the 'Lion's Den' last night. Taking part in a BBC TV programme called Lion's Den, held at the West Indian Centre in London ... He was attempting to expound his reasons for wishing to restrict the number of coloured immigrants to this country.

The piece goes on to mention 'Interruption' and that:

He had to shake his finger at the audience ... Mr Osborne said England should have the right to exclude the criminal, the idle and the sick - elements Jamaica already has ... He said he was expressing a personal rather than a party view when he said that he would wish Englishmen to have first chance at jobs in lean times. It was pointed out that the trades unions did not share his view.[21]

Both the *Chronicle* and the *Mercury* endorsed Osborne's views in several ways. First, he was given space to express his views at great length. Second, his views were printed without comment. Editorials were silent on the issue and Osborne's own claims that 'he has no racial hatred or antipathy and no colour bar sympathies at all' were reported by the paper as fact despite the evidence to the contrary provided in Osborne's writing. Third there is no reporting of the contempt with which he was apparently held in public at least by his own colleagues and party leaders in the House of Commons. We now know that views expressed in Cabinet discussions of immigration were closer to Osborne's than was admitted at the time.[22]

On occasions the language used in articles concerning Osborne expressed sympathy for his views. For example he was given 'rough treatment' by his opponents, he was attempting to 'expound his reasons', he is reported as 'explaining his reasons' and he '*had* to shake his finger at the audience' (my emphasis). Osborne was also given credibility by the respect he was accorded as an important member of Leicester's community, by being given a platform for his views at regular intervals and in that the papers carried stories about him on other issues. For example, he appeared in the *Mercury* of 21 April 1959[23] and 7 May 1959, complaining about trains from St Pancras to Leicester being late.[24] On 17 June 1959 he discussed industrial take-overs.[25] By contrast Leicester's own Members of Parliament, Barnet Janner, the Labour MP for Leicester West, John Peel, Conservative for Leicester South East, Sir A Ungoed-Thomas, Labour, Leicester North East and H W Bowden, Labour,

Leicester South-West appeared much less.[26]

Little real alternative to Osborne's argument was put before the public of Leicester. There was no attempt to inform the local community of Britain's role in relation to the land the newcomers were leaving, or to the role of immigrants in meeting labour shortages or in occupying property vacated by the falling indigenous population of the city. Articles, few as they were, which attempted to describe the origin of black migrants contained racist stereotypes and prejudices which did little to counter the ignorance encountered by immigrants about the geography and economics of Britain's former empire and the cultures of immigrant peoples. One exception was the one piece written by Rupert Fevier, a qualified chemist who came to Leicester from Jamaica in 1953. Under the headline 'West Indian answers Mr Osborne' he wrote:

> Contrary to Mr Cyril Osborne's land flowing with milk and honey all Jamaicans know too well that the UK is a poor country compared to the USA ... but West Indians have little chance of emigration to the USA.

> The British public should be enlightened about the state of affairs that compels West Indians to save their last penny, sell their belongings, borrow from family and pawn their jewellery to pay the expensive fare to come to England ... and shiver in the cold winter. It is possible for a coloured man to get a higher education in the West Indies usually through self sacrifice of his parents. The key jobs are held by Europeans and they continually bring replacements from Europe.

> Many of the West Indians coming to Britain are doctors, lawyers, teachers and other college educated men whose ambitions are continually frustrated in their own land. If our land could give us a life worth living we would gladly go back.[27]

However, opposition to the racist discourse led by Osborne and followed by others was generally confined to letters. The power of the arguments expressed in such correspondence was weak in comparison to those of the racists in that no prominent national or local politician provided a focus and lead comparable to that of Osborne. Arguments used were vague and general. They were based on moral principles of love for each other with appeals to good nature and human kindness, and lacked any discussion of historical or material circumstances. For example, in the *Mercury* of 27 February 1955 a reader wrote 'Why all this controversy about the colour bar? Did not Christ die for the black and white?'[28] or on

20 March 1959 another letter stated 'Why all this hullabaloo about West Indians? There is good and bad in all'.[29] Again on 14 May 1959 a headline read 'Black skin or white it's just a matter of where you're born'[30] and again 15 May 1959 'A Negroe's plea: Why can't we be brothers?'[31] On 19 January 1960 the *Mercury* carried a letter stating 'My best friend is smashing and she's black'.[32]

Crime

The second feature of the discourse of the Leicester local press discussed is the way that crime was handled. Crime was the largest single category of race reporting in the *Leicester Mercury* according to a study by Barry Troyna (1981) carried out between 1976 and 1978. Crime has always been important in the provincial press and the *Leicester Mercury* provided no exception to this. The *Chronicle* carried little crime reporting as it concentrated on issues behind the news rather than routine local day to day events.

There are several noteworthy features of crime reporting in the *Leicester Mercury* during the 1950s. First the use of adjectival racism is universal. There was no crime report in the newspapers studied, concerning a person who was identifiably black where their race was not made significant. In these reports white people were not identified as such, but rather defined in other ways.[33] Occupation is one such way. For example 'Coloured man is gaoled for biting policeman'.[34] Gender was another. 'Girl says Negro held her captive'.[35] Relationships too define white people as in 'Husband who attacked coloured man is freed'.[36] Interestingly while sometimes race was used alongside another descriptive form of identification for black people, for example 'Two coloured busmen are sent for trial'[37] or 'Coloured bus conductor is allowed bail',[38] more commonly race was the sole adjective defining black people. The use of adjectival racism in this way not only emphasises the race of black people above all else, but by not acknowledging the ordinary roles they may have in life, hinders the recognition of commonalties between black and white people: black people have jobs and families too.

Secondly whereas nationality is used to distinguish different groups of white people, black people are often referred to as 'Negroes' or more commonly 'coloured' regardless of nationality.[39] For example 'Coloured men and girls in raided house'.[40] The coloured men in this story were

United States servicemen. This compares to: 'Bench urged deportation of Leicester Pole'[41] or 'Boy put in hostel with Irish drunks and Poles.'[42]

Third, crime reporting was important in contributing to the invisibility of black women. Much of the press coverage of immigration tended to assume maleness: blacks *were* men.[43] Crime as a social phenomenon is a particularly male affair. Not only are the criminals predominantly male, but so are the professionals who deal with crime: the police, solicitors and judges. Only as victims do women have a strong presence (Heidensohn, 1985). This is reflected in crime reporting. There were no items of crime reporting in the newspapers studied involving black women. Perpetrators were either white men where race was insignificant and unacknowledged or were black men. Victims were white men or women. Given that crime reporting was one of the few ways in which black people appeared in the newspapers, the absence of black women is noticeable.

Ordinary People

The third feature of press reporting discussed here is what has been called 'human interest' stories. This category of race reporting was identified by Troyna (1991) in his study. In Hartmann's (1974) study of the 1960s, 'normal' stories were also the fourth largest category of race reporting. However he found that 'race or colour was subsidiary to the central interest of the story'. How are African Caribbean people presented in human interest/normal stories in the local press in Leicester in the 1950s? In the papers examined local African Caribbean people did not appear in the papers at all as ordinary members of the community. It is not possible to identify African Caribbean people by name and it could be that stories did include African Caribbeans without reference to race at all. However, there are two points to be made in relation to this. First there were no articles, reports or features which included local people who were identifiably of West Indian (or Asian) origin where no significance was attached to race. Nor did they appear in advertisements or letters or visual material such as photographs. Local black people appeared as immigrants or as criminals who were usually men. The second point is that if African Caribbean people are included but without any indication of nationality, ethnicity or race then the dominance of adjectival racism remained unchallenged: in the newspapers people were white unless stated otherwise. It was not only local black people who were distinguished in this way. Stories about black people from other parts of the United Kingdom and from around the world routinely acknowledged race. The one exception to this was stories of visiting celebrities such as black singers. When Louis Armstrong appeared at De Montfort Hall on 12 March 1959 and in an article about Sammy Davis on 14 March 1959 they were treated in the press in a way that was not different in kind from reviews of white artists.

Critcher et al (1975, p.77) in a study of local West Midlands press argued that even human interest/normal stories were 'racially charged'. Stories which had a 'human interest' dimension or which supported a position of tolerance on the issue of race relations and immigration often include stereotypes or negative value judgements about black people. This is true of the Leicester press of the 1950s also. For example the *Leicester Chronicle* of 29 April 1950 carried a piece by the Rev A H Kirby who in his regular column generally adopted a liberal position on race relations. This was about the Seretse Khama issue and told a story of a great lady during the war years who wanted to entertain US Servicemen as a gesture of good will, but requested no Jews. So she got 'six beaming sons of coal black mammies'. The intention was to ridicule racism but the description reinforced a stereotype of black people common in the press of the time.[44] Van Dijk's (1991, p.187) discussion of 'semantic strategies' in relation to race in the press is highly relevant to the three articles quoted below.

On 19 February 1955 the *Chronicle* carried a 'Background' article on the West Indies.

...Mr Paul Collinson proprietor of a Leicester manufacturing woodworkers business visited Trinidad for two weeks he found it be a land of striking contrasts... Port of Spain - busy streets lined with sweat shops and tree filled outskirts where millionaires live in Sunset Boulevard type villas ... The other aspect is the shanty town where the Negroes live in huts and 'lean-to's of waste wood and iron and spend much of their lives doing nothing. To Mr Collinson the Negroes need not be as poor as they were. They only worked for short spells... He was impressed with their enthusiasm for getting their whites whiter.[45]

It was followed on 5 March by 'Topic of the Week: Leicester's Coloured Nurses'. This is one of the few stories about black women.

Student nurse Dorothy Turner ... was a stranger, one of six coloured nurses training at Leicester General Hospital... They pay their own fares and they are determined to go back with a British State Registered Nurse Certificate, one of the soundest nursing qualifications in the world... Leicester General Hospital has been training coloured nurses under colonial sponsorship for ten years. But more applications than ever are pouring in from Africa and the West Indies.

Why? Because the Colonial Office recently decided not to vet applications. It is possible now for coloured girls to come to Britain 'on spec' without reference to the government and hundreds are.

Student nurse Ernie Romeo ... 'I came over with other West Indians in the hope of taking up nursing... I am lucky to have been accepted.'

Matron of Leicester General Hospital, Miss G E Prior told me 'we find them easy to teach. They are adaptable and eager for knowledge. In practical work they are a little slow but sure. And they are kind and gentle with the patients'.

Miss C K Banks, Matron of West Coates Maternity Home has had several coloured nurses learning midwifery in her hospital. 'I have always found them highly intelligent ... The only fault I can find with them is their easy going attitude to life. They regard childbirth as such a natural everyday thing... and mothers have told me they are a great comfort on the labour ward... In all the years I have trained coloured nurses I have never had one complaint from a patient.'[46]

Being 'easy going' and 'natural' but also 'slow' are familiar stereotypes for West Indians both men and women. Other stereotypes were found in a piece on 11 February 1956 in the *Chronicle*. This time the stereotypes were no less familiar. This item was headlined 'Nigeria the land of "colourful" people'. It went on to describe 'happy, excitable, generous people'... the writer grew 'attached to the natives' who lived in primitive conditions with 'wide happy smiles on their faces'.[47]

While these articles can be seen as an attempt to present a positive view of black people and do indeed contain positive descriptions, they included an element of surprise that for example West Indian girls should be 'highly educated' and went on to refer to the need to 'check their qualifications'. These positive articles were also few in number compared with the overwhelming presentations of black people as problems. Apart from contrasting views of black and white migrants one aspect of the reaction to the arrival of settlers in Leicester, was to raise questions about how racialised relations should be organised. The reporting of 'race' in the local newspapers illustrated the lack of recognition or acceptance of the idea that Britain could or should become a 'multi-racial' society. The implicit question raised was should the 'races' be kept apart?

South Africa

The fourth and most remarkable feature of the coverage of racialised groups in the local press in Leicester during this period was the amount of attention given to South Africa and the developing apartheid system. South Africa was referred to in all kinds of reporting in both the *Chronicle* and the *Mercury*.

Apartheid was presented as a legitimate way of organising racialised relations with which to compare the 'laissez-faire' approach in Britain. Some space, usually in the correspondence columns, is given to opponents of apartheid to express their views explicitly but apartheid was often the pivot on which debate took place. In addition a powerful sub-text making implicit comparisons was created by continual references to South Africa in all kinds of race reporting.[48] Barry Troyna (1981), in his study of local and national papers of the late 1970s, argued that ideas expounded by the right wing National Front were used as a boundary marker for discussion of race in editorials in the *Leicester Mercury*. It seems that the apartheid system played a comparable role in the 1950s. However, rather than a boundary marker per se the South African system was presented as a legitimate model for organising 'race relations' with which to compare the laissez faire approach in Britain.

On 14 February 1950, on the front page of the *Mercury* the headline '250 Africans held after riot' led a story concerning events which took place in Johannesburg.[49] Then, on 8 March 1950, the front page of the *Mercury* was dominated by the story of Seretse Khama under the headline 'Seretse is banished for five years'.[50] On 9 March 1950 the front page read 'Seretse: Negroes in UK stage protest meeting'. The story included extracts from *Die Burger,* the South African paper.[51] The Seretse Khama issue continued in the *Mercury* until 10 June 1950.[52]

On 15 February 1955 the front page of the *Mercury* carried the headline 'More Africans moved', a story describing trouble when blacks were moved out of Johannesburg. There were 30 arrests.[53] Cyril Osborne in his piece in the *Chronicle* of 8 January (already quoted above)[54] and in another of 29 January 1955[55] made explicit comparisons with South Africa. An article on 19 February 1955 in the *Chronicle* was introduced thus:

John Chatham talked to two men about racial problems ... The *Illustrated Leicester Chronicle* has recently taken an interest in the colour problems. I've had a chat with two people who have interesting views on coloured people.

On a short visit to Leicester this week a professor of theology who has recently been in South Africa and has strong views on Apartheid.

Dr Horton Davies came to see his friend Rev A H Kirby and gave his address at Victoria Road church. The Negroes are not ready. No matter how eager they might be to vote in general elections. When we see coloured students in Leicester we think of them as representatives of their peoples, but this is a mistake.

The Africans we see in England are the most westernised of their races - those they have left at home are often 2,000 years behind us in social development and education.[56]

The issue of 14 February 1958 carried a piece about the operation of a colour bar in a public house in Coventry.[57] This prompted letters in the issues of 19[58] and 27 February 1958[59] all of which centred on Apartheid as a possible solution to the 'colour problem'. One such letter of 19 February 1958 began 'Was Jesus white?' and included the following:

I am a South African of Scandinavian descent. We have many Jews in South Africa and I have never seen a black one ... I do not wish to belittle the efforts of many black people in England to acquire education for the first time as they have a long and dreadful history of barbarian and backward ways.[60]

Replies on 27 February 1958 included one under the headline 'Racial Equality' which continued 'Have we, of the white race much to be proud in our present history which is full of barbarity? ... I wouldn't call South Africa's present attitude to the races civilised'.[61]

A letter in the *Mercury* of 21 August 1958 was signed anti-apartheid with the headline 'Joint effort needed to save South Africa'.[62] A further letter on 25 August 1958 was under the headlines 'Apartheid - aim the common good'. The piece continued:

time is required to educate the African both socially and culturally. The time will come when the African will reach a stage of development when he will be able to shoulder the greater responsibility of government.[63]

The *Chronicle* carried an 'Investigation' on 28 June 1958 on the front page. It continued on page three under the headline 'The problem of Leicester's coloured population'. The article discussed the 'mess of slums being created causing colour prejudice' and declared that 'Highfields is now know as Leicester District number six - a reference to the native slums of Cape Town'.[64]

At the height of the Nottingham and Notting Dale white 'riots', on 27 August 1958 the front page of the *Mercury* used the headline 'Nottingham riot - a case of the biter bit'. This piece carried extracts from South African and Rhodesian newspapers commenting on the riots. For example the *Bulawayo Chronicle* was quoted to the effect that:

Now that the people of Britain have to focus on something at home perhaps they will know of the background and realise that there is more to the colour problem than just colour.

The race riots have had the impact of a sociological atom bomb on the reading public in Rhodesia. No sensible person will gain any satisfaction from signs that the colour problem is now erupting in Britain. Nevertheless we are entitled to hope that this will bring home to the people of Britain the problems and complexities.[65]

The issue of 30 August 1958 contained follow up letters. One letter claimed that:

White South African newspapers are right... We white people need not be ashamed of our prejudices, they are natural ... Advocates of equality are responsible for the degeneration of the white race.[66]

A letter on 8 September 1958 declared that the South African way was right. 'The great thing about Imperialism is that it enables backward races to advance under the rule of a better power ... All men are not equal.'[67]

Clearly not all references to South Africa were favourable to the apartheid system. An article in the *Mercury* of 2 February 1958 described a meeting at Leicester's Anglo-Overseas Centre. This Centre had been established by local African Caribbeans to counter the ignorance and racism they encountered in Leicester. At the meeting Canon Eaton, who was a founder member of the Leicester Council of Churches and the Leicester Diocesan Newsletter, and who had previously lived in South Africa for twenty years, was quoted as saying 'The West Indians are not being assimilated into the community because they have nothing in common with the community'.[68] This produced a response in letters on 17 February 1958 including one stating 'How would the European react in Africa or the West Indies if having spent ten years as a carpenter he were told he was not wanted in his trade?' Another letter included 'I begin to wonder whether the apartheid doctrine of South Africa has not penetrated the Canon's ideology during his twenty one years in that country'.[69] But as in the case of the immigration issue the arguments were weak and based on moral principles only. An article in the *Chronicle* of 3 January 1959, which was one of several reports of unrest in South African townships, refers to a charge in South Africa by police on 'native women'.[70] On 12 March 1959 the *Chronicle* carried a piece about Rhodesia with the headline 'Witchcraft used in terror reign - governor says'.[71] But one of the most revealing pieces about South Africa appeared on 12 May 1959 in the *Mercury*. The headline read 'Black nannies should not hit white child - African servants have too much control protest'. This concerned a meeting of the South African Women's Federation in Johannesburg. A debate was held about the problems of black servants smacking white children.

> Too many children are influenced by servants who belong to a primitive people and whose background and way of life are alien to those of a European culture... In many families black nannies are drawn in as a member of the family. This is not a good thing. Smacking is the duty of the father alone. It is not for black servants to do it... It would be a good thing if there were no servants so white mothers would stay at home and care for their families and be good mothers... The Rev D F De Beer said 'if mothers are forced to go out to work she should leave her child in a European crèche'.[72]

That the proceedings of this group should be reported in the *Leicester Mercury* is remarkable in itself and it is hard to see the purpose of the inclusion if not for its ideological content. The paper gave voice to the perceived threat to white society which was posed by over familiar contact with black people as well as the supposed threat to patriarchal family forms posed by mothers working outside the home.

By 1960 the *Mercury* began to contain articles and editorials critical of South Africa. For example on 21 January 1960 a report was included on South Africa's divorce rate.[73] On 22 January 1960 an article headed 'Church calls for Higher pay for Africans' described poverty in South Africa and on the following day, after a mine disaster in which almost 500 Africans died, an editorial asked:

> How shall they square the African's risk of life with apartheid's legal robbery of his most elementary freedom? Many today must be thinking of Shylock's 'If you prick us do we not bleed?' ... There is no substitute for experience, but the Commonwealth exhibition billed for Leicester in four months time may mean that it is not left to tragedy to arouse our concerns for our native peoples.[74]

On 30 January 1960 the *Mercury* contained a report of a Leicester University undergraduate meeting which had backed a boycott of South African goods. 'Those against it', it was reported, 'thought it would hurt South African natives'.[75] Letters on the boycott issue continued into February. The criticism of South Africa in the *Mercury* was developing.

On 4 February 1960 an editorial declared 'No literate person can doubt British disapproval of Apartheid'.[76] These moral judgements about South Africa contrast with the benign references and covert comparisons which appeared through the 1950s. But it was the Sharpeville massacre which precipitated change in the paper's approach to South Africa. While a racist discourse continued, South Africa no longer provided a respectable model for racialised relations: a model that could be contrasted with the problems deriving from Britain's disorganising developing 'multi-racial' society.

The report of the Sharpeville massacre itself on 22 March 1960 took an interesting form. It carried the headline 'Why I got out of South Africa by City Midwife' and described a meeting of Leicester's Anglo-Overseas Association during which 'Mrs L Koza a native of Basutoland who is a midwife at the Westcoates Maternity Hospital' gave a report.[77] The editorial was headlined 'Massacre'.

> ...It is a massacre that will not be forgotten or forgiven either in Africa or in the more civilised world. What brought it about? It was a rebellion against injustice, against the single denial of human rights, the more immediate cause being South Africa's pass laws which require coloured people to carry identity cards ... His [Vervoerd's] cold blooded cynicism rests on Apartheid - a pretext for the white man's continued enjoyment of a higher material standard of life than is to be found outside the United States.

> Fear now hag-rides the white South African, not because his black brown and coloured serfs cast envious eyes upon his domestic luxuries, his gleaming motor car, his fine clothes but because the coloured man prizes something he cannot gain by robbery, cannot buy in money; civic pride, the vote, recognition as a human being.

The lesson has been written in blood. It is not quite too late for the white South African to learn the lessons - unless he wished to teach the rest of the world that in his country barbarianism originates from the white side of the colour bar.[78]

The dramatic and emotive language of this editorial seems to reflect the disillusionment and sense of betrayal felt by those who had once held South Africa as an example for Britain to follow, the bitter disappointment at being let down by our 'kith and kin'. It is this enforced abandonment of the South African example rather than a commitment to equality for black people which provided the emotional driving force of the editorial.

This editorial was followed on 23 March 1960 by a front page story on the 'TUC's Horror at South African shooting'. This same issue contained an editorial which attempted to come to terms with the implications of international condemnation of apartheid and at the same time seemed to support the British government's failure to condemn the South African system.

After the Slaughter
The first flash of horror at the ghastly day's work at Sharpeville and Langa dies away and it is followed by an emptiness. What, the individual asks, is to be done? Mr MacKenzie's mild criticisms of apartheid have already created an unexpected hullabaloo.

What the American government can say is not necessarily the correct official line here although each and every member of the Cabinet might wish to endorse it on a personal level.

The British government's silence might be misunderstood in a few quarters but that is a calculated risk. Mr MacKenzie will be trying not to give offence to Dr Vervoerd and in this he is surely right. For as long as it is possible Dr Vervoerd should know that help is available to him within the Commonwealth.

Officially this country must - even against the evidence of eyes and ears - believe that modification of policy is possible. This is just as necessary to save the South Africans in spite of themselves as it is to help the coloured people.

And while the British Government is silent the people of this country is having plenty to say. Dr Vervoerd knows that British opinion is critical of his policy. That will harden at the knowledge of the speech he made yesterday when he said his first duty was to the South African police for the courageous efficient way they had handled the situation. We are back to our original question, what is to be done by the people? They are expressing the horror and disquiet at what happened in Sharpeville. They can only wait now and hope that Dr Vervoerd like them will come to see that it is a direct result of a policy of racial division and oppressive brutality applied. It is Dr Vervoerd's last chance in the civilised world.[79]

On 24 March 1960 the paper called for South Africa to be expelled from the Commonwealth.[80] On 25 March 1960 an article by Stanley Lemon described a visit he had made some four years previously when he was shown around Sharpeville by a South African official. The article reported without comment the wonderful conditions for Africans described by the official: 'He could not think of a single thing the natives could complain about... .'[81]

Articles describing the continued resistance to Pass Laws in South Africa continued on 26 March 1960[82] and an editorial followed on 28 March 1960.[83] The sense of disillusionment continued in another condemnation in the editorial headline of 29 March 1960, 'And Now Kenya'.[84] The bitterness at loss of Empire and the more critical approach towards Apartheid continued in articles throughout 1960.

A year after Sharpeville the *Leicester Mercury* gave explicit recognition to the changing role of South Africa in discussions of racialised relations in Britain:

This event has reshaped our thoughts on the colour problem and has led to South Africa's withdrawal from the Commonwealth... As for South Africa's possible return to the circle, this could not be until Sharpeville has been blotted from the memory by the ending of apartheid.[85]

By the 1970s South Africa had lost its role in relation to issues of race in Britain in the pages of Leicester local papers. In an analysis of local and national newspapers' coverage of race, including the *Leicester Mercury*, Barry Troyna (1981, p.17), writing in the late 1970s, did not include South Africa as being relevant to the discussion of race in Britain. At this time it was the policies of the National Front which provided a 'boundary marker' for writing on race relations. Barry Troyna examined the daily national press, and two local papers, the *Manchester Evening News* and the *Leicester Mercury*. He found that after categorising the coverage, 47% of reporting came under four topic headings. These were the National Front, crime, immigration and human interest/normal. Race relations and white hostility comprised an additional 13% of material. Little attention was paid to housing, education, health or employment. In the *Leicester*

Mercury, crime was the largest single category of coverage at 16.8% closely followed by the National Front at 16%. Human interest/normal was covered in 12.2% of items and immigration in 7.6%. Race relations accounted for 9.9% of coverage.

Conclusion

While consciousness of national identity among the British has long been recognised and its racism has been acknowledged, there has in fact been little exploration of the development of racialised identities of British whites. It is argued here that a consciousness of empire was present in the discourse of the local newspapers in Leicester of the 1950s. This consciousness took several forms. First, stories about white emigrants moving to the colonies and Commonwealth countries of the old British Empire, particularly the Dominions, suggest an awareness of these societies as being white, as belonging to 'us': men and women in happy families. In contrast, black members of the Commonwealth living in Leicester were seen as undesirable, - 'them' they appeared as male criminals and problems. These contrasting views suggest a consciousness of whites as a racial and ethnic group which has not been sufficiently recognised as part of the racism of British society. Discussion of black people as criminals and their lack of appearance in human interest stories presented a distorted picture of black people.

Finally, the constant references to South Africa presented an implicit comparison with Apartheid as a way of organising race relations which was contrasted positively with the developing multiracial nature of parts of the country. The Sharpeville massacre was a watershed in this regard. After the events of 21 March 1960 Apartheid was no longer presented as a possible model of race relations in the Leicester press.

These aspects of the discourse in the papers were linked by the sense of fraternity with the white communities of the former British Empire. The racism in British society of the 1950s was deeply embedded not just in attitudes and behaviour towards black immigrants but also in the very identity of British whites as a group. There were token attempts to describe the experiences of Black people coming to Leicester, but more often Sir Cyril Osborne's anti-immigration speeches were the source of information on black immigrants to Leicester. Contrasting presentations of white emigrants and black immigrants appeared alongside each other without any sense of incongruity or comparison ever being made. While these negative views of black migrants were appearing in the Leicester press, the people themselves were struggling to find decent homes in the city. This is the subject of Chapter Four.

Notes

1 The Leicester Mercury Blue Book, the *Leicester Mercury*, George Street, Leicester.

2 Ibid.

3 During the period before the 1964 general election editorials became more strident in support of the Conservatives. This may have been a response to the likelihood of a Labour victory.

4 *Leicester Mercury*, 7 October 1959.

5 *Leicester Mercury*, 17 February 1959.

6 Ibid, 19 February 1959.

7 Ibid, 19 March 1959.

8 Ibid, 6 April 1959.

9 Ibid, 10 April 1959.

10 Ibid, 1 May 1959.

11 Ibid, 26 May 1959.

12 Ibid, 2 June 1959.

13 Ibid, 17 June 1959.

14 Ibid, 20 June 1959.

15 *Leicester Mercury*, 27 August 1958.

16 Ibid, 20 January 1960.

17 *Illustrated Leicester Chronicle*, 8 January 1955.

18 Ibid, 15 January 1955.

19 Ibid, 29 January 1955.

20 Ibid, 5 February 1955.

21 *Leicester Mercury*, 11 October 1958.

22 See Chapter Two.

23 *Leicester Mercury*, 21 April 1959.

24 Ibid, 7 May 1959.

25 Ibid, 17 June 1959.

26 A story was included in the *Mercury* about Barnet Janner on 21 November 1958 under the headline 'Let more aliens in pleads Mr Janner' and Mr John Peel made a speech in the House of Commons on 27 July 1959 in defence of the colonial civil service in the Hola Camp killings in Kenya. *Hansard* (Commons), 5th Series, Vol 610, 191-7, 27 July 1959. This was mentioned in an editorial in the *Leicester Mercury*, 5 August 1959.

27   *Illustrated Leicester Chronicle*, 15 January 1955.
28   *Leicester Mercury*, 27 February 1955.
29   Ibid, 20 March 1959.
30   Ibid, 14 May 1959.
31   Ibid, 15 May 1959.
32   Ibid, 19 January 1960.
33   The examples that follow are all headlines. These are read more often than the text and influence the way the report is interpreted by the reader. (Tannenbaum, 1953; Van Diyk, 1991, p.50).
34   *Leicester Mercury*, 20 July 1959.
35   Ibid, 12 August 1959.
36   Ibid, 5 January 1959.
37   Ibid, 8 December 1958.
38   Ibid, 24 November 1958.
39   For a discussion of the difference between colour prejudice in relation to nationality see Hartmann, P (1975, pp.36-37).
40   See reports by Cyril Osborne and Rupert Fevier quoted above.
41   *Leicester Mercury*, 8 December 1958.
42   Ibid, 3 February 1955.
43   See reports by Cyril Osborne and Rupert Fevier quoted above.
44   *Illustrated Leicester Chronicle*, 29 April 1950.
45   *Illustrated Leicester Chronicle*, 1 February 1955.
46   Ibid, 5 March 1955.
47   Ibid, 11 February 1956.
48   Rich, (1994, p.124) argues that 'The close historical ties between Britain and South Africa indicate that a considerable body of British thought on race has been shaped by the South African example'. However his essay concentrates on ideas of opposition to apartheid at national level.
49   *Leicester Mercury*, 14 February 1950.
50   Ibid, 8 March 1950.
51   Ibid, 9 March 1950.
52   Ibid, 10 June 1950.
53   Ibid, 15 February 1955.
54   *Illustrated Leicester Chronicle*, 8 January 1955.
55   Ibid, 29 January 1955.
56   Ibid, 19 February 1955.
57   Ibid, 14 February 1958.
58   Ibid, 19 February 1958.
59   Ibid, 27 February 1958.
60   Ibid, 19 February 1958.
61   Ibid, 27 February 1958.

62   *Leicester Mercury*, 21 August 1958.
63   Ibid, 25 August 1958.
64   *Illustrated Leicester Chronicle*, 28 June 1958.
65   *Leicester Mercury*, 27 August 1958.
66   Ibid, 30 August 1958.
67   Ibid, 8 September 1958.
68   Ibid, 2 February 1958.
69   Ibid, 17 February 1958.
70   *Illustrated Leicester Chronicle*, 3 January 1959.
71   Ibid, 12 March 1959.
72   *Leicester Mercury*, 12 May 1959.
73   Ibid, 21 January 1960.
74   Ibid, 22 January 1960.
75   Ibid, 30 January 1960.
76   Ibid, 4 February 1960.
77   Ibid, 2 March 1960. The Anglo-Overseas Association was an organisation founded and led by local West Indians and by the Quakers and other local whites to counter prejudices and promote toleration and understanding of the growing West Indian population living in Leicester. See Chapter Seven.
78   *Leicester Mercury*, 22 March 1960.
79   Ibid, 23 March 1960.
80   Ibid, 24 March 1960.
81   Ibid, 24 March 1960.
82   Ibid, 26 March 1960.
83   Ibid, 28 March 1960.
84   Ibid, 29 March 1960.
85   Ibid, Editorial, 21 March 1961.

References

Carter, Bob; Harris, Clive and Joshi, Shirley (1993), 'The 1951-55 Conservative Government and the Racialisation of Black Immigration', in Winston James and Clive Harris (eds), *Inside Babylon*, Verso, London.

Centre for Contemporary Cultural Studies, *The Empire Strikes Back*, Hutchinson, London.

Cohen, S and Young, J (1972), *The Manufacture of News: Deviance, Social Problems and the Mass Media*, Constable, London.

Critcher, C; Parker, M and Sondhi, R (1975), *Race in the Provincial Press: A Case Study of Five West Midlands Papers*, Ethnicity in the Media, UNESCO, Paris.

Eysenck, J H J and Nias, D K B (1980), *Sex, Violence and the Media*, Paladin, London.

Foot, Paul (1965), *Immigration and Race in British Politics*, Penguin, Harmondsworth.

Gilroy, Paul (1987), *There Ain't No Black in the Union Jack*, Hutchinson, London.

Gordon, P and Rosenberg, D (1989), *Daily Racism: the Press and Black People in Britain*, Runneymede Trust, London.

Hall, Stuart (1978) 'Racism and Reaction: A Public Talk Arranged by the British Sociological Association, 2 May 1978', in *Five Views of Multi-Racial Britain*, Commission for Racial Equality, London.

Hartmann, Paul and Husband, Charles (1975), *Racism and the Media*, Davis-Poynter, London.

Heidensohn, Frances (1985), *Women and Crime*, Macmillan, London.

Herbert, Ray and Reuss, Carol (eds) (1986), *The Impact of Mass Media*, British Film Institute, New York.

Hiro, Dilip (1992), *Black British, White British*, Grafton Books, London.

Holmes, Colin (1989), *A Tolerant Country*, Faber and Faber, London.

Husband, Charles (ed) (1975), *White Media, Black Britain*, Arrow Books, London.

James, Winston and Harris Clive (eds), *Inside Babylon*, Verso, London.

Katz, E and Lazarsfeld, P (1955), *Personal Influence* The Free Press, New York.

Lawrence, Errol (1982) 'Just Plain Common Sense: The Roots of Racism', Centre for Contemporary Cultural Studies, *The Empire Strikes Back*, Hutchinson, London.

Layton-Henry, Zig (1984), *The Politics of Race in Britain*, Allen and Unwin, London.

MacKenzie, John M (1984), *Propaganda and Empire: The Manipulation of British Public Opinion 1880-1960*, Manchester University Press, Manchester.

Morley, D (1980), *The 'Nationwide' Audience, the British Film Institute*, London.

Rich, Paul B (1994), *Prospero's Return?*, Hansib, London.

Solomos, John (1989), *Race and Racism in Contemporary Britain*, Macmillan, Basingstoke.

Tannenbaum, P H (1953), 'The Effect of Headlines on the Interpretation of News Stories', *Journalism Quarterly*, 30.

Troyna, Barry (1981), *Public Awareness and the Media : A Study of Reporting on Race*, Commission for Racial Equality, London.

Van Dijk, Tuen (1991), *Racism and the Press*, Routledge, London.

4 Somewhere to Live: African Caribbeans and Housing, 1945-1981

While the nature of employment has the greatest explanatory power in relation to the development of African Caribbean communities, housing is also a central determinant of the quality of life and position in society for most people. Some sort of shelter is also a prerequisite for employment. Theoretical debates about causes of residential patterns of various racialised and ethnic groups revolve around ideas of choice versus constraint (Byron, undated). Theory is underdeveloped compared with that of the issue of employment and issues of choice and constraint are not confined to minority groups. Work in this area rarely pays attention to issue of gender. As Pritchard (1976) has argued:

> Very few people of any kind have complete freedom to choose there they live... every decision will involve the resolution of choice and constraint and of all the limits of that decision will be set by the actions of those responsible for the provision of accommodation.

Various positions have been adopted in relation to the relative weight assigned to choice or structure. For example Dayha (1974), in the case of Pakistanis has emphasised choice based on cultural considerations. Brown (1981) stressed the determining structures of class and race. Peach (1975, p.7) argued that economic factors such as employment influenced decisions at the macro level such as the area in which to live, but social factors may determine choice of the particular area. Panayi argued in relation to nineteenth century Britain, that immigrant neighbourhoods allowed the development of ethnicity (Panayi, 1994, p.78). The oversimplification of factors contributing to residential patterns represented by the choice/constraint dichotomy argued by some, has been challenged more recently (Byron, undated) where it has been argued that choice is made in the context of the constraints imposed by structures.

For some groups racism forms an important component of constraining factors. Perspectives on the housing patterns of immigrant groups on the one hand, emphasise the choice that migrants make to live in close proximity to each other and to emphasise the support this provides both in practical terms and in cultural affiliation. On the other hand others have pointed to the boundaries imposed on immigrants especially, black and Asian groups by exclusion and discrimination. In practice choice and constraint interrelate in housing as in employment: black people made choices in the light of knowledge about constraining factors. People did not apply for jobs they had good reason to believe they had no chance of getting and black people in Leicester tended not to apply to Building Societies for mortgages when they knew they would not have been granted; in view of what is known about 'redlining' discussed below these were rational 'choices'.

Byron (undated, p.7) has criticised Brown (1981) for giving 'causal power' to structures in the decision making process. She sees her work as lying within the framework of structuration theory. This sets out to show the complexity of the relationship between actions and structure, emphasising not just the constraints imposed by structures but the enabling function of structure. In her analysis of the housing decisions of Nevisians in Leicester she emphasised the initial intention of migrants to return home within three to five yeas. However the relationship between intention and behaviour is itself complex and the enabling aspects of social structure are different for different groups of people. The relationship between 'intention' and subsequent behaviour for the mass of ordinary people is most usually subject to continuous negotiation in the light of structural constraint. Indeed it could be argued that in matters of personal choice, the more powerless economically, politically and socially people are, the smaller is the level of decision making at which structural constraints impede: the very poorest make decisions on a day to day basis, the affluent can plan over a lifetime. Byron (1994, p.193) acknowledged, that despite intentions, a 'majority of Nevisians and probably other Caribbean migrants will continue to live in Britain'.

The spatial segregation of black and Asian minority groups has been seen as crucial in debates about race relations and spatial integration has been regarded as a prerequisite for good race relations (Luthera, 1988, p.103). Indeed harmony between racialised groups has been seen as a function of spatial integration and equality between groups has been seen as less important (Small, 1994). The historical examples of South Africa and the USA have seemed to suggest that segregation in practice appears to support inequalities between racialised groups. The situation of women in relation to men suggest that integration and harmony are insufficient to produce equality. There has however been little study of gender in relation to housing and such an analysis is not possible within the scope of this study. The relationship between harmony, integration and equality are complex and are complicated further when issues of migration, cultural difference and racialisation are conflated (Small, 1994).

Luthera (1988, p.103) has argued that the race relations debate has been devoid of any civil rights concept. Instead, dispersal was seen as the answer to race relations problems (Lee, 1977, p.2).

Of major influence in debates about housing has been Rex and Moore's (1967) study of Sparkbrook in Birmingham. In this study based on the 'Chicago' school of sociological analysis, Rex and Moore allocated people to five groups according to their relationships to the housing market. The classes were, owner occupiers, council house tenants, tenants of whole houses, lodging house proprietors and tenants of lodging houses. This study can be seen as a classic application of the Weberian perspective challenging Marxist insistence on the salience of the relationship of the means of production as the determinant of life chances. The study has made a significant contribution to the debate. However it has been recognised that the housing classes described by Rex and Moore (1967) may not provide a reliable predictor of life chances in every case. Owner occupation of cheap and rundown inner city properties, for example, may not bring financial rewards or status compared with middle class tenants of large out of town properties with high incomes. This has been true of African Caribbean owner occupiers in Leicester.

In the chapter on employment, it is argued that the choices made by black migrants to Britain were often made in the light of the well founded anticipation of discrimination and that therefore a proper consideration of the effects of such discrimination can only be made in an historical context. This is not to undervalue the important contribution made by sociological studies, like those of Rose (1990) and the P.E.P. reports (1967; 1968; Smith, 1974, Brown, 1984) in establishing racism at a given point in time, in a situation where both public and academics preferred to deny its existence. However the cumulative effect of racism in ever changing forms and in different areas of life together with the complex interaction of decision making made by those subjected to its consequences, are revealed over time. 'Choices' made by African Caribbeans in relation to housing can similarly be seen as being made within a context of the constraints of decisions made within prevailing racialised constructions. Once made, choices had long term consequences.

In 1978 Leicester Council for Community Relations complained that in spite of the fact that Leicester has been a major centre for black and Asian migration since the Second World War there has been no comprehensive study of the housing of black or Asian residents in Leicester as there has been of other cities.[1] The only studies of housing in Leicester in relation to immigrants are that of Pritchard (1976), which was a highly technical study focused on the issue of mobility and that of Byron (undated) which is a small study of Nevisians. Leicester has always been regarded as prosperous and housing conditions have been seen to reflect that prosperity:

> Prosperity and continuous building has meant that the city never accumulated the same legacy of large amounts of slum property that have in some cities. Indeed Leicester has been on of the best housed English cities (Pritchard, 1976, p.31).

Highfields

This is how Highfields was described in 1967:

> Despite the fact that immigrants are scattered throughout the city, an inquiry for the 'coloured' district will lead any stranger directly to the Highfields area. If one were to act on the assumption that the coloured community in any white city will live in the worst residential district, one would simply come out of the station, look around without asking any questions and take the road that runs back behind the station, apparently leading nowhere; and would arrive at Highfields. The district is nowhere near a hundred per cent coloured. It is not run down and decaying like Harlem or Notting Hill It is merely rather shabby and on a cold, windy day, a depressing kind of place (Grigg, 1967, p.4).

As the white population of Leicester moved out of the city centre during the 1950s, houses became available to rent or to buy. The area bounded by the old London Road, the Leicester Railway station to the west, Spinney Hill Park to the east, Humberstone Road to the north and Evington Road to the south became the centre of African Caribbean settlement. This area is called Highfields and many African Caribbeans have felt a great loyalty to it and its name (*Highfield Rangers: An Oral History*, 1993, p.7). Highfields is very close to the city centre and was also within a mile or two of some of the most important employers of black workers:[2] Imperial Typewriters on East Park Road and Copdale Road, John Bull on Ethel Road and also Metal Box and the British Shoe Corporation. The properties consisted of elegant, substantial terraced houses built in the late nineteenth century for professional classes (Marett, 1989, p.3). These generally lined the main roads and smaller streets consisting of terraced houses containing two rooms and a kitchen downstairs with or without a passage and two or three rooms upstairs. Typically these would have the stairs at right angles to the internal walls, a feature characteristic of terraced housing all over the city as is the absence of a front or back garden Even three storey, five or six bedroomed properties have only a yard at the back. This has contributed to the lack of greenery in an area with few open spaces. The schools have no fields and Spinney Hill Park is the only green area. Highfields was an attractive area to black, Irish, Polish and other Europeans as well as Asian workers. The latter group arrived rather later than that of the others whose migration was established much earlier (Irish) or linked to the war years (African Caribbeans and Europeans).

Experiences of Housing

The complexities of the way in which experiences and decision making interrelate are illustrated in the housing histories of African Caribbean people in Leicester. The operation of the 'colour bar' with respect to housing for black immigrants to Britain has been well documented elsewhere (Glass, 1960; Patterson, 1963; Foner, 1979). As in other areas African Caribbeans in Leicester found it difficult to rent accommodation. Typical were the comments of Roy Rowe:

> Accommodation, that was a big problem, a very big problem. When I came here first I had a cousin who used to live here. I came to the same house. But I left in 1958 to look for a house. I saw this flat in Western Road. I was in uniform... I saw a girl in the agency. She said she had to see someone or other about it. But she stopped half way up the stairs. He asked her something ...I didn't hear. But she said the flat had gone. I was quite sure she had said 'the man is coloured'. Anyway I didn't get it, but it still said in the paper, 'rooms to let'.

> You would see 'Rooms to Rent'... someone would look through the window and when they saw you they wouldn't entertain you. They wouldn't even open the door. But the next week the ad was still in the paper.[3]

Many Caribbean migrants found that Polish people were more ready to let to them. Elvy Moreton came to England in 1959 from St Kitts and moved to Leicester in 1961:

Polish people helped a lot of black people... My husband got us a place ... we rented a bed-sit until the second child came along and later we got a council place on Rowletts Hill. It was brand new it had just been built.[4]

Eric Hudson said that:

Once going door to door the door was slammed so hard that my fingers nearly got trapped.[5]

African Caribbean people, both men and women, often provided support for each other of various kinds. Housing was particularly important in this respect. Women who came as independent people were often able to rely on friends and relatives as were men. But women alone did have particular problems especially if they had children. Carmel Charles said:

When I got pregnant nobody wanted blacks. I had to foster my daughter out. We were all living separately for one year. I picked the baby up on Friday afternoon. Then I got a room.[6]

Carmell Charles ended up in a homeless unit.

It was heartbreaking... But when the second child was six weeks old we bought a house. [7]

Houses were cheap in Leicester and some African Caribbean people managed to buy. But this too was a difficult process. Lee Morris found that certain areas were hard to purchase in:

My cousin had bought a house in 1959 and I rented from him. Then I got a mortgage - no problem. I borrowed money from a building society. But when we were looking for a property we were put off ... I wouldn't put up with that treatment today. We were looking up Chesterfield Road. There were a lot of Polish people and Latvians up there. ...There was a concerted effort between the person selling and the building societies to put you off. One property I tried to get but I was sort of put off.[8]

Although Lee Morris got a mortgage easily this was not typical. It was hard for many to get mortgages from building societies and many people took out short term loans at a higher rate of interest from banks. Monroe Thomas went to a broker to get his mortgage:

> I wanted a house. They were going cheap -you could get a suit for £7 in those days. ... but they wouldn't give me a mortgage. They said what I'm working for can't cover me. I said 'I'm coming home with £18 a week. But a mortgage was based on your flat rate only which was £12....' A man in the tax office said I know a company what won't turn you down. It had only been there six months. They buy houses at a cheap rate then sell them to you. The house was £2500 and I beat the guy down to £2300. I paid to a mortgage broker £4.10 a week with the insurance and everything. I paid the money off in four years six months. I paid too much down as a deposit. [9]

Novelette Mackoy came to Leicester as a child but her father had been here since 1961:

> He never mixed outside of work. He never felt comfortable in the white community... Financially when they became better off he had the choice to leave Highfields but my Dad didn't want to risk it. He had a lot of friends who moved to Wigston, but they got a lot of racial abuse. His view was that he wasn't going to suffer racism at work and at home as well. [10]

This provides a very clear example of the way in which 'choice' is made within a context of expectations, founded on experience of the way in which black people were treated and also provides some understanding of why many African Caribbeans identified with Highfields. Indeed some black people who did move out of Highfields experienced problems. Doris Cope, who like Novellette Mackoy had come to Leicester from the Caribbean as a young teenager, moved out of Highfields to what had become the more middle class area of Clarendon Park by the 1970s. This was an area near to the city centre but was inhabited by that time by many professional people such as teachers, social workers and university lecturers . It was close to the University:

> Living in a white area I did feel uncomfortable and embarrassed going into shops. My kids have middle class white attitudes but they were still stereotyped as black kids. [11]

'Coloured' students also had problems getting lodgings and the University of Leicester itself was claimed to be operating a policy of segregation in its approved lodgings in the late 1950s:

certain houses on the lodging scheme tended to get institutionalised for the use of non-European students.[12]

The experiences of black people were mirrored by whites who were also strongly discouraged by estate agents and building societies from purchasing in Highfields. Mary Grigg (1967, pp.98-99) reported on this in 1967. Personal experiences of the author also confirm this, when in 1974 estate agents showed extreme reluctance to give information about properties they were selling in the Highfields area on the grounds that 'you wouldn't want to live there'. The assumption of shared racist attitudes among whites were common in Leicester until the 1980s.

As revealing as the snapshots of experiences are, it is only when the experiences of people are considered over a period that the relationship between choice and structure is illuminated. Percy Harding moved very many times during the first twelve years that he lived in Leicester. Then when he finally got a three bedroomed council house in 1970, Percy stayed in it for the next thirty one years.

My cousin came in the war. He married a Leicester girl... My brother came in 1955... I came in 1958 and my girlfriend, she came up in 1959.

Accommodation was terrible... We got a room, one room...We stayed until somebody moved out from the house my brother was living in, in Upper Charnwood Street. We heard that a man was looking for decent tenants. We had lived with Indians and this was another Jamaican. He had just bought the house... We moved then and we were surprised. We didn't get on well at all. We were trying to be respectable tenants, cleaning etc. ...But my nephew was coming up and I asked if my nephew could stay with us tonight... but he never came back to me... My nephew came and we talked till about 11 o'clock at night and when I took him to [the place where he was to stay], they could not take him... So he stayed with me... the [landlord] was upset... I managed to get a room in another place... That place was hell... The person bought the house specifically to let out... The noise was terrible, mostly young people... At weekends it was terrible... So we leave. We went to another Indian house...We lived there for a little while...They were quite nice people, business people. Then we got married... We used the room for the reception, it was Boxing Day, the 26th of December. We got married in the morning. At 5 pm in the evening on Boxing Day the police came and knocked on the door, saying we 'have had a telephone call' we were making too much noise. At 5 pm in the evening! ... I told the police we got married this morning... there had been a complaint...we were not making too much noise really. ...You could see that that was racist but we didn't let that bother us.

I lived there until the first child was born then no sooner had the child been born that we got our marching orders.   We came to a West Indian house. Another young lady lived there and another young man It was so close - cooking and eating from the same pot, but my wife got pregnant again so we had to move again. We never managed to get anywhere - I try and try. It was close to November. Then we move up to Highfields. This was rented by another Jamaican man and he sub-letted to us. This man was quite terrible. I couldn't describe him. He was a terrible landlord. He had the top half and we had the bottom. We couldn't get anywhere nice. We kept looking...

In 1962 when my wife was having a baby and we called the ambulance but they said it was too late to leave and she had to have the baby there... The landlord started to raise hell and said you didn't tell me your wife was going to have a baby here. You will have to pay me more rent. It was shocking. The same weekend someone came and said, 'I can find you somewhere to live'. It was November and it was cold. Anyway we got a house in Cobden Street and we move out...rented the whole house...And we were so glad. But the house was unfit to live in according to the authorities and we move to... we end up with a council house. We lived there for a little while until these houses were built. We lived in one house [on St Mathews Estate] and then these six houses were built.   We have been living in this house thirty one years... My happiest was at Forest Road, we were like one big family... When we got to Cobden Street we were so pleased.

It's a lovely house here. [when we were rehoused by the council] We had three choices according to them. I wanted to go to Evington actually. I was told point blank - she told me there is no way. They wouldn't send you, as a black person, to Evington. When she told me point blank... well it wasn't her policy... You have to take the next best thing. I was offered up by Wharf Street. I turned that down. It was nice here, quiet, quiet. We have another child. That was a two bedroomed house, so we applied to come across here. ...I came to live in this house. I'm the first person to live in this house. The policy was, you have to get a three bedroomed house [when you have three children]. I bought the house in 1980.[13]

Percy Harding's story illustrates the problems black people had in finding decent housing. It is a demonstration of the limitations of the 'choice' argument in relation to African Caribbeans. Once in comfortable accommodation, Percy Harding and his family felt settled and stayed there for thirty one years.

The shortage of labour in Leicester from 1945 until 1974 is discussed elsewhere in Chapter Five. But while many local employers were very keen to employ black workers, public opinion, as expressed in the local press and private actions of individuals indicated that the presence of black people was not wanted.

Reactions to the Arrival of Black People

The housing problems that black people had, during the 1950s and 1960s were little understood by the rest of the local population. The two local papers in Leicester, the weekly *Illustrated Leicester Chronicle* and the daily *Leicester Mercury* presented a picture of bad housing conditions which were largely of the 'immigrants' own making.

Some attention was paid to the problems black people had in finding accommodation, but this was often presented alongside myth and prejudice about West Indians. For example in February 1955 the *Chronicle* reported that:

> One of the biggest problems they [Jamaicans] presented was to find suitable accommodation. He had heard cases of ten Jamaicans living in a small house a £1 a week each. When municipal inspectors ordered them to be moved on they often jumped the housing queue.[14]

The *Chronicle* of 14 April 1956 reported difficulties in finding lodgings for overseas students 'particularly if they are coloured'. But more common was the view that West Indians chose to live in overcrowded conditions. The *Leicester Mercury* carried an article in January 1955 headlined 'West Indians Crowd Eight to a Room'. It continued:

> The Minister of Health knows that overcrowding and unsanitary conditions exist in the London Borough of Lambeth where West Indians crowd eight people in a room and consider it 'paradise' but does nothing about it.[15]

A *Chronicle* investigation into the 'City's Coloured Population' in June 1958 reported the high prices the coloured families in Leicester were paying to live, but went on:

> And in some districts of the city a mess of slums is being created causing colour prejudice among white people living in the same streets. Let me make it clear that the African and Jamaican likes to keep himself spotlessly clean but I'm horrified at the condition under which many of them are forced to live and I mean forced. .... big crumbling houses unkempt with sacking and tattered

curtains drawn tight across the window containing anything up to thirty residents. Front doors which open to reveal blackened grimy walls and greasy floors. Houses where there are several beds in a room and where the cooking stoves are on the landings to be shared by all the residents on the floors. I contacted Deputy Medical Officer of Heath, Dr Ross. He promised 'immediate action by his department'. Dr Ross said his department was concerned about overcrowding by coloured people and has taken steps where possible to eliminate it. I asked Dr Ross if it was true that as many people allege that the City Council doesn't care too pins so long as it can pack the Negroes in to some sort of accommodation as so avoid having to find accommodation for them. He denied that. 'The regulations apply to all, there is no colour discrimination' he told me. But Mrs Lucy Turner of Stoughton Street told me that coloured people are packed like sardines into a leaky house. 'There are so many there coming and going that no one knows just how many. But in the recent hot spell there was a most unpleasant smell from the house' she told me.... Let's not beat about the bush. When Negroes move into a district property values fall. Many have a strong and emotional fear of Negroes. It's true that many tend to crowd together more than we would. By our standards they live poorly.[16]

This mix of apparent sympathy and understanding coupled with contradictory information, but laced with myth and prejudice was typical of the coverage of the issue in the local press throughout the 1950s. There was some recognition of unfair treatment but the responsibility for this was seen to lie with black people; their culture, attitudes and misunderstandings of British life. Indeed the presence of 'coloured immigrants' in itself was actually the cause of the problem. The solution was always to stop immigration, by which was always implied black immigration. The article quoted at length above ended thus:

Something must be done to stop these people being exploited, often by their own kind. Something must be done to prevent new slums in Leicester. Something should be done for their own sakes as well as ours to control the admission to this country of these unfortunate people.[17]

While it is not clear the extent to which the views expressed in the local press are representative of local opinion, they are one expression of it and are often taken to be 'public opinion' and are therefore powerful. This power was increased by the apparent support given to the racism of the newspapers by public figures and local officials in particular. In September 1958 at the time of the Nottingham and Notting Hill Riots - events which were clearly of concern to people in Leicester,[18] the *Leicester Mercury* carried a long article based on the Pubic Health Inspector's annual report.

Mr G A Hillier is reported to have said.

> The influx of foreigners and West Indians and Pakistanis help to make the situation more difficult.[19]

The leader of the same issue said:

> Leicester's colour problem is not one of skin but of living standards and hygiene. ... overcrowding and failure by some coloured people to understand the British way of life leads to bad neighbourliness and unfortunate incidents.

The piece continued:

> these were contributing factors in the Notting Hill riots. Indians Pakistanis and West Indians and others ...will never be accepted enough to achieve integration while there are such wide gaps in social and domestic standards.[20]

In the mid 1960s the first PEP report (1967) established what African Caribbeans had known since their arrival; that racial discrimination existed in Britain. As understanding developed over the next two decades it became clear that the structural disadvantages experienced by black and Asian people were not simply a function of individually made discriminatory decisions, based on prejudice. Structural disadvantage arose as a result of the complex interaction of discrimination, the unintended consequences of traditional practices and procedures, a racialised culture and the class position of racialised groups. Debates centred on how to understand and therefore counteract what has been commonly called 'institutional racism'.

The relationship between the public and private sectors in the provision of housing creates particular problems in any attempt to explain the residential position of African Caribbeans. In employment the state allowed employers control over the allocation of jobs subject only to weak and largely ineffectual race relations legislation. The effect of this in Leicester is discussed in Chapter Five. On the other hand, in relation to education, the state through local authorities, had direct and overwhelming control. The small private sector was important in terms of inequality for the society as a whole, but small in terms of the number of people it served. In Leicester the local education authority adopted policies which reflected a pervasive racialised perspective concerning black and Asian immigrants. This is discussed in Chapter Six. In housing however, responsibility was shared between the public and private sectors. Evidence such as the statements of decision makers in housing such as that of Mrs Irene Pollard quoted below suggests that powerful people in the Leicester local authority during the 1950s and 1960s, shared the same negative views of African Caribbeans as those responsible for policy in matters of education. Indeed, personnel as in the case of Mrs Pollard, overlapped. She was chair of governors of Moat School who refused to accept 'immigrant' pupils.[21] In practice inequalities in employment education and housing interacted. Smith (1989, p.38) has argued that:

> The disproportional disadvantageous residential circumstances of black people reflect first their position in the labour market, second their treatment within the housing system and finally the relating independent effect of location on both employment and housing opportunities.

The partial nature of responsibility for housing has meant that local authorities were not forced to make decisions concerning the housing of African Caribbeans. The housing conditions of black people were not seen as related to local authority decisions until the mid 1970s. Under the policy of renewal, initiated at that time by the government, Highfields was among the first areas improved by LCC. While these polices had a positive impact on the housing conditions of African Caribbeans, they were insufficient to change the basic inequalities in housing already established. There was no planning by central or local government to meet the needs of immigrants moving to Britain in this period and this allowed those making decisions with varying degrees of power in society to make them within racialised frameworks of understanding. Estate agents, building society managers and local council officials operated policies which discriminated against black people. These decisions had profound effects on peoples' lives.

Government Policy

The policies of local authorities were constrained and influenced by central government. Initiatives by local authorities related to legislation which were controlled through financial management. In housing as in other matters the government did nothing to encourage or help local authorities assist immigrants with housing.

Central government policy has been subject to varying views on the role of public housing. However, governments have defined their role in much more restricted terms than that considered appropriate towards, for example, education. The responsibilities of government to meet housing needs have been confined to those who were not able to house themselves through the market. Notwithstanding the changes in policy of successive governments since 1945, public provision of housing and intervention in the private sector has been led by the need to ameliorate perceived problems in the private sector and to house those for whom the market would not provide (Burke, 1981, p.17).

This, as Luthera (1988, p.107) argued:

Allowed the indigenous population to do its utmost to exclude black people from acquiring decent accommodation, developing good equity in property and consequent mobility in terms of employment and economic mobility in general.

Public policy was clearly not developed with the explicit intention of limiting access to particular types of housing for black people. However this is not to suggest that this would not have happened if the state at both national and local levels had been conscious of the consequences of policy for black people in the 1950s and 1960s. Indeed not only does evidence from the way the local authority acted in relation to the education system, suggest that black people would have been excluded, but the statements of local officials in Leicester exemplified above and below suggest that their actions in relation to housing were based on attitudes that were racialised and indeed racist.

Central policy until 1949, dictated that public housing was provided for the 'working classes'. This idea gave way to that of 'housing need' (Burke, 1981, pp.16-17). The period between the end of the Second World War and 1969 was characterised by slum clearance and rebuilding, facilitated by legislation giving local authorities powers to compulsorily purchase. However this policy failed to keep up with demands. By the 1960s one solution was seen as the creation of multi-occupied high rise blocks and Leicester City Council adopted this option, albeit in a limited way. Terraced housing such as that described above in Leicester City was demolished and replaced by tower blocks:

Between 1945 and 1966 the local authority in Leicester built over 16000 new dwellings, in a scheme to replace the estimated 18000 substandard dwellings.[22]

As is the case with other authorities, council houses in Leicester were allocated according to a residence rule of five years except in the case of returning sailors, soldiers and airmen for whom it was waived. This apart, housing need was the basis of allocation.[23] But not everyone who was in need got a house and there was a great deal of scope for judgement in selection. Applications for tenancies included information about details of occupation and earnings and sometimes included comments by housing visitors on the cleanliness and care of existing accommodation.

The role of the housing visitor has been crucial and the criteria for allocation used in public housing was not required to be published. Notions of deserving and undeserving tenants were widespread in local authorities (Burke, 1981, p.179). Prejudice towards black people by housing visitors has been hard to establish but is recognised as a problem (Rex and Moore, 1967, p.22). The operation of the allocation of council housing, in Leicester in the 1950s and 1960s was consistent with what was known about other local authorities.[24] In 1973 LCCR, aware of the importance of eliminating prejudice and discrimination in allocation, offered to help train housing visitors in Leicester. [25]

As the proportion of people living in council housing increased to around 32 % in the mid 1970s the alternatives were reduced for those who were not selected (Burke, 1981, p.179). The effects of these policies were that African Caribbeans did not become council tenants in Leicester and this is consistent with the situation in other cities, described for example in Birmingham (Rex and Moore, 1967, Burney, ??). Merlyn Rees, the Labour Government's Junior Minister responsible for Race Relations visited Leicester in December 1969. The City Council produced a confidential 'case book' of information for Mr Rees, which was leaked to the press. The casebook was reported as including the following:

> The immigrant population do not seek accommodation on council housing estates and do not wait to be re-housed from clearance areas. Out of 28,000 council dwellings there are only 160 immigrant tenants and of 8,000 families waiting to be rehoused from clearance areas only 12 are immigrants. In the two years to April 1969 45% of applicants for local corporation funds to house purchases were for immigrants.[26]

Many people knew of, but did not understand, the residence rule, assuming that names could not go on to the waiting list until the residence period was complete. Certainly nothing was done to inform people of their rights in Leicester. Not only were West Indians unaware of their rights in relation to public housing but many knew nothing of the rent tribunals which might have eased conditions in the private rented sector.[27]

The worst housing conditions were found, nationally, in the private rented sector (Burke, 1981, p.45). Under the 1965 Act a landlord or tenant could apply to have the rent of a dwelling reviewed and a fair rent fixed. Effectively excluded from public housing, and finding bad conditions as tenants many African Caribbeans tried to buy.

Building societies were unwilling to give mortgages on properties in Highfields. The proportion of rented accommodation meant that the area was seen as high risk.[28] They were also unwilling to give mortgages for houses which opened straight on the street, a situation common for the smaller terraced houses throughout Leicester.[29]

Highfields was 'redlined'. Redlining has only recently been openly acknowledged by building societies (Burke, 1981, p.40). The Leicester Building Society was finally persuaded, by LCC, to abandon redlining in 1978 and other building societies followed suite.[30] Prior to 1978 black people were then forced to apply for loans from banks and other sources which charged higher rates of interest over shorter periods and required higher deposits. This also had an added financial penalty after 1963 when tax relief on Building Society mortgages was introduced. A Shelter study showed that in 1970 only 24 % of mortgages to 'coloured' households had been provided by building societies. This was despite the fact that 48% had savings accounts with building societies. Banks had provided 45% of all the mortgages with repayment terms of less than eight years. 35% had been on council house waiting lists but had waited so long that they had bought for themselves (Jansari, 1981). In the white population mortgages and house ownership were nearly always in the hands of men whether single or married. While it is hard to establish through sources it is likely that this was the case with black people too.

The situation in Leicester between 1961 and 1971 were described in another project carried out for Shelter on housing conditions in Leicester. It concluded that the housing shortage in Leicester had not been eliminated between 1961 and 1971 and conditions had actually worsened. There were some improvements: more households enjoyed a fixed bath, indoor WCs and hot water. But the report singled out Highfields and Spinney Hill together with North Braunstone Council Estate as having 'appalling and often worsening conditions'. Overcrowding had increased with the proportion of the population sharing dwellings rose from 3.7% to 4.2% over the period and the proportion of people living to a density of more than one and a half people per room had risen from 4 to over 5%. Owner occupation had increased very little but the proportion living in council housing had risen from 23.2% to 30%. This was accompanied by a falling supply of rented accommodation from 30% in 1961 to 25% in 1971 and 27000 homes still had no inside WC at all. The report concluded that by eight indicators of housing conditions, Highfields and Spinney Hill were in a worse state in 1971 than in Leicester as a whole with the gap widening. Overcrowding which implied at least ten people in a three bed roomed house in these areas had doubled to 18% by 1971. Despite these conditions the recently set up Tenants Association of Spinney Hills and Wycliffe claimed that rents in the area were the highest in Leicester.[31]

Despite the existence of the reports such as that of Shelter, the Select Committee on Race Relations and Immigration in its 1970-71 session investigation into housing was to report that:

> The problem of immigrant housing is not known either to central government or to local authorities. They were hampered by the inability to get facts.[32]

The passing of the 1962 Immigration Act increased public discussion of the issues and the local press in Leicester continued to focus on the 'problems caused by [coloured] immigrants'. Articles on overcrowding among West Indians were carried by the Leicester Mercury during 1962 and continued throughout the decade, presenting a very similar view.[33] Alongside issues of housing the decade saw 'panics' over education, health and crime as well as articles which focused on numbers of immigrants coming into the country. Some of these issues are discussed elsewhere in this book.[34]

Increasingly officials of the City Council were drawn in to public debate as the growth of far right organisations, which had a high profile in the press, set the terms of the debate about immigration. Public pronouncements lent support to the view that bad housing conditions were the result of the choices made by immigrants. Mrs Councillor Irene Pollard of Spinney Hill Ward and Vice-Chairman (sic) of the Housing committee having been criticised for not 'enforcing regulations on overcrowding' said:

> West Indians who are living in overcrowded houses don't often grumble. They seem to like being together. They are loath to bring complaints because they know they will be turned out of their homes... I should have thought we could have had an organisation to teach West Indians if they cannot be taught before they leave their own countries what is here and how we behave. That is the cause of this trouble and why they like to live together. West Indians in my experience love living together. I know a house in the Melbourne Road area where the beds are never cold - they sleep in them in three shifts.[35]

The view that immigrants were causing bad conditions was given particularly powerful legitimisation when Dr B J L Moss became Chief

Medical Officer of Health in 1960. Dr Moss's term of office was characterised by a significant change in the nature of Annual Health of the City of Leicester Reports, from then until the reports changed their nature in 1972. The problems 'created by immigrants' received special attention in his reports. Of all the many health issued raised in the reports, which were around 200 pages long, 'Immigrants' were mentioned in relation to housing and particular diseases. They were adding to the problems of overcrowding in the city and some individual 'immigrants' were arriving with TB reversing the downward trend in the incidence of this disease in Leicester which had been a feature of the 1950s. On one occasion this was reported in the *Leicester Mercury* under the headline 'Immigrant diseases causing alarm' –claim made by Councillor S A Barston.[36] Of particular interest is that Dr Moss's reports gave figures for the numbers of people treated for Gonorrhoea and Syphilis broken down into two groups – 'immigrants' and locals. This began when Dr Moss took office. These were the only diseases subject to this kind of analysis and in 1964 venereal diseases were given by each separate country of birth. In 1962 there were two cases of leprosy among immigrants and this was made much of by the *Leicester Mercury.*

In 1963 it was reported that poor housing conditions led many West Indian mothers to request hospital places to deliver their babies. The proportion of such requests granted is not known although less than half of all applications for hospital confinements were allowed. Despite these problems Dr Moss claimed that there was no necessity to adapt local authority services to any great extent to meet the needs of immigrants.[37] This suggests that this highlighting of the problems of 'immigrants' served purposes other than medical needs and health provision. Dr Moss did not report on the proportion of hospital beds allocated to West Indian mothers. This did not stop the *Leicester Mercury* reporting:

> Immigrants and the post-war bulge put strain on city's mother and baby services. Women forced to give birth at home because there are not enough hospital beds.

And continued:

> Immigrants live in terrible conditions and have to have their babies in the hospital.[38]

The influence of Dr Moss's view can be seen in that the 'problem of immigrants' in relation to health and housing was so often highlighted by the *Leicester Mercury*. These press reports contributed to the hysterical tone of much of the press coverage of 'immigration' issues and illustrates the importance of key officials in influencing public debate.

By 1969 the government found the 'demolition and rebuilding policy too costly' (Burke, 1981, p.124). Although formally it was the local authorities who controlled Council housing the government has, in effect, controlled the amount of building through the loan sanction machinery. The 1964 Housing Act had given local authorities powers to force landlords to improve their properties (Burke, 1981, p.124). But take up was low so in 1969 LAs were given power to declare General Improvement Areas (GIAs) (Burke, 1981, p.125). This enabled grants to be made to landlords with fewer conditions attached and for LAs to make general environmental improvements. Burke has suggested that the fear of racial conflict induced the government to tackle the problems of the inner cities (Burke, 1981, p.124).

The first GIA in Leicester was the Clarendon Park area. This was a white working class district of small terraced homes to the south of the city centre and on the west side of the main A6 London Road. It was bounded to the north side by much larger properties overlooking Victoria Park and to the east by even grander houses along London Road itself. The result of Clarendon Park becoming a GIA was gentrification of the area. It became a magnet for young professionals; lecturers, teachers and social workers, with some working class people remaining. By the early 1970s the problems of the 1969 Improvement Programme had become apparent to the government and LAs. Investment in privately rented houses had not been achieved and the gentrification of GIAs was widespread. A report by LCC in 1976 recorded that between 1969 and 1974 work in the GIAs had actually been most successful in areas of low social stress. The policy had less benefit for people in the worst areas of housing in Leicester such as Highfields.

In addition the problems of high rise developments of the 1960s were already becoming obvious, although Leicester had never embraced this strategy so enthusiastically as many other authorities such as Nottingham or Birmingham.[39] Leicester had, as a result, relatively few high rise blocks. One of the few, however, was the St Peter's Estate in the heart of Highfields. People were already applying for transfers from St Peter's by the early 1970s.[40]

In 1973 government housing policy became subject to a rethink. In

June of that year the government published a White Paper *Better Homes, the Next Priority*. This initiated a policy of improving the worst homes first and was enacted in the Housing Act of 1974. Local Authorities had increased powers to lend money, housing associations were encouraged and provided for security of tenure in rented properties. It also made provision for the setting up of Housing Action Areas (HAAs). Local authorities were given wide powers to improve these areas through a variety of means including compulsory purchase for enforcing improvements. Older stocks of houses were no longer pulled down but renovated. In Leicester as in other places this would have the effect of preserving the environmental characteristics of those parts of the city which had stood since the nineteenth century. At this time Highfields and Spinney Hill were among the worst housing areas in the city. Conditions were poor and the houses had generally not been improved. There were about 200 empty houses, 4.5% of all properties. This had partly been a consequence of planning blight. Two schools, Medway and Highfields Junior had wanted to expand their sites and there was also a new road proposal which, although it was eventually dropped, affected property.

The city was divided into improvement zones in a 15 year programme of renovation. Details of the programme were outlined in Leicester's Renewal Strategy Programme Report of 1976. The city was divided into 53 zones which were then subdivided into three bands by 'social stress'. This was indicated by housing, social and environmental conditions. The 1971 census identified areas with high proportions of rented accommodation, overcrowding, and empty properties and other factors were used to band areas. The band of 17 high social stress included six areas in Highfields. The policy adopted involved an ambitious project of action on a variety of fronts. There were powers of compulsory purchase which were used to persuade owners to make use of empty properties. Housing associations were also involved in improving properties. Housing Action Areas were sub divided into smaller areas of several streets and a policy of involving the residents in these small areas in an apparently democratic process to improve the areas began. A meeting was set up with residents in the area who were encouraged to elect representatives to meet with council officials on a monthly basis to discuss issues. The aim was to publicise grants and involve residents in the process. Housing advice centres were set up in empty houses and tenants were moved out of their houses while they were improved. There was some demolition of the worst properties. The problems of the needs of very different groups of people were hard to balance as the area included white residents, some of them elderly, as well as black people and Asians. It was acknowledged that the programme often created great social turmoil.[41] There was some minimal recognition of the special needs of different groups of people[42] for example, the elderly, the handicapped, single people particularly students and 'immigrants'. These special needs were identified in the review of the policy. This period was also one of cuts in council house building. In Leicester the number of new starts dropped from 1000 to 500 to 425 from 1974 to 1977. There were 12,500 people on the waiting list.[43] While LCC was aware to some extent of the way in which the policy impacted on various groups of people, there was no systematic monitoring of the effects of the policy on these different groups. The view was that improvements would benefit all.

That the renewal policy had a positive effect on housing conditions in the Highfields area is not open to doubt. But many problems remained. Preserving the characteristics of this part of the city built in the nineteenth century also tended to preserve the negative features such as lack of open space or few safe play areas for children. Such absences are known to have a detrimental effect on children's health. LCCR along with Shelter, were the only organisations critically monitoring Leicester City's housing policy, particularly with respect to its effects on black and Asian people in the city. It continued to identify housing problems in the light of the renewal strategy in the second half of the 1970s.

The LCCR has been described as the main forum for discussions on race relations between its establishment in 1965 and the late 1970s. It had a very large membership of representatives from a wide range of organisations from all over the city including officers of LCC. It had problems in reconciling conflicting functions as a channel of communications between minority organisations and LCC and its objective to promote good race relations[44] and its African Caribbean representatives became impatient with these problems.[45] Its sub committees produced reports on housing conditions of black and Asian people in Leicester and had been critical of the Council's policy.

In 1978 the LCCR's report on Leicester's urban renewal scheme showed that virtually the whole of Highfields had become part of a HAA or GIA and a report of the LCCR Housing Officer in March 1979 pointed to the need for special provision for elderly Asians, black and Asian women, West Indians and alienated black youth, the problem of social cultural and community facilities, play areas for children and the need for special provision for low income owners, among others. A further problem was that of the young homeless which had been an issue for some time.

Earle Robinson reported to the Select committee on Race Relations and Immigration in December 1975 of:

> The situation where we had to start counting heads and find who was actually sleeping in a launderette or sleeping in a park or dossing down somewhere else. There were quite a few. There are a couple of hostels that we are trying to recommend people to go to.[46]

One such hostel was set up in 1975 by Youth Foundation, an organisation which grew from the Black Peoples' Liberation Party (BPLP). Later it received grants from the British Council of Churches and funds from Urban Aid. The aims of Youth Foundation were to provide temporary accommodation for young black men, to provide for rehabilitation of youths returning from Approved Schools, to co-operate with projects to create a better understanding between races, to provide facilities for multiracial studies and to act as an advice centre for young black people. The centre was led by a group including T. Zampaladus, 'Minister of Information'[47] of the BPLP. Youth Foundation later evolved into a housing association which specialised in the provision of housing for black people.

In November 1977 the City Council had been designated an Inner Area programme Authority and Leicester's programme under this scheme began in April 1979. Leicester obtained one of the highest Inner Area allocations of any programme authority. The first urban programme was announced in May 1968 after Enoch Powell's 'Rivers of Blood' speech. The aim was to provided funds to areas identified as having problems in housing, education, health and welfare (Smith, 1974, pp.67-69). While attention to the needs of black and Asian was central to the Programme in practice the funds went to geographical areas rather than groups of people. Studies of other areas have suggested that black people did not do well from this funding (Smith, 1974, p.71). A second phase of the programme followed a government review in 1977,[48] and economic, industrial and environmental issues became the focus of the programme. Once again, a justification of the policy was 'the fear of racial tension and subsequent loss of social control' (Smith, 1974, p.70).

However this policy can be seen as a move towards minimal recognition of the need to address the specific needs of ethnic minorities (Smith, 1974) and in Leicester some minimal ethnic monitoring was carried out from 1978. The 'racial' background of applications for council houses, mortgages and grants were recorded.[49]

In 1980 the LCCR in a document titled, *Access to Housing*, criticised the authority for lack of comprehensive ethnic monitoring. The Select Committee on Race Relations and Immigration had drawn attention to the lack of records in relation to housing of ethnic minorities in 1971. It had also pointed to the 1969 Cullingworth Committee which had called for an end to residential qualifications for access to council housing. Leicester had steadily reduced its residential qualification from five years but maintained an employment or residential qualification of one year. The LCCR continued to point to the disadvantages experiences in housing conditions of all parts of the city.

By 1981 the City Council's renewal programme had been hampered by the reduction in the government's Housing Investment Programme. While the renewal programme improved the housing conditions in Highfields, basic inequalities in housing conditions between Leicester's black and Asian residents remained.

Conclusion

Exclusionary practices by private providers, together with collusion in public policy makers resulted in African Caribbeans living in poor housing conditions in the 1950s and 1960s. While it is clear that like white people, African Caribbeans wanted decent and appropriate accommodation, many others attributed poor conditions to the choice of African Caribbeans people themselves. Key decision makers within the LA concurred with this view. By the mid 1970s racial discrimination was beginning to be acknowledged and Leicester City Council implemented changes which benefited African Caribbeans and Asians. The adoption of the renewal policy, the reduction of the residence rule and the persuasion of building societies to end red lining, marked the change in this approach. The renewal policy improved housing conditions in Highfields which has contained the largest concentration of African Caribbean people in the city and has continued to do so through the period.[50]

In its policies LCC was following policy at Government level. In the 1950s and 1960s the Government did nothing to assist, or deal with the problems in housing of black and Asian immigrants. The lack of planning was consistent with the policy on entry to the country as a whole and cannot be seen as a product of a 'laisez faire' approach. By the late 1970s, Government policy towards the housing inequalities of black people showed some evidence of change. But it was characterised by weak and ineffectual race relations legislation and uncoordinated, inconsistent and unsystematic policies. Ameliorative projects were led by fear of racial tension and often failed to benefit the groups for which they were intended (Smith, 1974, p.75).

While it has not been possible to establish a direct relationship between policy in housing in Leicester and the disadvantages experienced by African Caribbeans, housing policies for different areas of Leicester have been described. We know the approach to housing adopted in Highfields. The experiences of African Caribbeans described above and information concerning conditions in Highfields provided by reports of organisations such as Shelter can be linked with this policy.

It was in the early years of the 1980s that LCC began a more systematic and positive approach to racialised disadvantage. For example racial harassment on council estates was addressed in 1982 (Fitzgerald, 1988) and the Survey of Leicester which analysed the population of the city in terms of ethnic groups, was carried out in 1983.[51] These more positive policies were insufficient to remove inequalities created by complex and cumulative interaction of past policies and disadvantages arising from the class position of African Caribbeans. It is the class position of African Caribbeans to which we now turn.

Notes

1   *LCCR News*, May 1978.
2   See Chapter Five.
3   Interview with Roy Rowe, 6 September 1994.
4   Interview with Elvy Moreton, 12 December 1994.
5   Interview with Eric Hudson, 28 April 1994.
6   Interview with Carmel Charles, 13 July 1994.
7   Ibid.
8   Interview with Lee Morris, 5 September 1994.
9   Interview with Monroe Thomas, 4 October 1994.
10   Interview with Novelette Mackoy, 17 August 1994.
11   Interview with Doris Cope, 19 January 1994.
12   J Eldridge, 'Race Relations in Leicester University', MA Thesis, University of Leicester, 1959.
13   Interview with Percy Harding, 30 November 1994.
14   *Illustrated Leicester Chronicle*, 5 February 1955.
15   *Leicester Mercury*, 27 January 1955.
16   *Illustrated Leicester Chronicle*, 28 June 1958.
17   Ibid, June 28 1958.

18   See Chapter Three.
19   In fact there were negligible numbers of Pakistanis in Leicester at that time. Mr Hillier was presumably confusing Pakistanis with Indians, or East African Asians.
20   *Leicester Mercury*, 22 Sept 1958.
21   See Chapter Six.
22   Survey to City Development Policy, LCC, 1952.
23   LRO, DE 3277, City of Leicester, Housing Committee Minutes, 17, 7, 1958.
24   Ibid, pages 26-27.
25   Valerie Marett Archive (VMA), Minutes of the Housing Sub Committee, LCCR 23 3 1973.
26   *Leicester Mercury*, 12 December 1969.
27   L Mitchell, 'Accommodation Patterns of West Indians Immigrants In Leicester', MA dissertation, University of Leicester 1967.
28   VMA, Renewal Strategy Programme Report, LCCR, 1974.
29   S D Yates, 'Spinney Hills - Housing Satisfaction and Opportunity Among Native and Immigrant Residents', MA dissertation, University of Leicester 1969.
30   Interview with John Perry, Team leader for the Renewal Programme, Leicester City Council 1976-1990, 18 May 1997.
31   *Leicester Mercury*, 17 July 1964.
32   VMA, *Housing*, Vol 1, Report HMSO 1976.
33   *Leicester Mercury*, 18 November 1962, 15 March 1963, 14 September 1963 which concentrated on 'Health problems created by coloured people' 25 September 1963, 28 November 1963, 7 February 1964, 13 December 1964, 19 October 1965, 27 October 1967, 2 July 1968, 16 December 1968.
34   See Chapters Three and Six.
35   *Leicester Mercury*, 19 November 1969.
36   Ibid.
37   LRO, L 641, Health of the City of Leicester, 1962.
38   *Leicester Mercury*, 7 February 1964.
39   Interview with John Perry, op cit.
40   VMA, Howard Baker, 'St Peter's Estate – Some Problems of an Inner City Housing Estate', April 1971, Scarman Centre, University of Leicester.
41   Interview with John Perry, op cit.
42   Housing Policy Paper Renewal Report, LCC, undated.
43   *Leicester Mercury* 7 October 77.
44   VMA, Constitution, LCCR, undated.
45   Interview with Valerie Marett, 16 May 1997.

46	House of Commons, Sessional Papers 1975-76, Select Committee on Race Relations and Immigration, 4 December 1975, HMSO, London, para 35.
47	See Chapter Seven.
48	Cmnd 6845, Policy for the Inner Cities, Department of the Environment.
49	House of Commons, Session 1980-81, Fifth Report from the Home Affairs Committee, Racial Disadvantage, Evidence of Mr P Graham, Director of Housing, LCC, 13 March 1981, HMSO, London.
50	*Survey of Leicester*, LCC, 1983.
51	*Survey of Leicester*, op cit, 1983.

References

Brown, Colin (1984), *Black and White*, Heinemann, London.

Brown, K (1981), 'Race Class and Culture: Towards a Theorisation of the 'Choice/Constraint' Concept', in P Jackson and S J Smith (eds), *Social Interaction and Ethnic Segregation,* Academic Press, London.

Burke, Gill (1981), *Housing and Social Justice*, Longman, London.

Byron, Margeret, *The Housing Question: Caribbean Migrants and the British Housing Market*, Research Paper 49, School of Geography, University of Oxford, undated.

Byron, Margaret (1994), *Post War Caribbean Migration to Britain: The Unfinished Cycle*, Avebury, Aldershot.

Dahya, B (1974), 'The Nature of Pakistani Ethnicity in Industrial Cities in Britain', A Cohen (ed), *Urban Ethnicity*, Tavistock, London.

Fitzgerald, Marian (1988), University of Warwick, Centre for Ethnic Studies, Resource Centre 'Racial Harassment in Leicester', *Black Housing*, Federation of Black Housing Organisations, Vol 4, No 3.

Foner, N (1979), *Jamaica Farewell*, Routledge and Kegan Paul, London.

Glass, R (1960), *Newcomers*, Allen and Unwin, London.

Grigg, Mary (1967), *The White Question*, Secker and Warbur, London.

Highfields Rangers An Oral History, Leicester City Council, Leicester 1993.

Jackson, P and Smith, S J (1981), *Social Interaction and Ethnic Segregation,* Academic Press, London.

Jansari, A (March 1981), Research Officer Shelter, 'Coloured Households and Owner Occupation A study of the pattern of house purchase of ethnic minorities in Leicester'.

Lee, T (1977), *Race and Residence: the Concentration and Dispersal of Immigrants in London*, Clarendon Press, Oxford.

Luthera, M S (1988), 'Race, Community, Housing and the State: A Historical Overview', in Ashot Bhat, Roy Carr-Hill and Sushel Ohri (eds), *Britain's Black*

Population: A New Perspective, Gower, Aldershot, (2nd ed).

Marett, Valerie (1989), *Immigrants Settling in the City*, Leicester University Press, London.

Panayi, Panikos (1994), *Immigration, Ethnicity and Racism in Britain 1815-1945*, Manchester University Press, Manchester.

Patterson, S (1963), *Dark Strangers*, Tavistock Publications, London.

Peach, C (1975), 'Introduction: the spatial analysis of ethnicity and class', in C Peach (ed), *Urban Social Segregation*, Longman, London.

PEP (1967), *Racial Discrimination in England*, Penguin, Harmondsworth.

Pritchard, R M (1976), *Housing and the Spatial Structure of the City*, Cambridge University Press, London.

Rex, John and Moore, Robert (1967), *Race Community and Conflict: A study of Sparkbrook*, Oxford University Press, London.

Rose, E J B et al (1990), *Colour and Citizenship*, Oxford University Press, London.

Small, Stephen (1994), *Racialised Barriers*, Routledge, London.

Smith, D. J. (1974), *Racial Disadvantage in Britain*, Penguin, Harmondsworth.

Smith, Susan, J (1989), *The Politics of 'Race and Residence'*, Polity Press, Cambridge.

5 Race and Class: The Operation of the Colour Bar and its Consequences for the Class Position of African Caribbeans, 1945-1981

Introduction

Employment is at the heart of any consideration of the development of the African Caribbean Communities in Britain. Whether it was the 'push' of unemployment and the consequent poverty in the sending societies or the 'pull' of job opportunities in the industrialised countries, employment has been central to the debate about the causes of migration. Of those who have argued for the importance of the labour needs of the advanced economies in the post war period Ceri Peach (Peach, 1963, 1965, 1968, 1991) has been the most influential. His thesis, supported by international comparison (Peach, 1991), is that the number of immigrants coming to Britain from the former colonies was a function of vacancies in the economy. Castles and Kosack's (1973) detailed and comprehensive examination of international migration also places the need for labour at the centre of an explanation for post war migration albeit from an opposing Marxist perspective. Both provided an economic determinist perspective. While for Castles and Kosack it was the logic of the capitalist system which turned black migrants into an industrial reserve army, Peach presents the economic system as given, as almost outside human agency. Government intervention to control Commonwealth immigration in the 1962 Act interfered with what could otherwise have been a naturalistic process where the free movement of labour reflected the demands of the economy in Western Europe. While Peach has maintained and developed his argument since the mid 1960s, debate has recently begun to focus on human agency as a factor in creating the employment and settlement patterns of African Caribbeans in Britain.

The extent to which those in positions of power, government policy makers and officials such as labour exchange officers and employers utilised racialised prisms through which to make decisions concerning black (and white) workers has been increasingly recognised (Duffield, 1988). Clive Harris (1993, pp.29-30) has argued that it was not inevitable that black workers should occupy jobs at the bottom of the occupational hierarchy doing jobs which white workers would not. There were vacancies throughout the occupational structure and the occupational distribution of black workers could be most adequately explained by racism.

Marxists such as Castles and Kosack (1973) have seen racism as a tool with which the employing class divided the working class. The racist views of individual employers do not, from this perspective, interfere with the historic task of the bourgeoisie to pursue profit. Racism is seen as instrumental rather than the result of employers acting on widely held cultural beliefs about the suitability of different groups of workers, for different jobs. While racism can be seen as beneficial to the employing class at the level of the whole society, Marxist explanations give insufficient attention to the role of cultural beliefs in influencing individual employers and others with the power of hire and fire decisions at the level of the individual workplace. Such cultural beliefs lead to decisions which are not always economically rational, for example when vacancies are not filled because of a view that black workers are not suitable in jobs which involve dealing with the general public.

This argument also applies to government policy. Early post war studies of black and Asian migration to Great Britain argued that Government policy in the 1950s could best be described as laissez-faire and that the change of policy embodied in the 1962 Act was a result of popular pressure particularly following the 1958 Notting Hill and Nottingham 'race riots'. This has been challenged by research making use of now available government documents of the 1940s and 1950s. This has revealed the extent of the racist perspectives held by members of the Cabinet, and other policy making officials. The Labour government of the late 1940s and Conservative governments of the 1950s did not want black workers in Britain and their views were often reinforced by the opinions of servants of the state at all levels who used racist stereotypes and assumptions in consultation exercises (Harris, 1993, Carter, Harris and Joshi, 1993).[1] For example in the survey on unemployment among 'coloured workers' conducted for the Ministry of Labour in June 1953, the report from the North Midlands Regional Officer in Nottingham which covered Leicester, wrote that it was agreed that:

Opportunities are however becoming less owing to reduced demand for labour in occupations which are particularly suitable for coloured workers.[2]

Labour exchanges influenced both the occupational and consequent geographical distribution of black workers by directing them into particular jobs and in doing so reflected and contributed to the maintenance of cultural beliefs about black workers which were held throughout society by workers, trade union officials, employers and the general public. This understanding provides a modification of Peach's thesis which seeks to explain both the occupational distribution and pattern of settlement of black people in Britain as a 'replacement population'. Vacancies in jobs and housing created in cities by the exodus of white people and their replacement by black and Asian workers can no longer be regarded as a naturalistic process. Mark Duffield's (1988) study of the role of immigrant labour in foundries highlights the political role of the labour movement in the subordination of immigrant workers. He argues that:

The dispersal of black workers, encouraged by the Ministry of Labour and helped by the trade unions had most effect in relation to West Indians. The success of the dispersal policy can be judged from the fact that, until the present recession at least, the profile of West Indian employment was distinct from that for Asians. The former tending to be more thinly spread over a wide range of industries whilst the bulk of the latter concentrated in just a few such as iron foundries or textiles. The difference between dispersal and concentration would have a significant effect on the struggle against racism that West Indians and Asians could wage in the industrial sphere (Duffield, 1988, pp.28-29).

At the highest level government policy was influenced by a racialised perspective of Britishness which both Labour and Conservative governments sought to maintain through their policies of recruitment of European white workers, British emigration to the dominions and black colonial immigration to Britain (Paul, 1995).

An increasingly sophisticated understanding of the racialised nature of British culture and society in the second half of the twentieth century has developed in research and scholarship over the past ten years and with it has come an understanding of the way this has influenced the lives of black people in material terms and in producing the racialised identities through which people understand their lives. Attention is now beginning to focus on the consequences of racialised white identities too.[3] Work in the area of race and employment can be seen to parallel developments in the area of gender and employment.[4] Employers have used culturally determined attitudes concerning the suitability of posts for men and women in order to allocate jobs (Beechey and Perkins, 1987; Walby, 1986). While notions of appropriateness of jobs for women may change one time, levels of segregation by gender remain high. But while the study of the use of gender as an organising principle by employers based on culturally held beliefs about the capabilities of women workers is established, it has yet to be taken up in historical or sociological research with respect to race. As Harris (1993, p.21) has written, the operation of the 'colour bar' has not been properly explored. Explorations of the salience of gendered categories of workers has provided a challenge to human capital theories by, for example, demonstrating through gender the social construction of the concept of skill in the workplace. It is increasingly realised that a view which suggests that women tend to work in occupations that are less skilled has to be modified by an understanding which sees jobs which women do, classified as unskilled: that skill categorisation is related to notions of the type of workers who do the jobs rather than an objective measurement of skills or knowledge required.

This chapter examines the employment of workers from the Caribbean from 1945 in Leicester. African Caribbeans were able to find work in Leicester easily where labour shortages were particularly acute.[5] However, their occupational choices were circumscribed by the operation of the colour bar, by gendered and racialised notions of their suitability as workers. Two very important employers of black workers in Leicester, Polymer Engineering and Imperial Typewriters, have been shown to operate discriminatory practices. The fact that employers did make choices and had the power to influence job opportunities for black people is also illustrated by the case of Grattons, the Mail order clothing retailer, with offices in Leicester. The manager, Graham Brown[6] set out to structure the workforce in his business according to a set of values concerning who should and should not be employed. The firm adopted a policy, from 1966 onwards, which countered the more common practises of local employers towards black people and was unusual, possibly unique. This case does illustrate the power and ability of employers to choose the kind of people who are employed. This chapter describes this remarkable policy. Trades Unions have had a dual and contradictory role in relation to black people and the relationship of African Caribbeans to Trades Unions in Leicester is raised. Finally the chapter also considers, the possible consequences in terms of the social class position of Leicester's black population of the de-skilling which was a feature of many employment histories.

Leicester's Industries

Leicester used to have a reputation for prosperity dating back to the beginning of the twentieth century. The basis of that reputation lies in its unusually high levels of employment for women which produced a high average household income.[7] Women have traditionally been employed in greater proportions than men in the hosiery industry which was the main industry in the region until the mid nineteenth century (Nash and Reeder, 1993, Chapter Two). From that period the manufacture and distribution of footwear became important and during the 1920s Leicester became known internationally as the greatest boot and shoe distribution centre in Britain and the largest centre in the world for the production of knitted goods (Simmons, 1974, p.5).

The late nineteenth century saw the development of light engineering and also the production of machinery to serve the hosiery and footwear industries (Nash and Reeder, 1993). During the inter war period engineering experienced rapid expansion. In 1939 the three traditional industries still dominated the local economy. Of 135,000 factory workers nearly two thirds were employed in these industries. There were 34,000 workers in hosiery, 21,000 in boot and shoe manufacture, 15,000 in distributive trades and 13,000 in engineering (Leicester Official Industrial Handbook, undated, p.57).

By the end of the war engineering had become the most important industry employing between 30,000 and 40,000 workers (Leicester Official Industrial Handbook, undated, pp.35-36). During the Second World War footwear and textiles began to decline. Between 1939 and 1945 10,000 women workers left the hosiery industry, many directed to work in munitions and the 14,000 men who previously worked in boot and shoes entered the armed services.[8] These industries never recovered their lost workers, despite a post war boom.

Leicester ceased to be a major footwear centre. Manufacturers such as Stead and Simpson, Brevitts, Freeman, Hardy and Willis also engaged in retailing. In the 1950s a series of take-overs led to the formation of the British Shoe Corporation which became the largest footwear retail organisation controlling 40% of all outlets (Nash and Reeder, 1993). The largest knitted textile employers, Corahs, which was owned by Courtaulds also controlled thirteen other companies in the 1960s.[9] Leicester remained relatively prosperous. From 1948 until the mid 1970s unemployment levels were consistently lower than the national average. The engineering industry continued to manufacture textile and footwear machinery, typewriter machine tools and also made vehicle products, heavy engineering, stone crushing and foundry equipment, metal products and cement mixers. The main manufacturers included Stibbe, Bentleys, and Wildt Mellor Bromley, Imperial Typewriters, Jones and Shipman, Adcock and Shipley, Metal Box and 'John Bull' Rubber company. Other important manufacturers were Frears Biscuits, Foxes, the sweet manufacturers, and Walkers Crisps. Many of these firms made extensive use of black and Asian workers, both men and women, from the 1950s onwards.

Shortage of Workers

In March 1946 Leicester had no women and one hundred men registered as unemployed from a population of 263,000.[10] The shortage of labour in Leicester was part of a national shortage that was a major problem for the Labour government immediately after the war (Joshi and Carter, 1984). Locally there were over 4,000 job vacancies for men and 1,500 for women. The manager of the local labour exchange claimed that this represented a smattering of the jobs really available. 'Men and women pass through our hands almost immediately. It is quite phenomenal' (Leicester Official Industrial Handbook, undated, p.37). The shortage of workers was so great that 'manufacturers are at their wits end to cope with the rush of trade'. There was a

> boom in fact, in every trade, but at the same time there is this awful brake of the shortage of labour and materials, and the slowly-to-be-lifted restrictions which further add to the troubles of the manufacturers (*Leicester Official Industrial Handbook*, undated, p.45).

Representations were made by the Leicester and District Hosiery Manufacturers Association to the North Midland Regional Board of Trade concerning the shortage of workers in the industry (*Leicester Industrial Handbook*, p.59). They were given 'valuable assurances' by the government. There were particularly acute shortages in boot and shoe manufacture and engineering.

> The shortage is being particularly experienced in the foundry sector of the industry, a fact which is causing a bottleneck in production.

It was to foundry work that many male West Indians in Leicester were directed. Despite the 'valuable assurances' given by the government, the shortage of labour was much discussed in the pages of the *Leicester Mercury* and the *Illustrated Leicester Chronicle* into the 1950s. In an article in the *Leicester Mercury* of 1 April 1950, it was stated that 'vacancies far exceeded numbers of unemployed'. In January 1950 the *Leicester Mercury* had described how a scheme providing for the introduction of foreign female workers into the hosiery industry had been held up due to lack of suitable housing. Local manufacturers were considering providing a hostel for German 'girls' selected by the Ministry of Labour.[11] This scheme is consistent with government policy of preferring white European workers to fill vacancies rather than Caribbean or Asian migrants, demonstrated in research at national level and discussed elsewhere in this book (Paul, 1995). The report also mentioned the lack of day nurseries, a deficiency which if put right would enable women with children to take up employment. On 17 November of the same year the *Mercury* reported 1100 vacancies for men in Leicester in engineering, banking, civil engineering, railways and passenger transport and 1,000 for women.[12] The persistent shortage of women in textiles led to manufacturers offering financial inducements to existing employees to recruit others and paid people to walk about the town in sandwich boards advertising vacancies (Nash and Reeder, 1993, p.59).

This situation continued into the 1950s. In the government's count of unemployed 'coloured' workers in June 1953, it was reported that there were no 'colonial' men registered as unemployed or claiming National Assistance. There were just two Indian and Pakistani men registered.[13] In a *Leicester Chronicle* piece entitled 'Leicester's Coloured Nurses' on 5 March 1955, Mr L H Dearne, Secretary of Leicester's Number One Hospital Management Committee said:

> We would gladly take more coloured girls if we could. Nearly all the hospitals in the county are short of staff.[14]

In 1956 the shortage was still acute. There were five jobs for every boy leaving school.[15] But by 1958 the *Chronicle* was reporting the difficulties of school leavers in finding work [16] and reports of the 'slump' appeared in 1959.[17]

However by the end of the decade Leicester was once again experiencing shortages of workers. Foreign workers were needed to fill jobs in agriculture,[18] there were vacancies for 9,000 miners in the East

Midlands and concern was being expressed in the editorials of the *Leicester Mercury*.[19] There were high levels of vacancies of all types. In 1961 hospitals were desperate for nurses and had posts which were left vacant for months.[20] Beds were being closed because of staff shortages.[21] At Imperial Typewriters the Director's Report for 1963/4 reported:

> In Leicester it is very difficult to recruit new labour owing to the very high level of employment; we are not alone in this city in suffering from a chronic shortage of work people of all types.[22]

Sometimes even acute shortages would not persuade employers to take on black workers. In an unusual statement which both acknowledged and opposed the colour bar in Leicester, workers at a hosiery firm wrote to the Leicester Mercury:

> The large hosiery firm which we work for is advertising for factory labour. But at the reception office all coloured applicants are turned away and consequently there are often vacancies which could easily be filled at once. We cannot understand why no workers are better than coloured workers. All of the younger girls here who have had to do temporary reception work lately (including me) are disgusted and very disillusioned.[23]

In 1970 Leicester was chosen by the Department of Employment as an area to be investigated as an example of labour shortage in engineering. Leicester was known to have 'a record of persistent shortages in skilled engineering occupations'.[24] In large firms labour shortages were said to have restricted production and caused overdue delivery dates.[25] Unemployment was not a problem in Leicester until the mid 1970s. It was then for the first time that black and white workers had serious problems in obtaining employment. However, even in the 1970s unemployment in Leicester was lower than in many other parts of Great Britain.

African Caribbean Experiences - Men

The desperate need for workers in Leicester for most of the period between 1945 and 1974 is reflected in the experiences of Caribbean migrants. Most found jobs of some description easy to obtain. Monroe Thomas came to Leicester from Barbuda in 1961 aged twenty nine. In Barbuda he had been a 'guide for tourists... I used to do skin diving and scuba diving'. In the

1950s he spent one month each summer in Guadaloupe. He also fished. Between 1954 and 1958 he spent ninety days a year cutting sugar in the Virgin Islands. He arrived in Leicester on a Tuesday and on the following day he had secured a job stacking milk cartons at Kirby and West, the Leicester Dairy. After working there for nine months on a flat rate of £7 per week he got a job in 'the hosiery'. Then he moved to a dyers where he stayed for one year. 'I worked hard.' But by the mid 1960s 'they had no work coming in and I got no pay'. Monroe then moved to a foundry where the basic pay was £12 per week but he earned £18 because 'you could work as long hours as you wanted'.[26]

Monroe Thomas's ability to move from job to job in order to acquire better pay and conditions was typical of the experiences of many Caribbean workers. As Eric Hudson said:

> There was so many job vacancies that if you didn't like a job you could move from one to another.[27]

However, moves did not always produce an improvement. Jobs were easy to get but they were often of the least desirable kind in unpleasant conditions. Monroe Thomas eventually became ill with pneumonia at the foundry.[28] The type of jobs male workers obtained in Leicester reflected national patterns of employment of black labour (Harris, 1993, pp.21-23). It is hard to establish the extent to which local labour exchanges influenced these patterns of employment [29] Most Caribbean workers in Leicester managed to get jobs without visiting the Labour exchanges. More often, jobs were obtained through contacts with friends or relatives already in employment and this contributed to the pattern of occupational distribution of black workers.

Jobs per se were not a problem but black people in Leicester experienced discrimination. Understanding of the factors which create the different employment patterns of racialised groups has become increasingly sophisticated, as it has with understanding gender segregation at work. The nature of the way in which perceptions of both race and gender interact is however underdeveloped. In the 1950s the expression 'colour bar' was used to describe the total exclusion of black people from particular categories of work. Many white people in Leicester supported this. Mr PJ Murphy in a 'Mock Parliamentary Debate' on what was described as the 'Midland Number One Talking point' held in February 1955 in Leicester's Guildhall, said:

> I realise there is a colour bar in Britain and up to a point I support it. It was
> wrong for us to have to live cheek by jowl with coloured immigrants.

The report of the debate in the *Chronicle* began:

> Can you imagine primitive Zulus working as conductors on Leicester
> corporation buses? No? Neither could members of the Leicester Parliamentary
> Debating society ... they were warned that the trickle of Jamaicans now
> entering Britain might develop into an overwhelming flood of Indians, Burmese
> and African savages unless restrictions were imposed on colonial
> immigration.[30]

The term 'colour bar' was not used to describe situations where quotas
were in operation or where promotion, advancement and development at
work were only available to whites.   So for example, Mr L H Dearne
Secretary of Leicester Number One Hospital Management Committee, said
of 'coloured' nurses in March 1955 'There is no bar on colour or creed in
any of our hospitals' but in the same speech he also said 'we must limit the
intake of colonials to 25% of each training class'.[31]

The 'colour bar' was simultaneously supported and denied. This placed
a complex double burden on black people who were well aware of
discrimination yet found it hard to demonstrate.   Overt admissions of
discrimination were rare.   More common were what Mark Duffield
described as 'gentlemen's agreements' between employers, trades unions
and local labour exchanges in informal understandings on the placement
and control of black workers (Duffield, 1988, p.28).   These agreements
included quotas, promotion barriers and first dismissal in times of
redundancy. Duffield suggested that Leicester was one of the few places
where such agreements were formally recorded. An agreement was made
between the Transport and General Workers' Union (TGWU) and the
Leicester company Tubes, to limit the number of foreign and colonial
workers employed. The agreement restricted numbers, insisted upon union
membership and stipulated that these workers would be the first to go in
cases of redundancy. It also made provision 'that blacks should not be
promoted to supervisory posts or transferred to piecework jobs' (Duffield,
1988, p.28). This agreement resulted from the company recruiting five
Jamaicans in 1954. Such documentary evidence of agreements is rare.
Systematic evidence of an experimental and statistical nature concerning
discrimination against black people was not collected until the mid 1960s
confirming what black people already knew but was previously denied

(PEP, 1967; Smith, 1974; Brown, 1984). This kind of evidence was important in that it demonstrated the fact that black people were being denied jobs and advancement, but failed to examine the longer term consequences.

Research at national level, noted above, about the stereotypical and prejudiced view of governments and officials concerning black workers has only been explored more recently. These attitudes were shared by many employers and others in Leicester. This is not surprising given the pervasiveness of racism in the national culture. For example, Jamaicans were described as only half as efficient as the average British worker in the *Leicester Chronicle* in 1955.[32] But it is through the employment experiences of West Indian workers in Leicester that some of the effects and long term consequences of the racism embedded in British culture can begin to be revealed.

African Caribbeans at work in Leicester were treated differently from white workers in a variety of ways. A participant observation study of the Midland Red Bus Garage in Leicester carried out in 1971 described a range of ways in which opportunities arose to discriminate against West Indian and Asian employees. For example the training officer was heard on the telephone to a garage manager. He said 'We've got one for you, but it's all right he's white.' Other ways in which the black and Asian workers were badly treated included the use of discriminatory testing procedures, insulting language and harassment by fellow workers.[33]

Many black people were able to recall events in their employment history when they felt they were discriminated against. Sometimes this was clear but often it was not. Black workers faced a burden of being unsure as to whether they had been badly treated and this insecurity had an effect on later decisions.

Reuban Nelson came to Leicester from Jamaica, where he had worked in farming, in 1961. He got a job at William Barsby Engineering as a labourer. He stayed for four years. He believes that he was discriminated against but he had not realised it at the time. On occasions he was told there were no vacancies or sometimes that the vacancy had gone.

> I never knew it was because of the colour of my skin... I went to one place and asked for a job. The foreman came and told me I must wait. A vacancy is there. I wait and the receptionist told me the vacancy is gone. I never knew what was going on.

Years later Reuban Nelson met the foreman.

The foreman came to my house. I was upstairs sleeping because I was working nights at Jones and Shipman. [When I came down] The foreman was playing cards with a friend and he says 'I know you, you came for a job... he then said 'The other workers were asked if they would work with a black person and they said no'.[34]

This consultation with white workers was not an uncommon occurrence. Roy Rowe who came to England in 1949 described this to a reporter on the *Chronicle*:

White people don't like us really. They say things behind our backs. They are too ready to pick quarrels and when it comes to getting a job a coloured man is up against it. The boss simply won't engage a West Indian unless he's found out first how the [white] workers feel. Unless they agree there's no chance. It's so unfair. If people could only realise that we're human like themselves and that we're fighting for the same things they are fighting for. It's only the colour of our skins that is different. [35]

The staff manager of one of Leicester's biggest firms again blamed others:

People complained that when their children answered the door and found a coloured man standing there they were frightened. So we had to take them off our delivery services... the men had been absorbed into other jobs but were victims of circumstances beyond their control. They are the victims of the ignorance of the people who complain. If the idea of the coloured man being a bogey man had not been put into the mind of the child they would have no groundless fear.[36]

Reuban Nelson said:

What can you do? You can't do nothing... It's hard to decide ... not easy... it can be there but you don't know. I got on all right with many of them... one or two blacks, one or two Asians but mostly whites. I get on all right with my work mates.[37]

Reuban Nelson worked at Jones and Shipman.

I never liked the job - labouring. I worked there eight years. I asked the gaffer for a transfer and was refused. So I leave. But then I went back. [38]

After being unable to get another job Reuban Nelson returned to Jones and Shipman where he worked for another six years in the same job. He was never granted his request for a transfer. He needed a hip replacement operation and so had to leave. His last few years working were spent as a Park Attendant for Leicester City Council.

Roy Rowe came to Leicester in 1956 aged twenty six. He worked for Leicester City Transport as a bus conductor. His decisions about employment were influenced by an anticipation of the problems he might face as a black man in an occupation which had inherent conflicts in relationships. He had been a prison officer in Jamaica and he did at one time apply for a job in the prison service in Leicester.

> I told them what colour I was. But they were mostly white people in the gaol. I applied for the fire service but they said there were no vacancies...The first job I had was on the buses. I came on the Monday ... We went to somebody who said 'I think I'll give you a chance'. He gave me the papers [for a test]. He said that's very good, but you're a farthing out. But I said 'look at that figure. It looks like a half penny'. I was told 'you're a clever bloke'.[39]

Roy Rowe picked up the job so quickly and they were so short of staff that his training period was cut short. Four months after starting the job he was training others.

> In them days there was a lot of colour prejudice. I used to be abused on the buses...I would have stuck it for a long while but the irregular hours were upsetting my stomach.[40]

He got another job at John Bull.

> I was abused by the foreman. I told him 'the days of slavery are over'. Then I went back on Midland Red as a conductor and I learned to drive the buses. You had half hour practice and they expected you to drive. Then I went into engineering at Imperial Typewriters. I was signing on getting £11.10s. My wife was sick. But the money was not very good, just the same as the dole. I got so cheezed off staying at home I wanted to go to work. It was piece work.[41]

One occasion Roy Rowe was quite sure that he was discriminated against.

> During a time of unemployment I went to sign on. One day I was given a letter to go down Abbey Lane. I walked in the office - at that time I had a letter. I

have been given it from the Labour Exchange, but I didn't give it to her. She said 'Sorry there's no job at all'. I said 'Are you sure? I've been sent by the labour exchange'. When I showed her the letter, she turned blue, man.[42]

Roy Rowe spent his last fifteen years at work at Corahs, the hosiery company. He made good friends and became the union representative in the Knitters' Union where he was involved in negotiating wages.

Black people who came to Leicester possessing professional qualifications or craft skills were often unable to obtain work which made use of these qualifications, abilities or skills. Sometimes people struggled for years to get the chance to exercise skills they had learned, but with varying degrees of success. Ronald Rochester worked for himself in Jamaica as a car trimmer. His first job in England after leaving the RAF was in a foundry in Dudley in 1949. He then moved to Syston just outside Leicester in a mattress factory. He took what he could get. He then moved to Imperial Typewriters and then to John Bull. But he again got a job working with cars about which he felt happier.[43] Ramdin writes of the bitter disappointment of migrants which was the result of a long and slow adjustment to accepting inferior positions (Ramdin, 1987). West Indians only occasionally got the opportunity to express this resentment in public for example in the local press.[44] On one such occasion a West Indian expressed concern about deskilling in the *Leicester Mercury*.

How would the European react in Africa or the West Indies if having spent years as a carpenter then were told they were not wanted in their trade?[45]

The policies of British Governments in the early post war period in attempting to consolidate influence through encouraging white emigration to the Empire/Commonwealth while simultaneously discouraging black immigration into Great Britain (Paul, 1995) are expressed in the personal experiences of African Caribbeans. Rupert Fevier, a qualified chemist came to England in November 1953. He was employed by a Leicester firm of manufacturing chemists.

It is possible for a coloured man to get a higher education in the West Indies usually through the self sacrifice of his parents. But his qualifications once he has attained them are useless. The key jobs are held by Europeans and they continually bring replacements from Europe...

Many of the West Indians coming to Britain are doctors, lawyers, teachers and other college education men whose ambitions are continually frustrated in their own land. If our land could give us a life worth living we would gladly go back.[46]

Downward occupational mobility has been discussed in the literature on African Caribbeans in Britain (Ramdin, 1987; Glass, 1960, p.96; Smith, 1974; Foner, 1979; Bryon, 1995). Margaret Byron in her study of Nevisians in Leicester noted that occupational status was reduced after migration (Byron, 1995, p.100). She gives the example of a teacher who was not accepted as qualified in Leicester (Byron, 1995, p.102). The position of black and Asian teachers in Leicester is discussed in Chapter Six.

An illustration of the talented nature of many Caribbean migrants to Britain can be shown in Mervin Ishmael. Son of a policeman, he had joined the British army in 1942 from Barbados. He transferred to the RAF and served as a wireless operator until 1948 when he settled in Leicester. He spent four years at Leicester College of Technology and went on to Leicester University College. He was awarded an industrial relations scholarship at London University where he received a diploma in Industrial Relations. He became secretary of the shop steward's committee at the factory where he worked and was a member of Leicester Trades Council. He was also secretary of the Anglo-Overseas Association. He married a white woman.[47]

An example of what happened to many educated and talented people in Britain lies in the work history of Carlton Sweeney. It is only when this history is considered as a whole and over time that the long term consequences for him are revealed. The cumulative effect of the discrimination and prejudice West Indians met needs further research. Such experiences can be seen as a powerful influence on the class position of West Indians as a group.

Carlton Sweeney tried hard to enter his chosen profession in accountancy, to have a career path and to earn his living by his obvious skills and talents. He had some success through perseverance but he was unable to achieve his career aims through professional advancement. He continued to develop his considerable talents outside paid employment.

Carlton Sweeney came to Leicester from Antigua in 1953 as a young man of twenty four. He had attended a College in Trinidad where the Headmaster had been grooming Carlton as a teacher. His parents owned shops and his mother had offered to set him up in business with a shop or perhaps a music studio where Carlton could teach music. He played guitar and piano or organ.

I said no, I'd rather concentrate on economics. I always liked music ... I just wanted musical pleasure. I didn't see it as a way to make a living... I had a misconception of England actually, just like many of us. During the war it was a different atmosphere. When we got into civilian life... In a way I was so pro-British - that we felt our place was here rather than America. I heard you could work and study. I wanted a degree in economics majoring in accountancy. I wanted to get into an office but it wasn't easy. In an office sometimes they were talking about £3 per week. I would be ashamed to send to Antigua to say I was working for £3 a week. I got my first job at £5 10s. There were chaps my age over there [Antigua] in masonry and other craft trades making that money anyway... Actually although we weren't all that industrialised, we were more rural, you had very good woodworkers, the standard of education was quite high; equal to anything here.

The racial overtones were done in such a manner that they weren't obvious. It was not until you've left and turned you back that you realised. We had the impression [before we came] that we wouldn't have any problems racially. Sometimes we would 'phone up for a job and my English was good, they would say the vacancy was there. But by the time you got to the factory, they would say it has been taken. It happened to me. One of the things was that I gave it back to them actually.

At my first job this fellow was always making racial taunts. It was an industrial chemists. I worked on the production line. I asked if I could go into the laboratory because I always did well in science. But they said no. In the factory although I saw the conditions I thought I would take a correspondence course.

A man at the Labour Exchange told me there was work at Imperial Typewriters. The Personnel Officer said there was no vacancy. I said thank you very much and left. The next day I went back and said. 'You have a job here and I want it.' He was amazed at my direct approach. He said 'when can you start?' I was there fourteen years.

I was the only coloured person in two thousand. I earned respect. I was always annoyed when some of the people say thing like 'we come from the trees'. We didn't tell our parents. We didn't want to upset them.

But working and studying wasn't easy at all. I found working forty-four hours a week, I couldn't do anything at all... I used to leave Imperials at 6 o'clock for a class at the College of Technology. It was advanced work. I was studying chemistry and accountancy. The class started at half past six. One of the classes - the teacher had already started.

[At Imperial's] I was in the finishing section. I got transferred. I started in the portables. I always liked doing things with my hands. My Dad was a furniture maker. He let me use his tools. The assistant foreman wanted to make me a handy-man for the whole production line to fit into any section. I wanted to make more money in the finishing section. I was fast. They used me to time parts, to set the time for the new factory opening in Hull. They used the fastest person to set the time rates so I went slower. There was hanky panky. They were taking advantage and I didn't like it ... I took any opportunity to take a course. ... I got a grant to go to Teacher's Training College but it was only three hundred pounds a year. I had the children - two little ones.

I belonged to the Trade Union. They introduced a day release course in public relations. I only got on because Imperial didn't do the choosing. Seven of us were sent up from Imperial. We had to overcome certain remarks in the factory every time we got off the course.[48]

Carlton left Imperial and worked in an engineering firm. But he wanted to go to business college. A person at the Labour Exchange helped him to secure a place at a college in Nottingham in 1968. 'I was getting somewhere. I got a grant and expenses.'

Later he worked for Leicester City Council preparing accounts. It was suggested that he moved to manage the books for the newly opened Leicester United Caribbean Association (LUCA) Centre in the late 1970s, which he did 'for a couple of years'. He then helped to set up the Highfields Workshop with Balunda.[49] From there he moved to another community project as volunteer co-ordinator for Caribbean Court.[50] Although Carlton Sweeney had become an accountant he still faced prejudice. He was interviewed for a job in local government.

I was the only West Indian that was accepted. During the interview the lady who was chairperson was antagonistic from the word go... She was so abrupt. The other man on the panel was embarrassed. The others were given twenty minutes but I was in and out in five. I found out what happened later but I don't believe in making too much noise. I was asked 'as a common man, how would you feel about having to discuss with business men?' I said 'I never thought of myself as a common man. By the way I've been to school with people like you and I'm not overawed by the English. ... My father was one by the way.' I'd made up my mind I wouldn't get it. Later a friend of mine found out, it was prejudice.

Carlton Sweeney was an early and prominent member of the Anglo-Overseas Association. Later he became a member of the Board of Visitors of HM Prison. He became treasurer of the Caribbean Credit Union, treasurer of the African Caribbean and Asian Forum.[51] He has written and published a book about his experiences in Leicester[52] and was the British correspondent of the *Antiguan Times* and later the *Daily Observer* of Antigua. In retirement he has taught music. He was unable to use his abilities and talents fully in a professional capacity. While the existence of discrimination has been demonstrated statistically and in case studies of organisations since the mid 1960s, the effects of racism on individuals over their lifetime has been explored much less. The relationship between the deskilling experienced by individuals and the consequences this has had for the class position of West Indians as a whole is under researched.

African Caribbean Experiences - Women

Women migrants from the Caribbean, like their male counterparts, had no difficulty in getting employment in Leicester. The way in which women have been excluded, ignored and marginalised in discussions of migration has been discussed in Chapter Two. Women as paid employees is an under researched area and little systematic research about the employment patterns of women was conducted until the early 1980s. Even less is known about the structural position of black women workers although there has been some attention to this subject in recent years (Phizacklea, 1982; Morakvasic, 1983; Bryon, Dadzie and Scafe, 1985; Mirza, 1992; Byron, 1995). Previously adopted paradigms used to analyse the role of black women in society, for example that of the pathology of black family structure, have been criticised (Lawrence, 1982, pp.116-122). However, knowledge of black women workers has not been integrated into theories of migration nor of discussions of the class position of black people in Britain to produce gendered understandings. Instead the differential place of black women workers has been addressed separately and has not yet penetrated the models used to theorise the social class position in relation to race.

This is not to argue that black female workers have not been theorised at all. Annie Phizacklea (1982) in her study of West Indian women workers in Britain has used the concept of class fraction developed in relation to male and female workers to describe the position of black women workers. She argued that West Indian female migrants faced triple oppression as workers, migrants and women.

Early studies of migration have tended to assume that women migrants from the Caribbean came as dependants upon men. More recent research focused on Caribbean women have shown that a primary reason for migration was access to paid employment. Phizacklea's study of West Indian women in North West London in the 1970s, shows that before migration:

> Women's access to regular paid employment is even more limited and sporadic than it is for men because they are confined to sectors of women's work...Money making activities included dressmaking, domestic service, small-scale trading and certain agricultural tasks, but such work rarely enables a woman to achieve financial independence (Phizacklea, 1982, p.100).

This view is supported by Byron's (1995, Bryan, Dadzie and Scafe, 1985, p.250) study of Nevisians in Leicester and is reinforced here.

Elvina Prince came to Leicester in 1963 having left Antigua in 1959. She had 'no job' in the Caribbean. 'I did housework for other people. I worked for a Chinese lady.' In Leicester she became a cleaner and later worked at John Bull and Walkers Crisps. Then she moved to a clothing factory.[53] Veronica Williams also had not had paid employment in Barbuda before she came to Leicester in 1959. 'I worked the ground - helped father with the vegetables.' Her father sent her to Leicester when he heard that other members of the community were over here. 'He hoped I would help him out.' She got a job in a shoe factory.[54]

West Indian women sought paid employment in Britain. Stone reports that:

> West Indian women valued the greater opportunity for a regular weekly wage and thus financial independence in Britain (Stone, 1983, p.37).

Davison (1962), Foner (1979), Carby (1982) and now Byron (1995) show this as the primary reason given by Caribbean women for coming to Britain.

> A remarkable discontinuity revealed in this analysis of Caribbean migration is the high level of gainful employment among the female members of the sample in Britain compared with their marked lack of waged employment in Nevis prior to migration. Women migrated primarily to engage in paid labour per se (Byron, 1995, p.120).

Black women experienced the prejudice of an ethnocentric view of such employment of women. It was widely held during this period that children whose mothers worked in paid employment were somewhat disadvantaged compared with those whose mothers were full-time 'housewives'. This view was reflected in discussion held by the Select Committee on Race Relations and Immigration held in May 1973. Mr William Deedes, in the Chair said:

> The national figure is that thirty-three per cent of married women are working outside the home and one third of the labour force is women; that is your comparison. You [Brian Piper] are saying that in Leicester it is 40%. I think that does constitute a problem.[55]

Earlier Mr Deedes had received a positive answer to the question:

> Do you think that more mothers from the New Commonwealth have to go to work proportionately than mothers in our own country...is it more?

One feature of black female labour consistently reported in the literature is the fact that the characteristics are closer to that of white female labour than is the case for black and white men. The primary disadvantage is gender. Anthias and Yuval-Davis (1992, p.119) argue it thus:

> The disparities are lower because sexism already disadvantages women in the labour market to such an extent that the effects of race are not so apparent.

Caribbean women enter a labour market already segregated by gender. Phizacklea (1982, p.103) examined the position of West Indian women compared to white in terms of economic activity rates, hours worked, occupational distribution and unemployment levels. She suggested possible reasons why West Indian women were more likely to be in the labour market than white women. Factors include the material disadvantages of black people in general, that for West Indian women the concept of motherhood involves an economic responsibility and the importance of financial independence (Phizacklea, 1982, p.102). Indeed differential activity rates for black and white women become even greater where mothers of young children are concerned (Stone, 1983, p.35). West Indian women are more likely to work full time. Part time work is a way in which white women have combined child care with paid employment and have coped with the demands of the double day. Caribbean women have addressed this problem by working shifts (James and Harris, 1993, p.76). Caribbean women have higher average earnings than white women but this is a product of longer hours worked as pay rates are lower.

Occupations by sex are highly segregated but West Indian women have a slightly different occupational distribution than whites. While 27% of white women are clerical workers only 11% African Caribbean women work in this area and whereas 11.6% of white women are in sales, only 1.3% of African Caribbean women are. Only 11.7% of white women are professionals but 25% of black women fall into this group. This is misleading however because a high proportion of black professionals are nurses where they are concentrated in the least desirable areas of mental and geriatric nursing and are more likely to be State Enrolled Nurse (SENs) rather than State Registered Nurses (SRNs) (Ramdin, 1987, p.310). In manufacture West Indian women are also more likely to be in engineering and clothing than white women. It is interesting that in Leicester, those employers listed above who were well known as employers of black labour, maintained the gendered segregation of their workforces. There is also evidence that black women are more likely to be unemployed than whites. Irene Breugal (1994, p.192), dissenting from others, argues that the existing literature presents a false picture of the position of black women in relation to white and that racism is as important in determining black women's place in the labour market as gender. This is in major part, she suggests, as a result of the categories used to collect statistics on employment, which obscure differences between groups. However Breugal herself creates some confusion because she does not consistently distinguish between different groups of black women which sometimes include Asian women and sometimes do not. There are great differences between different racialised groups in terms of employment patterns.

Knowledge gathered in existing studies of black women workers is confirmed by the experiences of West Indian women who have come to live in Leicester since the Second World War and interviewed for this study. Women came as independent migrants or came primarily to get a job whether they were joining partners or other family members. Like men they found jobs easy to get.

Sometimes it was men who came to join their wives or girlfriends rather than the other way round. Roy Rowe came in 1956, 'I was twenty six. I had two sisters in Birmingham... my wife (girlfriend then), she was here'.[56] Herdle White came on his own to meet his wife in Leicester.[57] Linda Herbert worked in a shop in Nevis to finance her trip. She travelled with her cousin and got a job a week after arriving, in a knitwear factory.

I took what I could get. I worked there then at Imperial Typewriters on East Park Road and I left there in 1964. Then I went to British Telecom as a telephonist. I became a supervisor. I stayed twenty eight years.[58]

Elvy Moreton came to England in 1959 and to Leicester in 1961 aged twenty four. She had been a teacher in St Kitts and came to train as a nurse. She travelled on her own but joined family- a brother and a cousin.[59]

The higher activity rates of West Indian women are confirmed by the experience of people in Leicester. In Robinson's study of sixty families of primary children in Leicester conducted in 1964, he found that forty two of the families had two parents and in all of these except four, both parents had paid employment.[60] Women were subjected to the same kind of prejudiced and stereotypical attitudes as male black workers and those who had skills or professional qualifications or experience acquired in the West Indies found they, like the men, were unable to use them in Britain. Margaret Byron (1994) in her study of Nevisians in Leicester characterises this deskilling process as a horizontal move. For example a skilled seamstress in the Caribbean became an unskilled hosiery worker in Leicester. Byron does not see this as de-skilling and agrees with Foner (1979) that a paid wage and higher standard of living for women in Britain produced satisfaction. She has argued that her data does not show evidence of downward mobility. However, this presents an oversimplified view of the relationship between pay and social class position. Historically, there are groups of manual workers whose pay levels have been higher than those of non manual workers, particularly if male manual workers are compared to female non-manual workers. The issue is further complicated for the position of married women in that their social class position has been given by their husband's occupation rather than their own. Whether the change from being a skilled seamstress with low remuneration in the West Indies to higher paid but unskilled hosiery worker in Britain represents downward occupational mobility is perhaps less important than the fact that skills acquired in the West Indies did not promise an opportunity for upward mobility in Britain. There were job vacancies throughout the occupational structure in Britain but all but a few West Indians in Great Britain became confined as members of the working class.

The experience of women who came to Britain with the intention of career advancement as nurses demonstrates that prejudice and discrimination hindered progress. Many women came from the West Indies to train as nurses at Leicester General Hospital which had an arrangement with the Colonial Office from 1945.[61] Referring to the

Leicester area Mr LH Dearne, Secretary of Leicester Number One Hospital Management committee said:

> Most of these girls are only interested in state registered nursing training.... three hospitals in Leicester the Infirmary, the General and Loughborough General ran courses to become state registered nurses but 'colonials' were limited to 25% of each course.[62]

One such nurse who came to Leicester was Ernie Romeo from Antigua.[63] She said she felt lucky to have been accepted. Mr Dearne complained that 'colonials' would not fill vacancies where they were short staffed but wanted State registered training. Although he admitted that 'all those we accept are highly educated girls we write to their homeland to check their qualifications'.[64] The stereotypical attitudes expressed by the Matron of Leicester General Hospital in 1955 and by Miss C K Banks, the Matron of Westcoates Maternity Hospital were described in Chapter Three.

These attitudes are reflected in the experience of African Caribbean women who wanted to be nurses. Doris Cope came to Leicester from Barbuda in 1964 aged nine. When she left school aged fifteen she started working at Cherubs, a clothing manufacturer in Leicester. She then changed jobs and worked in the laundry of a children's nursery. She began training as a nurse at nineteen years old at Leicester General Hospital.

> That's where I really came across racism. I had low status. Doctors looked over your head. Even the patients didn't look at you. I felt stupid. I didn't do very well, but I worked really hard. I became an SEN. I really wanted to be an SRN but two white women were chosen. They're Sisters now. I was resentful at times, but I didn't see it as racism then.
>
> I did two years training and went to Markfield, the TB hospital for the terminally ill. It was a bit heavy.[65]

Novelette MacKoy came about ten years after Doris Cope, in 1972, aged twelve. After school she went to work in a knitwear factory.

> I went to the careers officer but she had nothing positive to say. I wanted to be a nurse but the best they gave me was work in a factory... I didn't get on with my Dad and I wanted to be financially independent. ... the job was boring, extremely boring. I was stuck at this machine, it was so boring, full of middle aged women. I thought, what am I doing here? I did that for one year. Then I went to British Shoe. British Shoe had a lot of black workers. But the black

workers never got promotion. I questioned it with the Works Manager. We were stuck in the same job while the white workers moved on.

Then Novelette MacKoy moved to the Leicester Royal Infirmary as a nursing ancillary with the intention of training as an SRN.

I really enjoyed it. I didn't really see any racism. The patients were great. I worked in Orthopaedics. It was very hard work, very stressful but we all supported each other.

Experiences of black women confirm both commonalities and differences in the working patterns of black and white women. Both groups faced the problems of the double day of unpaid domestic responsibilities in addition to badly paid employment. After having a premature baby, Novelette MacKoy began part-time working at night. Her second child was also born prematurely and needed a lot of extra care so she gave up paid employment. But later she found a part-time job as a Community Nurse working 8.00pm -11.30pm, on three evenings a week. But she gave that up and joined the Community Care day nursing service. She was given a lot of responsibility - more than an ancillary should have.

The elderly were very racist. I never saw a middle aged white woman smile at us. They were wary. But it did change once I started speaking. One said 'You speak very good English. You're just like us aren't you?' - once the human barriers were broken down.[66]

Motherhood and caring responsibilities held back career advancement too. Elvy Moreton came to England in 1959 from St Kitts where she had been a teacher. She arrived in Leicester in 1961 aged twenty four to join her husband. She wanted to train as a nurse and began her training in Birmingham. She tried to continue her training in Leicester.

I got pregnant and the Matron told me straight away that the patients came first and I couldn't stay on the training... I had done about two years eight months of the three years... The matron did write to me and ask me to return but I had no baby sitter and I gave it up. I went to work in a factory. Like everybody else I wanted to stay five years. But you get caught in a trap. You've got to look after yourself and you've got to look after your family back home. I could hardly make ends meet here but I had to send money home to my mum. [In the factory] I had Saturday and Sunday off but my husband didn't think it right for him to look after the baby. They still had the mentality that a woman's place is in the home. They couldn't see that it was 'us' rather than a man and a woman. That limited a lot of black women like myself and men couldn't see any further than that. You should be in the home looking after the little ones while they can go to the pub and do whatever they wanted.

Elvy Moreton moved to Parkers in Queen Street where she worked for nine years.

I was always interested in catering. I started to take an interest in that, especially Caribbean catering. I used to do a bit of catering on the side for functions. A job came up at the Highfields Workshop Centre. There was no Caribbean style cooking then. The Colleges were all geared to teaching French cooking. I wrote a letter to the Highfields Newspaper.

As a result of this letter she began a year's research in Caribbean Catering at Southfields College in Leicester and began to help teaching the students. Eventually Elvy Moreton gained a City and Guilds Qualification in the teaching of adults and began to teach evening classes in Caribbean cooking.[67]   Elvy Moreton was a pioneer member of the Anglo/Caribbean Association in the 1960s. She helped initiate the Supplementary School for African Caribbean children and became involved in many community organisations. But her most memorable achievement was as founder of the Leicester Caribbean Carnival.[68]

Imperial Typewriters

Imperial Typewriters has been considered one of Leicester's most important companies throughout the twentieth century. In 1953 the firm went public and attracted a full front page report in the *Illustrated Leicester Chronicle*[69] where it was described as the 'largest [producer of typewriters] in the British Empire'. The Company employed both men and women and until the time of the strike in 1974 women received around two thirds of the hourly and piece work rates of pay for men.[70] Successive Annual Reports from 1953 until its take over by Litton Industries in the mid 1960s consistently mention the shortage of labour as a major problem.   For example in 1960/61 the Chairman's Review reported that 'production has not kept pace with orders received, the limiting factor being shortage of labour at Leicester'.[71] It is not surprising therefore to find that Imperial was an important employer for black and Asian workers in Leicester. It would be difficult to find a black family in Leicester who would not have had a member working at some time or another at Imperials.

The Imperial Typewriters strike which began on May Day in 1974 has been widely written about and is regarded as highly significant in the history of black industrial struggle in Britain (Dhondy, 1974, pp.201-205; Moore, 1975; Wilson, 1978; Braham, Rhodes and Dearn, 1981; Ramdin, 1987; Sivanandan, p.139). This is at least in part because it illustrates the collusion of trades unions with management in operating racist practices in British industry. It is also used as an example of immigrant workers 'fighting back' against their use as cheap labour and of women debunking the myth of passive Asian women workers. Ramdin describes it as an 'extraordinary strike' (Ramdin, 1987, p.278). Sivanandan describes it as 'The apotheosis of racism and therefore the resistance to it' (Sivanandan, pp.139-140). The strike attracted media attention and it has been claimed that this was because the workforce was 'coloured' and had received attention from the National Front (Bentley, p.234). It is also well remembered as Leicester has a reputation for the absence of industrial conflict.[72]

The strike at Imperials began as part of strike action at four Leicester firms on May Day. Three hundred workers at British United Shoe Machines, three hundred at Bentleys, two hundred at General Electrical Company in Whetstone and thirty-nine Asian workers from Imperial walked out. The strikers at British United, Bentleys and GEC quickly returned to work but those at Imperial not only stayed out but within a few days had been joined by another five hundred mostly Asian workers. While the initial grievance had been with regard to bonus levels, this was quickly radicalised with a revolt against racism and racist practices at work. The strike was not made official by the trade union concerned (the TGWU), indeed the union sided with the management against the strikers. This was in Ron Ramdin's words 'an extraordinary strike' with the Asian workers and their supporters sustaining a protracted dispute against all the odds. By the end of July most of the strikers had been sacked. Subsequently, the factory was to be closed by Littons, the parent company (Ramdin, 1987, pp.273-274).

The strike at Imperial has been viewed in the literature as an Asian strike involving a battle between Asian workers on the one hand and the employers supported by a white trade union officials of the TGWU on the other.[73] The role of African Caribbean workers at the factory has been largely ignored. One report by a female Asian worker described the position of West Indians at Imperial:

The West Indian women are treated just like us .... the West Indian women work like us but they go with the white women. Not a single West Indian in our section came out with us on strike. I don't know how they are in other sections. Even some of our own Asian women, who didn't support out strike have this same attitude. They don't want to take our side (Dhondy, 1974, p.205).

There is evidence that some West Indians in Leicester seemed to distance themselves from the strike describing it as 'an Asian strike'.[74]

Imperial employed West Indian people, both men and women until it closed and their non-involvement in the strike could be worthy of further investigation. The significance of this and its implications are not known. One problem with the use of the term 'black' to describe all people of colour who are subjected to racism is that it can obscure differences between groups (More, 1975, pp.77-85; Ramdin, 1987).

Polymer Engineering

An important employer for black people in Leicester was Polymer Engineering, a division of Dunlop Ltd., referred to locally as 'John Bull', 'Dunlop' or 'Metalastic'. Polymer Engineering was one of seven operating divisions of the Industries Group, itself being one of four groups of Dunlop Ltd., the principal operating subsidiary in the UK of Dunlop Holdings plc. The firm in Leicester manufactured, marketed and sold coolant and brake hose for the motor industry and metal and rubber bonded components (metalastic products).

This employer was subject to an investigation by the Commission for Racial Equality carried out between 1977 and 1981.[75] The investigation concluded that the company indirectly discriminated against black and Asian employees in promotion to the position of foreman. Criteria for selecting foremen were used which were not relevant to the job and these procedures had the effect of discriminating against black and Asian workers. Two of the most important firms in Leicester have been shown to operate discriminatory practices with regard to black and Asian employees. This is something which has been described and understood by black people in Leicester. However not all employers operated such policies.

Grattons and Graham Brown

Grattons the mail order clothing firm through its manager, Graham Brown, [a pseudonym] operated a remarkable and perhaps unique, policy from 1966 until it closed in 1988 of what might now be described as positive discrimination. Graham Brown came to Leicester from Bradford in 1966 where he had worked for Grattons, since 1954. He became the new manager of Grattons' large premises in Gedding Road. At that time Grattons employed 350 people in Leicester nearly all of them women. Many were part time and tended to be older. The youngest worker was about forty and some were over sixty years old. Graham Brown made some important decisions about the composition of the work force based on his beliefs. He wanted to employ 'youngsters' and because the office required reorganisation he had the opportunity to change the composition of the staff.

> One of the earliest things I did was to recruit a young girl into the typing department. At that time the existing manager from whom I was taking over the firm was still on site and the first day that this girl started she was on another floor from where we were in the office, and said 'Have you seen a coloured face in the office?' and I said 'if you mean - in the typing department, I suppose you have why?' He set off on a tirade which I don't need to go into... I'd seen Leicester here and it was fairly clear even at that time that there was a fairly big coloured population, if you want, and if they fitted the bill as far as I was concerned they were good enough to employ. ... It was clear to me that if I was going to run this office we've got to have youngsters. We've got to have a mix of staff because you can't do it with ... I looked around the Highfields area and could see the faces round about ... I did two things, I made contact with a head I knew and talked about school leavers and possibilities etc and the other thing was I went to the Community Relations Office ... I said, I don't want to get involved in politics but I wanted to know a bit about the Community I'm living in.
>
> I was building up the office. At the peak there were over 700 people... The Asians were coming in - mostly young girls and it built up. I insisted right from the start they were coming in on an absolutely equal basis... I also insisted we would hear no language in the office except English. It helped them because a lot of them did not have very good English at this stage and they needed it in the office to do the work. ... The thing built up and the West Indians came in. I made absolutely sure that they too (were treated equally), because there were more problems in terms of whites especially for them, the white population didn't really expect them to be in the office ...they're all right

for nurses and punching tickets on the buses but not in the offices. I tried to delegate.

Graham Brown had close contact with schools and offered opportunities to leavers who were judged to have poor chances in the employment market. Graham Brown 'took them on'.

Some people were closing their eyes to the real difficulties people were having and you've got to work out what the problems were.

By 1971 out of 658 employees, 83 were black or Asian. Graham Brown kept detailed records of the ethnicity of people working in the various departments and the percentage who were Asian or black. All the black and Asian workers were full time, usually youngsters whereas there were many older part time white women workers. While the percentage of black and Asian workers was less that 16% overall they made up about 50% of the young full time workers. By the 1980s Graham Brown felt that such detailed records were unnecessary.

At one stage when the National Front was in its heyday we had a supervisor who used to support them...she was a leading light of the National Front. I said 'I would defend to the last your right to belong to any political party but the first time it entered the office you're out'. They weren't militant.[76]

The office closed in 1988 when Graham Brown retired and the work was moved up to Bradford.

The case of Grattons under the leadership of Graham Brown deserves attention for a number of reasons. His policy illustrates the power that employers had in influencing the lives of people through the opportunities that are opened or closed through employment. Second, it is often argued that because racial discrimination was widespread that individuals were powerless to do other than adopt 'normal practice'. Graham Brown shows that discrimination was not inevitable. Systematic attention to monitoring the nature of the workforce and policies designed to make the composition of the workforce reflect the community outside provides a challenge to the inevitability of black workers being confined to jobs which white workers would not do.

Trades Unions

Trades Unions have played a dual and contradictory role in relation to racism and sexism in the work place. While on the one hand, trade unions have been a vehicle for opposition to racism and immigration control (Duffield, 1988; Miles and Phizacklea, 1978, pp.90-98) they have also failed to address the specific needs of black and women workers (James and Harris, 1993; Chessum, 1989) and have on occasions actively colluded with discriminatory practices of employers and have instigated such practices (Duffield, 1988; Miles and Phizacklea, 1984). Despite this, African Caribbean workers, both men and women, have joined trades unions. Evidence here supports the view that the pattern of commitment to trades unions among disadvantaged workers, for example women, black and Asian workers is similar to other groups.[77] A range of involvement occurs; paper membership only, involvement on specific issues and full commitment including the holding of official positions. The experience of Leicester African Caribbean migrants in this study are consistent with the findings of Phizacklea (1982, p.111) in her study of African Caribbean workers in North London. Some African Caribbeans in Leicester have received help from their unions over specific problems, but were otherwise involved little. Others have ambivalent attitudes towards trades unions as a result of their experiences. Ronald Rochester found little support from the union when he experienced racist abuse at work and did not act to help him when the management of Jaguar Cars in Coventry incorrectly calculated his wages which resulted in a loss. However, his union, the Amalgamated Union of Engineering Union (AUEW), helped him get a job on one occasion and despite these problems Ronald Rochester remained a member for thirty five years.[78]

Some people have shown strong commitment to their unions. One such person is Herdle White. He came to England from Jamaica in 1959 and then moved to Leicester in 1961. He began working at Freemans Shoes and later went to Bentleys, the Leicester engineering company. He stayed there twenty years becoming shop steward for the AUEW, active in the anti racist campaigns of the 1970s and involved in the Labour Party.[79] Women expressed their support for their unions but also raised the problems for women particularly mothers, of being active. Elvy Moreton had wanted to be more involved:

I was always a trade union member. I asked to be a representative. But [it involved] a lot of time going to meetings and when you've got two young children you can't do it. It takes up so much time.[80]

In Leicester, trades unionists have been among those opposing immigration controls, calling for anti discrimination legislation. For example, in September 1958, the Trades Council held a meeting to discuss immigration controls. The meeting was addressed by Mervin Ishmael, a Barbados born rubber worker and member of the TGWU. Mervin Ishmael was one of the pioneers of the African Caribbean community in Leicester and was a committed and active trade unionist. The meeting passed an anti 'colour bar' resolution and called for racial discrimination to be made a punishable offence. Leaflets were given out calling for black and white workers to unite and 'sweep the racialists off the streets'.[81] However, some Leicester trades unionists have also supported immigration controls and discrimination against black workers. A meeting of the Trades Council, which at the time had an Indian President, held in May 1961, illustrates this. Male members of the Boot and Shoe Union called for the 'limitation of colonial immigration' to Britain. This caused 'bitter outbursts' and the resolution was referred back to the executive committee of the Trades Council by delegates representing 80,000 workers, some of whom were 'coloured'.[82] The debate was both emotional and acrimonious. One speech quoted a report concerning a 'planeload of illiterate Pakistanis' coming to Britain and met the reply:

For heaven's sake the press is here. We must make it clear that the Trade Union movement stands for no discrimination on colour or any other grounds.[83]

The *Leicester Mercury* carried a full report of the debate and it continued:

Mr Alfred Stanley for the Boot and Shoe Union read the resolution which called for people allowed into [Great Britain] to be skilled and to have the necessary finance. It also called for an inquiry into the living accommodation which most of these people are prepared to accept...Coloured people are infiltrating into the lower paid workers not into the upper tax classes... The difficulty is that concentrated in these lower jobs they will have difficulty in keeping up their standard of living. Mr Joseph Hall replied that without the coloured worker many essential services would be in trouble. He said it would be dangerous to accept the resolution and perhaps a sub committee could work with established immigrant organisations on housing problems. Mrs A E

Adams of the Leicester Women's Boot and Shoe Branch said that sometimes coloured people had wept when unable to find jobs. [84]

Conclusion

African Caribbeans in Leicester as in other areas of Britain are overwhelmingly working class. As Clive Harris has argued, labour shortages existed in the post war period throughout the occupational structure but black workers, male and female were channelled into particular occupations within the unskilled manual strata. Women were also accepted as nurses but were kept at the bottom of that particular occupational ladder. Both men and women experienced occupational segregation vertically and horizontally. Black people found it very difficult to achieve middle class status and this was true of Leicester. Very few people were able to maintain professional or skilled status which they may have had on arrival or achieve it over their occupational lifetime in Leicester. African Caribbeans were confined to a limited range of jobs designated as suitable through racialised and gendered constructions of identity. The practice of recruiting workers through word of mouth, evident here in the accounts of African Caribbeans in Leicester exacerbated the concentration of workers among a relatively small number of employers. The working class profile of black people in Leicester then contributed to a racialised construction developed from the 1970s onwards, through which this working class profile has been seen as evidence of African Caribbean failure as an 'ethnic group' particularly in relation to the Asians who are seen to be more successful economically. The few exceptions to the class profile of African Caribbeans has not challenged this construction.

One notable exception to the general pattern of work histories was Robby Robinson.[85]   During the 1970s, a small group of middle class African Caribbeans in Leicester has been created to a large extent through Leicester City Council's involvement with the African Caribbean community. Through its support for a variety of 'community' projects the Council has created opportunities for a few African Caribbean people to enter professional services. But this group remains small. The majority were denied the opportunity to express their skills and talents through employment. This is not to say, however, that people have not found other means of personal development. The racialised construction of identity evident in public discourse and operating in the work-place informed public policy when black children began to appear in schools in Leicester from the late 1950s. Chapter Six shows how the pervasive racialisation impacted on the experiences of children.

Notes

1   For a discussion of Winston Churchill's racism see A. Roberts 'Winston Replied that he Didn't Like Blackamoors', *The Spectator*, 9 April 1994.
2   PRO, LAB /8 /1898.
3   Some aspects of the construction of white identity are discussed in Chapter Three.
4   It is a pity that scholars have not adopted identical terminologies in describing labour market differentiation.   The terms 'vertical', and 'horizontal' segregation are used by Hakim (1979) to describe differentiation with respect to gender.
5   Harris, (1993, p.15) argues that 'labour shortage has been presented as a natural phenomena divorced from the capitalist system of production'.
6   This is a pseudonym.
7   Nash and Reeder ,1993.
8   Leicester and Lille were listed as Europe's two most prosperous towns by the League of Nations after World War Two. *Daily Mail*, 12 April 1946.
9   Ibid.
10   Ibid.
11   *Leicester Mercury*, 6 January 1960.
12   *Leicester Mercury*, 6 January 1950.
13   PRO LAB /8/1898.
14   *Illustrated Leicester Chronicle*, 5 March 1955.
15   Ibid, 30 June 1956.
16   Ibid, 28 June 1958.
17   Ibid, 20 June 1959.
18   *Leicester Mercury*, 10 January 1961.
19   Ibid, 14 January 1960.
20   Ibid, 25 January 1961.
21   Ibid, 23 February 1961.
22   LRO, L658, *Imperial Typewriters Director's Report 1963/64*.
23   *Leicester Mercury*, 25 September 1964.
24   LRO, L620, 'Skilled Engineering: Shortages in a High Demand Area. An Inquiry into the Leicester Area', Department of Employment, Manpower Papers, No 3 May/June 1970, page 3.
25   Ibid.
26   Interview with Monroe Thomas, 4 October 1994.
27   Interview with Eric Hudson, 28 April 1994.

28   Monroe Thomas, op cit.
29   Despite considerable effort I was unable to obtain any records from the Labour Exchange in Leicester.
30   *Illustrated Leicester Chronicle*, 5 February 1955.
31   Ibid, 5 March 1955.
32   *Illustrated Leicester Chronicle*, 5 February 1955.
33   J R Hewett, 'Race and Work: An Investigation in Race Relations in a Bus Garage', MA Thesis, University of Leicester, 1971.
34   Interview with Reuban Nelson, 6 July 1994.
35   *Illustrated Leicester Chronicle*, 1 October 1955.
36   *Leicester Mercury*, 11 February 1959.
37   Reuban Nelson, op cit.
38   Ibid.
39   Interview with Roy Rowe, 6 September 1994.
40   Ibid.
41   Ibid.
42   Ibid.
43   Interview with Ronald Rochester, 10 August 1994.
44   See Chapter Three for a discussion of coverage of the black presence in Leicester.
45   *Leicester Mercury*, 17 February 1959.
46   *Illustrated Leicester Chronicle*, 15 January 1955. Rupert Fevier's view is shown in the pages of the Leicester Mercury in a story about the editor's visit to Jamaica. The issue of 15 February 1960 carried a headline 'Jamaica's Own Little Leicester'.
47   *Leicester Mercury*, 11 February 1959.
48   Interview with Carlton Sweeney, 4 August 1994.
49   Balunda was a founding member of the Black People's Liberation Party. See Chapter Seven.
50   Caribbean Court is the name of complex of sheltered accommodation and a day centre catering for elderly residents of Leicester of Caribbean origin. The Centre was set up by members of Leicester's African Caribbean community and is now partly funded by Leicester City Council.
51   Interview with Carlton Sweeney, 4 August 1994.
52   Carlton Sweeney, *Flight*, Eureka Press, Leicester, 1979.
53   Interview with Elvina Prince, 15 August 1994.
54   Interview with Veronica Williams, 8 May 1994. This is a pseudonym.
55   House of Commons, Sessional Papers, 1972-73, Select Committee on Race Relations and Immigration, 24 May 1973, HMSO, London, paras 878 and 873.
56   Interview with Roy Rowe, 6 September 1994.
57   Interview with Herdle White, 28 September 1994.

58   Interview with Linda Herbert, September 1994.

59   Interview with Ely Moreton, 12 December 1994.

60   C E B Robinson, ' A General Survey of West Indian Children in the Primary Schools of Leicester', M.A. Dissertation, University of Leicester, 1964.

61   The *Leicester Mercury* of 13 April 1950 carried a piece describing how hundreds of nurses were needed in the Leicester area. Ramdin, (1987, page 103), shows that many nurses came from overseas to work in British hospitals. In 1959 overseas nurses entering Britain numbered 6,000 and by 1970 the numbers had risen to 19,000. 'Black Women and Nursing: A Job Like any Other', *Race Today*, August 1974.

62   *Illustrated Leicester Chronicle*, 5 March 1955.

63   Ibid.

64   Ibid.

65   Interview with Doris Cope, 19 January 1994.

66   Interview with Novelette MacKoy, 17 August 1994.

67   Interview with Elvy Moreton, 12 December 1994.

68   The Leicester annual Caribbean Carnival was started mainly by Elvy Moreton in 1984 and is a very important event for both the African Caribbean community and for Leicester as a whole.

69   *Illustrated Leicester Chronicle*, 24 January 1953.

70   LRO, L658, Imperial Typewriters Co Ltd., Imperial Typewriters Branch, (5/221) of the Transport and General Workers Union, 10 May 1970.

71   LRO, L658, Imperial Typewriters Director's Report and Accounts 1960/61.

72   *Economist*, 16 December 1972, page 30.

73   The issue of Equal pay for women has received insufficient attention in discussions of the strike. Wilson (1978), is one of the few writers to give this any prominence.

74   This expression was used by two interviewees. Interview with Eric Hudson, 28 April 1994; interview with Roy Rowe, 6 September 1994.

75   LRO, L658, *Polymer Engineering Division of Dunlop Ltd Leicester, Report of a Formal Investigation*, Commission for Racial Equality, London April 1984.

76   Interview with Graham Brown, 8 February 1995. Grattons in Leicester closed in 1988 when Graham Brown retired. The work was transferred to Bradford.

77   All interviewees in this study were asked about their involvement in trade unions. The majority were or had been members of unions. A minority were actively involved.

78   Interview with Ronald Rochester, 10 August 1994.

79   Interview with Herdle White, 28 September 1994. Herdle White later became the presenter of a music programme, 'The Herdle White Show'

and producer of a magazine programme aimed at African Caribbean listeners called 'Talking Blues', both on local radio in Leicester. His involvement arose because Herdle responded to a programme produced by Mary Beasley about minority groups in Leicester. See M Beasley, 'Racial Integration, A Comparative Study', MA dissertation, University of Leicester , 1969.

80   Interview with Elvy Moreton, 12 December 1994.
81   *Leicester Mercury*, 15 September 1958.
82   Ibid, 17 May 1961.
83   Ibid.
84   Ibid.
85   Clifton 'Robby' Robinson died in March 1996. See Chapter One for brief biographical details.

References

Anthias, Floya and Yuval-Davis, Nira (1992), *Racialised Boundaries*, Routledge, London.

Beechey, V and Perkins, T (1987), *A Matter of Hours: Women Part-time Work and the Labour Market*, Polity, Oxford.

Bentley, S (1981), 'Industrial Conflict, Strikes and Black Workers: Problems of Research Methodology', in Braham, op cit.

Braham, P; Rhodes, E and Dearn, M (eds) (1981), *Discrimination and Disadvantage in Employment: The Experience of Black Workers*, Oxford University Press, London.

Breugal, I (1994), 'Sex and Race in the Labour Market', in M Evans (ed), *The Woman Question*, Sage, London.

Brown, Coin (1984), *Black and White*, Heinemann, London.

Bryan, B; Dadzie, S and Scafe, S (1985), *The Heart of the Race: Black Women's Lives in Britain*, Virago, London.

Byron, M (1995), *Post War Caribbean Migration to Britain: The Unfinished Cycle*, Avebury, Aldershot.

Castles, S and Kosack, G (1973), *Immigrant Workers and the Class Structure in Western Europe*, Oxford University Press, London.

Chessum, Lorna (1989), *The Part-Time Nobody: Part-Time Women Teachers in West Yorkshire*, West Yorkshire Centre for Research on Women, University of Bradford.

Dhondy, M (July 1974), 'The Strike at Imperial Typewriters', *Race Today*, pp.201-205.

Duffield, M (1988), *Black Radicalism and the Politics of De-Industrialisation: The Hidden History of Indian Foundry Workers*, Avebury, Aldershot.

Foner, N (1979), *Jamaica Farewell: Jamaican Migrants in London*, Routledge and Kegan Paul, London.

Glass, Ruth (1960), *The Newcomers*, Allen and Unwin, London.

Hakim, Catherine (1979). *Occupational Segregation: A Comparative Study of the Degree and Pattern of Differentiation between Men and Women's Work in Britain, the United States and Other Countries*, Department of Employment, Research Paper No 9, London. Hakim's terms are reversed in the case of black workers, James (1993).

Harris, Clive (1993), 'Post-War Migration and the Industrial Reserve Army', in Winston James and Clive Harris (eds), *Inside Babylon: The Caribbean Diaspora in Britain*, Verso, London.

Lawrence, E (1982), 'In Abundance of Water the Fool is Thirsty: Social and Black Pathology', Centre for Contemporary Cultural Studies, *The Empire Strikes: Back Race and Racism in 70s Britain*, Hutchinson, London.

Leicester Official Industrial Handbook, Leicester corporation, E.J. Burrow, undated.

Miles, R and Phizacklea, A (1978), 'The TUC and Black Workers 1974-1976, Discrimination and Disadvantage in Employment', *British Journal of Industrial Relations*, Vol 16, No 2.

Miles, R and Phizacklea, A (1984), *A White Man's Country: Racism in British Politics*, Pluto, London.

Mirza, H S (1992), *Young Female and Black*, Routledge, London.

Moore, R (1975), *Racism and Black Resistance In Britain*, Pluto Press, London.

Morakvasic, M (1983), 'Women in Migration: Beyond the Reductionist Outlook', in A Phizacklea, *One Way Ticket: Migration and Female Labour*, Routledge and Kegan Paul, London.

Nash, David and Reeder, David (eds) (1993), *Leicester in the Twentieth Century*, Alan Sutton Publishing, Stroud.

Paul, Kathleen (1995), 'British Subjects and British Stock', in *Journal of British Studies*, Vol 34, No 2.

Peach, C (1963), 'Factors Affecting the Distribution of West Indians in Great Britain', *Transactions of the Institute of British Geographers*, Vol 38.

Peach, C (1965), 'West Indian Immigration to Britain, The Economic Factors', *Race*, Vol 71.

Peach, C (1968), *West Indian Migration to Britain, A Social Geography*, Institute of Race Relations, Oxford University Press, London.

Peach, C (1991), *The Caribbean in Europe: Contrasting Patterns of Migration and Settlement in Britain, France and the Netherlands*, Research Paper in Ethnic Relations No 15, ESRC Centre for Research in Ethnic Relations, University of Warwick.

PEP (1967), *Racial Discrimination in Britain*, Penguin, Harmondsworth.

Phizacklea, A (1982), 'Migrant Women and Wage Labour: The Case of West Indian Women in Britain', in J West (ed), *Work, Women and the Labour*

Market, Routledge and Kegan Paul, London.

Phizacklea, A (1983), *One Way Ticket: Migration and Female Labour*, Routledge and Kegan Paul, London.

Ramdin, R (1987), *The Making of the Black Working Class in Britain*, Gower, Aldershot.

Simmons, Jack (1974), *Leicester Past and Present: Modern City, 1860-1974*, Eyre Methuen, London.

Sivanandan, A (1981/1982), 'From Resistance To Rebellion: Asian and Afro/Caribbean Struggle in Britain', *Race and Class*, Vol 23, No 2/3.

Smith, D J (1974), *Racial Disadvantage in Britain*, Penguin, Harmondsworth.

Stone, K (1983), 'Motherhood and Waged Work: West Indian, Asian and White Mothers Compared', in Phizacklea, *One Way Ticket*.

Walby, Sylvia (1986), *Patriarchy at Work*, Polity Press, Cambridge.

West, J (ed) (1982), *Work, Women and the Labour Market*, Routledge and Kegan Paul, London.

Wilson, A (1978), *Finding A Voice: Asian Women in Britain*, Virago, London.

6   Too Many 'Immigrants': The Schooling of African Caribbean Children, 1960-1981

Introduction

This chapter recounts some experiences of a number of African Caribbean children in Leicester schools in the 1960s and argues that these can be understood in relation to cultural attitudes and the policies of the Local Education Authority (LEA) which were, in turn, related to government policies of the time. It is argued that policies in relation to West Indian children in schools are characterised by the use of the racially defined category of 'immigrant' which resulted in a failure to meet the needs of pupils, a focus on 'immigrants' as a problem and an assimilationist perspective towards cultural difference. The LEA attributed the lower attainment of West Indian pupils to aspects of West Indian culture rather than to the inappropriate educational experiences offered in schools.

Recent work on the differential educational attainment of different ethnic groups and the very high rate of exclusion of black boys has drawn attention to constructions of racialised and gendered identities in schools. Powerful notions of the supposed problems posed, particularly by black boys, but also by the presence of all black and Asian children in schools, can be seen in the policies of the LEA in the period. However, this chapter focuses primarily on the way in which the perceived problems created by black and Asian children in schools arose through a racialised construction of 'immigrants'. Gendered constructions of the various racialised groups in schools have not been addressed here.

Black Teachers

Some migrants who had arrived from the West Indies after the war came with professional qualifications. One such person was Clifton Robinson.

He had served in the RAF from 1944-1949 and formed one of the group of original pioneers of Leicester's African Caribbean community. He gained two scholarships: one from the RAF to do a degree in educational psychology at Birmingham University and as a colonial scholar he trained to become a teacher. After teaching for a year in Jamaica, he returned to Rugby in Leicestershire to join his wife and son. While working on the production of turbines in a Rugby factory, Robinson applied for a teaching post. He was told the post had been filled. Three weeks later the job was still being advertised and Robinson applied again.

> I didn't put that I was from Jamaica ... they invited me for interview. I told them that I was the same person who had been told [previously] that the job was filled. I knew an MP who was Labour and I passed the information on to him... but there were no legal procedures... nothing could happen about it... they offered me the job, but I didn't take it.[1]

Robinson subsequently applied for a teaching post in Leicester and gained a job at Mellor Street School in 1951 where he worked until 1961.

> They [schools] were heavily into streaming... the usual thing - which was awful - was to give the probationers the worst classes. The first year pupils that I had, several moved from the D stream upwards. The Head said that if you can do that with those children what can you do with the scholarship class? I stayed there for a very long while. I was happy there. I was the first West Indian teacher in Leicester... From Mellor there was a post in a unit for children with emotional and learning difficulties.[2]

Robinson was at St Peter's School for three years and then moved to Charnwood Primary as Deputy Head, where he remained until 1968. During this time he was invited by Mark Bonham Carter to serve on the conciliation committee of the East Midlands Area Race Relations Board.[3] Then he became Head of his old school, St Peters.

Finally he was appointed as head of a new school in Highfields, Uplands Junior School in 1970. He was awarded the OBE in 1973 and a CBE in 1985 and was Deputy Chair of the CRE from 1977 to 1985.[4] He was described as an 'extremely eminent member of the profession' by Leicester's Director of Education, J A Davis in 1973.[5] He is thought to be the first West Indian to become head of a school in Britain. He later became President of the Leicester United Caribbean Association (LUCA) and a JP.

He became an important figure in education in Leicester, where he observed ignorance among teachers in Leicester in the 1960s about children who Robinson described as West Indian, and their background. In 1964 he conducted a study of these children in Leicester primary schools which must be one of the few written sources of contemporary opinion of Leicester West Indians concerning education in the city.[6]

He remained one of only a handful of black teachers to work in Leicester schools. Leicester LEA made little attempt to recruit teachers from the immigrant communities through the 1960s and 1970s. They remain a tiny proportion of the teaching workforce. Evidence suggests that West Indian teachers took non-teaching jobs in Leicester. Valerie Marett (1989, p.130) in a study of the arrival of Ugandan Asians shows how the city failed to employ twenty three qualified teachers from Uganda who came to Leicester despite advertisements in the *Leicester Mercury* of 10 May 1973 advertising for teachers to teach immigrant children. The Association of Teachers of Ethnic Minorities in Leicestershire conducted a survey on the employment of black teachers in Leicester schools in 1979. There were held to be 65 teachers from ethnic minorities from a workforce of 8500. The children at this time were 18.9% ethnic minority. A report presented at a one day conference held in Leicester on 31 March 1979 quoted the case of a scale three post for Mathematics and Science development in a primary school where the pupils were predominantly from ethnic minorities. Although ethnic minority teachers with appropriate qualifications and experience applied the post was given to a Physical Education trained teacher with substantial experience in a secondary school and who had not even 'O' levels, in either mathematics or science.[7] The failure of Leicester and after 1974, Leicestershire LEA to employ teachers from among the black and Asian population has not only had implications for the education of children from the groups, but has also contributed to the construction of the social class profile of African Caribbeans in Leicester.[8]

Children

Children were among the earliest arrivals from the Caribbean. A common pattern was for the adults, either one or two parents to get established and then to send for their children later. Often children came one at a time as finance allowed. Children arriving in Leicester experienced a dramatic change in their lives. They encountered the same cultural shock which greeted their parents and many had other changes to cope with too.

Editha Drew who arrived from Dominica in 1962 said her first impression was 'What a place'. Her father had arrived in 1960 and her mother in 1961. Editha travelled with her cousin. Her first comment to her parents on arrival (which she later recalled with regret) was not 'Hello' but 'Why did you bring me here? ... I resented my parents'. Her memory of Dominica was of a happy life,

> bathing in the river with friends, having a picnic, cooking outdoors and there was no planning... Houses in the Caribbean all had verandas. They were wooden houses. That was my idea of a house.[9]

Editha Drew was sad to leave her granny behind in Dominica, who had cared for her, 'She had been a constant thing in my life until then'.[10]

Oscar Frank spent his childhood in Barbuda.

> In a sense I am more fortunate than my brothers and sister ... because I experienced the culture and way of life [of Barbuda] before I came to England. My experience in Barbuda was close to nature ... the innocence. I used to till the land, cultivate vegetables, keep goats and sheep. I went to the school in Barbuda ... there was only one. There is one of everything. There were only 1200 people ... one village and most people live in one area. ... All the tall buildings [coming up the hill of St Saviours Road, Leicester] ... I thought it looked grim and dismal. In the Caribbean it was all open spaces and the beach.[11]

Oscar Frank was cared for in Barbuda from the age of ten months until he was fourteen years by a great aunt. He had grown up separately from his five brothers and sisters. 'I didn't see much of mum'. By the time he was eight or nine the caring role had been reversed and he was looking after his ageing aunt.

> That was normal in Barbuda ... Meeting mum was a bit weird. I had a sense of alienation ... I had a sense of loss because unfortunately my great aunt didn't get on with my mum. She passed away three or four years after I came to England.[12]

Children do not always understand the reasons why their parents make the decisions they do. June Grey who had left her mother behind in the Caribbean came to join her dad and stepmother.

It was difficult with my dad. It still is. I don't know him ... My mum ... I was a pet ... I didn't think much of my dad. I missed my mum. It was very hard. I wanted her to come to England but she wouldn't.[13]

Robinson's study of West Indian children in primary schools in Leicester in 1964, showed two cases in which mother came to England first leaving the child with the father. But this was unusual. The average period of separation from the mother was two years nine months. There were seven examples where the absence was five years and four years and thirteen of three years. Some children in his study experienced the move to England as traumatic. For example Robinson wrote:

There were some problems ... letters arrived late and children arrived in England without anyone to meet them having travelled some 5000 miles unaccompanied. One mother sent her child all white clothing so that she could recognise the child on arrival but the child was not wearing the outfit when she arrived.[14]

Joan Riley (1985)[15] in her novel *The Unbelonging* describes misery and abuse at home and at school when arriving in Leicester from Jamaica in the late 1960s. However, many children had positive experiences.

On joining their parents in England some children owing to more favourable circumstances were able to move into the new environment fairly easily.[16]

Robinson found that in Leicester half of the children's parents were married. Fifteen children lived with their mother only and six with their father only.[17] For most children, being cared for by people other than their natural parents was a normal and acceptable part of family life.

children whose mothers cannot look after them will be readily 'taken in' or adopted by another family. This common form of informal fostering of children is a significant feature of social life.[18]

The pattern of child care illustrated by these Leicester children demonstrates the relationship between family structure and the migration process. Population movement has been a feature of Caribbean societies since emancipation (Thomas-Hope, 1977). In her study of Barbadian migration to Britain, Mary Chamberlain (1994, p.122) wrote: 'One important characteristic of Barbadian families is the generational leap-frog of childcare.' Family identity was the primary loyalty. Chamberlain argued:

In this family the pattern of childcare and family support enabled the migration of three generations of its members. At the same time migration assisted in the maintenance of the family back home. It was a reciprocal pattern ensuring family loyalty and a continuing family identity across the generations and across the sea.

This aspect of the social structure of Caribbean societies has been misunderstood and pathologised in studies of migration. For example, Margaret Byron (1995, p.54) in her study of Nevisians in Leicester criticised Davison (1962) in this respect. Davison's study of migration conducted in the early 1960s has been influential in subsequent debates.

[Davison] applied a standard which was largely inappropriate to the groups being studied as it was based on an upper class West Indian norm of the nuclear family which was itself modelled on that of the colonial power. Conformity to this model represented organisation, difference was equated with inferior levels or organisation, inefficient, disorganisation.

The complex pattern of family relationships has been compared with the nuclear family, held to be the norm in western industrialised societies and has been judged to be inferior. The nuclear family was accorded a central position in the maintenance of the social structure in the dominant functionalist school of social science in Britain and America of the 1950s and 1960s. This lent support to an analysis which saw the African Caribbean family as inadequate. Such a perspective fed into a racist view which saw black culture as both inferior and responsible for the low attainment of Caribbean children in British schools. The demise of the functionalist perspective in sociology, the development of the feminist critique and anti-racist discussions of the family as well as the spread of more diverse family forms in western industrialised societies has produced a challenge to this view (Lawrence, 1982; hooks, 1982).

What happened to children when they arrived at school in Leicester? Editha Drew went to Moat Girls' School.

In a way it was terrible. It put me right back. ... The West Indian children were seen as dunces who didn't know anything ... Children from the Caribbean had already passed what we were given to do. If we said we have done this we were told 'sit down you haven't reached that stage yet'. We were put in a class by age rather than by standard. I found that when I came here I forgot everything I had learnt. My mum would have helped me but she was working in an elastic factory and didn't have time to help me. The first day at school we did subtraction in the morning and I thought 'this work is for seven year olds. I can do this'. Back home we had dictation where the teacher would read from a book ... we would have homework every night and you got lines if you didn't do it. Here there was no encouragement. It demoralised me. ... there was one West Indian girl who had arrived before me. She didn't know what I knew. She latched on to me... Plus the Asian children who didn't know a word of English. A lot of time was spent with them. No Indian child could speak English. Black children got forgotten. There were a few West Indian kids then. We got on all right together. We went around together and the white kids. We were all friends. One white girl stuck to me, the others took the mick. She was a lower level than the other white kids.[19]

Editha left Moat two years later when she was fifteen. Oscar Frank went to Moat Boys'. He was already fourteen so he only stayed eight months. He was:

...disappointed when I went to school... Mainly because I was into education in Barbuda. I was one of the top boys. I won prizes. I came to England and was put into a class.. a couple of weeks later I realised the status of the class... I was put back four or five years. It was a very damaging experience from an educational point of view. There were a lot of Indians coming in... We were all herded into one class or group. There was always some degree of racism. In our class of about thirty there were twenty Asian kids, about five English and five West Indians. So we were in a minority... there was friction... between West Indians and Asians too but it was not that unpleasant. There was lots of flack, but we gave it back... we all became friends eventually.[20]

Oscar Frank's experience of Moat Boys' School in 1965 is paralleled by John Taylor's who was also at Moat between 1962 and 1966. John Taylor is white, brought up in Highfields. He went to Moat after failing the eleven plus. Moat was a technical school which was amalgamated with the Secondary Modern Dale School the year after John Taylor started in 1962.

In my class there were all kinds of minorities. There were four Polish, six or seven black kids. We were streamed and I was in the middle stream. There were more black kids in the lower streams ...over the four years I was there, the number of black kids rose a lot. I remember the Head talking to the school ... there were about 650 kids. About 400 were minorities. We all tended to mix. There was some conflict. On one occasion two lads started to fight, one with a dustbin lid and the other with a belt like gladiators. ... All the whites were down one end [of the playground] and all the blacks down the other... the teacher stopped it... we generally got on well. It was peculiar. There was a lot of racist talk but the lads were friends. Later some decided it [the racist talk] was unacceptable. Most of the trouble was from the whites and the West

Indians. The Asian kids worked harder... there was trouble when we played other schools at sport. On one occasion we got banned from the Rugger league. We were playing at Castle Rock at Coalville.[21] ... A fight broke out and a bloke got injured. There was ill feeling in the changing rooms - a sense that our team was a black team ... The bulk of my mates were West Indian.[22]

The last comment is consistent with the research of Edwards who showed that although British children shared the low ranking in terms of status and academic potential accorded West Indian children by teachers, they did not share teachers' attitudes to West Indians in terms of personal considerations (Edwards, 1979).[23] Robinson in his study argued that:

UK children played with others despite instructions from UK parents not to do so. UK children were instructed by their parents not to change in the same cubicle as West Indians. But they continued to do so if they have West Indian friends ... In a free writing exercise one child, an English boy, wrote that his parents didn't like wogs and would be leaving the Highfields area to get away from them. But he was friends with a West Indian boy ... good relationships were expressed in their essays entitled 'My School'.[24]

Some children had to wait for a place in school, sometimes for many months. Doris Cope came to Leicester from Barbuda in 1964 aged nine. She described how bad she had felt watching the other children going to school. It seemed like a long time. Eventually she went to Medway Junior School.

I liked it. I loved school. I hated to be off. There was one other black kid - another from Barbuda. I felt different. We used to be called wogs ... The Asians were more picked on ... We had fights, physical fights and the teacher intervened. But they [the teachers] embarrassed me with their comments.[25]

Most of the children asked by Robinson to name likes and dislikes about their schools in the Caribbean and in Leicester, preferred school in Leicester. They named not having to bring absence notes and having lots of room to play in and trees to climb in the playground as some of their likes about schools 'back home'. They disliked muddy playgrounds, strappings, hard work and beatings and cross teachers. In Leicester they liked milk and the teachers. They disliked being called names like 'black'. One child was so upset by being called 'blackie' that she became ill.[26]

Asked about racist name calling 'several teachers' questioned by Robinson said that 'West Indians were rather sensitive'. Some teachers reported that it [name calling] upset the children considerably. Several of the fights between West Indians and non immigrants originate from this source.

> One teacher was upset by a West Indian child who came to him with a complaint about being called 'Nigger', because she felt rather sorry for the child concerned but felt powerless to do anything about it.[27]

Racist abuse among children has received little attention from academics. While it has been acknowledged, confusion surrounds its significance. Teachers have long been aware that racist name calling, for example, can co-exist with friendships which cut across racialised groups. This has led to a view which sees racist name calling as unimportant in a situation where relationships were otherwise good. Barry Troyna and Richard Hatcher (Troyna and Hatcher, 1992, p.25) conducted a detailed study of racist name-calling in three primary schools situated in two education authorities in 1992. The study provides a framework for understanding. They wrote:

> conventional wisdom does, of course, lead us to believe that inter-ethnic friendships are not only accompanied by, but are a signifier of, the absence of racial prejudice.

Troyna and Hatcher's detailed study showed that racist name calling may or may not indicate racist beliefs. Racist name calling was utilised to express racist attitudes but was also used by those who hold racially equalitarian beliefs. Conversely, the absence of racist name calling does not indicate the absence of racist attitudes although it may do. As Troyna and Hatcher argued this is not to conclude that racist name calling is not racist.

> We would argue that it is racist in two other senses. First it is a form of hurtful discrimination against black children. Second it trades on a racist frame of reference and this tends to reinforce its legitimacy within the children's culture (Troyna and Hatcher, 1992, p.25).

To go further, it is argued here that racist name-calling experienced by West Indian children in schools in Leicester in the 1960s has to be seen in the context of a cluster of attitudes which saw West Indian culture as inferior and 'immigrants' as a problem, attitudes fuelled by ignorance of the children's background. What did West Indian parents thinks of Leicester schools in the 1960s?

Parents

Robinson interviewed 138 parents from sixty families in Leicester primary schools in 1964. Of these, 122 were born and had been educated in rural areas of Caribbean islands and many had never visited a large city before coming to Leicester. Sixteen were born and educated in the city. Eight were illiterate. The parents in general were impressed by their contact with schools in comparison with their experiences of other public servants particularly personnel managers and doctors. Asked why they were not more involved in school activities most said pressures of work made this difficult. Apart from four families, both parents were in paid employment. Except for six or seven families there was little understanding of the English education system.

In their Memorandum to the Select Committee on Race Relations and Immigration, Leicester LEA had put difficulties in promoting parental contacts especially with mothers as second in their list of 'Social and Educational problems of immigrant pupils in Leicester Schools'. They also identified lack of parental support as a problem.[28] However, Robinson's study shows a different view of West Indian parents.

> Several parents of fourth year children had set their minds on professional careers for their children and were satisfied that the secondary schools to be attended were geared to this desire, when in fact they would be attending without exception a secondary modern school and had been informed to that effect by the Education Committee. Asked if satisfied 60.2% replied generally satisfied, 30.4% generally dissatisfied and 9.4% unsure.

Robinson continued:

> A common source of dissatisfaction was the level of work given and also the type of work given in schools. Coming from an educational climate which places great reliance on memory as opposed to comprehension and where religion is a vital aspect of life, such things as the memorisation of Biblical passages the Psalms are placed high on the parent's list of scholastic achievements. Since also, clerical work has a good status value and is recognised as a sign of upward social mobility, the ability to write and spell also assume greater significance than they would to an English parent.

> Ability to deal with 'big sums', really a matter of sheer repetitive mechanical ability, achieves a greater recognition than understanding or application in a 'problem' situation. Head teachers generally implied that the relatively low level of participation in school activities was due to a certain lack of interest.

The very ready, unhesitant comments indicated to me that a fairly large percentage of West Indian parents were taking an intense interest in their children's education, a greater interest than I anticipated or would be usual in their rural home backgrounds in the West Indies.

The interest in their children's education is reflected in the number who have fallen easy prey to the 'door to door' encyclopaedia salesman. I was repeatedly shown sets of expensive ones up to £25, bought in many instances for children who were unable to read or with only very limited reading ability.

As in the case of many English parents but to a much greater extent, the West Indian parent is not attuned to the contemporary school aims or philosophy in the primary school. Their educational scales of values are in many cases diametrically opposed to that of the schools, and the resulting conflicts cannot but be harmful to the child. Here we have both educational and cultural disunity, which is I think, worse than just educational disunity.[29]

Robinson recounts an incident when he arrived at a house in order to carry out his survey and of being met by a child. She was told to tell her mother. The mother on receiving the message had assumed the child had done something wrong. Only the intervention of an aunt stopped her being punished before his second visit. He commented that to a West Indian parent lack of discipline showed lack of love. White parents allowing children to do what they liked was evidence of lack of love.[30]

However, while cultural disunity between home and school for West Indian families clearly existed, cultural incongruence between home and school with respect to white working class families was being explored by sociologists in the 1960s. Path-breaking studies such as that of Jackson and Marsden (1962) and J W B Douglas (1967) demonstrated the gulf between working class culture and that of the Grammar schools. As in the case of Blacks this 'cultural deficit' model has been used by some as an explanation of low achievement. West Indians suffered negative judgements about culture with respect to race as well as to class. The idea that West Indian children were over disciplined tended to provide an easily available answer to a variety of problems including the low attainment of West Indian children. Errol Lawrence has shown how these views reflect 'common sense' racist ideas about discipline in black families (Lawrence, 1982). The way in which cultural differences are perceived are clear in the response of the Education Authority to West Indian and other 'immigrant' children in Leicester schools.

Head teachers in Robinson's study found West Indian parents to be co-operative, their only complaint being punctuality. Robinson explained this with reference to the cultural background of West Indian parents.

> Many children have domestic duties to perform before coming to school and dare not leave before they are completed... Some parents are unaware that unpunctuality is frowned on here... Other examples of parents thinking of school here in the same way as in the West Indies may be seen in reported cases of parents requesting children be allowed to leave school during lesson periods to do errands in town... discipline is strict in West Indian homes.[31]

Nine years after Robinson's study was completed a representative of the Jamaica Service Group in Leicester giving evidence before the Select Committee on Race and Immigration in May 1973 presented a different view. Parental attitudes could have changed in that period or more likely the importance of differences in approaches to discipline did not warrant the significance attached to them. Mr Arthur Bottomley, a member of the Committee said:

> In the report by the Education Committee which we have been considering it is said that West Indian children expect and respect corporal punishment.

Mr A [sic] Hudson replied:

> I do not think I can agree with this because probably parents back in the West Indies dished out a certain amount of corporal punishment. Parents in England are trying to adapt themselves to the society in which they are living here. I do not think this is the rule of today.[32]

The report had stated that this expectation and respect for corporal punishment was a 'recipe for violence in a society'.

How are the experiences of parents and children outlined here to be understood? Children are a relatively powerless group in society and their experiences have been neglected in historical studies. It has long been established that children of Caribbean origin do not achieve as good measured results as other groups in examinations (Tomlinson, 1980). The deficit model, which focused on the economic status, family organisation and other aspects of the culture of Caribbean people has been challenged. Particularly important in this was Bernard Coard's study (Coard, 1971). Since then a number of studies have developed this critique (Tomlinson, 1981; Stone, 1981; Mullard, 1985; Troyna and Williams, 1986; Carby, 1982; Nehaul, 1996).

The Response of the Education Authority

It is argued here that the failure to address the educational rights and needs of African Caribbean children was a feature of the educational provision in Leicester schools between 1945 and 1974. This failure was a consequence of a policy informed by a view which saw people who were most commonly described then as 'West Indian' as a problem with a culture that was inferior.

The Development Plan for Leicester Schools approved in 1953 under the 1944 Education Act formed the basis of school organisation until the reorganisation into comprehensive schools which took place after the control of education had passed to the County Council in 1974. The Plan proposed six selective Grammar schools and two selective technical schools which together would accommodate 25% of the age group. The technical schools were to replace existing 'intermediate' schools which accepted children whose performance in the General Examination at eleven was just below Grammar School level. The remaining 67% (sic) of pupils were to attend Secondary Modern School, all but two of which were single sex. The school leaving age was raised to fifteen (Mander, 1980).

The decline of Leicester's population from its peak of 287,300 in 1954 exacerbated a trend present since the early 1920s of a diminishing school population. The birth rate in Leicester between 1942 and 1956 was higher than for the country as a whole but the effect in schools was mitigated by emigration. Immigration in the 1960s reduced the number lost in schools by this emigration of Leicester families to suburbs and beyond. However, the increase in pupils in Leicester schools rose less between 1944 and 1974 than the national average. 10% of children born in 1947 in Leicester had moved away before the age of fourteen. The age group born in Leicester in 1955 was reduced by 20% in 1961 but by 1970 when these children were fourteen years old they had been joined by an additional 486 children as a result of immigration. So not all the children who left Leicester were replaced by immigrants. In 1970 the cohort was only 92% of the size of this age group had been in the year of their birth. Leicester was therefore in a favourable position in terms of pupil numbers (Mander, 1980, p.49).

There are three outstanding features of the response of Leicester LEA to the arrival of black children in schools. First black and Asian children were grouped together in a racialised category called 'immigrant'. Historians of any black or Asian minority community in Britain face problems arising from the use of documentary evidence which utilises racialised categories. The population of Leicester has long contained a diversity of ethnic groups.

But in popular and academic discourse 'immigrant' was understood to refer to people with black or brown skins. Despite widespread understanding in the academic disciplines of the social sciences that 'race' has no biological base, of the social construction of racialised categories, the purely physical characteristic of skin colour was seen as significant and relevant to every aspect of life.

The second feature of the response of the LEA to African Caribbean children in Leicester schools was to see immigrants, defined by the Authority as 'West Indians and Asians', as a problem. Part of this problem consisted of the need to keep the numbers of such children in each school low. The needs of the children themselves were not considered during the 1960s. Indeed many were denied places in schools altogether for many months. It has already been shown that the number of immigrant children never made up for children lost through emigration and the view that schools were being overwhelmed by large numbers of immigrant children putting pressure on resources is not supported by the evidence.

The third aspect of the LEA's response to the arrival of African Caribbeans in schools was to view the culture of the newcomers as inferior to that of the society which they were joining. Implicit in Education Sub-Committee reports and discussions was an assimilationist perspective which saw the task of the education system as being to achieve a cultural adaptation by African Caribbean children. In addition, aspects of the culture of these children were seen as responsible for low attainment in schools. The policies of Leicester's Education Authority were broadly in line with that of national government.

Chris Mullard (1985) has identified three phases in government policy towards black people in schools. The first phase which lasted from the early 1960s to the 1965 White Paper on Education[33] adopted an assimilationist perspective. The second phase which continued until the early 1970s he described as 'integrationist' and the third as cultural pluralist. In a radical critique of British government policy concerning the education of black students Hazel Carby (1982, p.183) has argued that, despite apparent changes in policy, from assimilationist through to multiculturalism:

> The educational response to the presence of black students in the British school system has been framed in terms of the 'problem' for the system that these students present.

The policy of the local education authority in Leicester at this time broadly corresponds to the pattern outlined by Mullard except that aspects of the assimilationist phase continued into the early 1970s, and moves towards integration took place alongside rather than replacing the assimilationist perspective.

Local studies carried out in Wolverhampton and Birmingham suggest a similar approach by the education authorities in those areas to that adopted in Leicester outlined below. For examples in Reeves' (1989, p.79) study of Wolverhampton children were dispersed and left without places in schools. Grosvenor (1987, p.305) agrees that in Birmingham the 'LEA never had an official policy of dispersal, it clearly operated an unofficial one'. Grosvenor also argues that the apparent change of policy from assimilation to integration marked a continuity of approach.

The three aspects of Leicester's response identified here were normally conflated to become a perspective which proved resistant to evidence that was at times presented to the various committees. The first two features are illustrated in a study carried out by John Mander (1989) who was Head of the Schools Branch of the City of Leicester Education Department for most of the period 1945-1974. He summaries the LEA's policy:

> It was decided in the beginning that the best solution to the problems of immigrant children and to the long term solutions of more general immigrant problems was to make no administrative distinction between immigrants and indigenous children. So, for the nine years from 1957-1966, the number of coloured immigrant children in Leicester schools was not counted. In 1965, this led to some differences of opinion between the LEA, the Home Office and the Department of Education and Science. The government departments took the line that the LEA could cater for its immigrant pupils only if it made a central count their numbers. The LEA countered that the only useful figures would be accurate forecasts of the future numbers of immigrant children who would need schools; and this the government departments could not give (Mander, 1989, p.49).

The issue of numbers of 'immigrant' children and the need to keep them low became the dominant focus of the General Purposes, and Secondary Schools' Sub-Committees of the Education Committee during the 1960s. The General Purposes Sub-Committee discussed immigrant children in both primary and secondary schools. The Primary Schools Sub-Committee did not discuss immigrant children until September 1967. The reason for this is not clear. The Primary Schools Sub-Committee may have been less pressurised by Primary School Headteachers.[34]

In September 1963, the two Dale Schools merged with the Moat Schools[35] and at a meeting of the Secondary Education Sub-Committee of

28 April 1964 it was reported that Moat Boys' and Girls' Schools were experiencing rising number of pupils as a result of immigration.[36] These four schools were all in the Highfields district of Leicester where the majority of black and Asian migrants had settled. Robinson reported that there was a special meeting in May 1964 held at the 'Porkpie Chapel' on Belvoir Street where concerns about immigrant children were expressed by teachers. In November 1964 the minutes of the Secondary Schools Sub-Committee stated that 'Numbers of immigrant children leads to overcrowding'.[37] This is despite the reduction in numbers of children as a result of emigration. The minutes continued:

> There is no problem so long as numbers are small, say 15% - as numbers build up, administrative action has to be taken.[38]

Secondary Heads were now refusing to accept 'immigrant' children in schools.[39] Minutes of the Secondary Education Sub-Committee meeting recorded that:

> For some time past immigrant residents in the catchment area of the two Moat Schools have been diverted to other schools in the Eastern part of the city in order that the Moat Schools should not have too large a number of immigrant pupils.

The minutes continued:

> The possibility of further re-distribution in schools in the Eastern area is now exhausted. The Crown Hills, Mundella Boys, Mundella Girls and Spencefield School cannot take more children from the Moat area. They are left practically no room to take in additional children who may come to live in their own areas. There is ample room to take more pupils in the two Moat schools. The average size of classes in the two schools are set out below.[40]

Table 6.1   Average Class Size in the Two Moat Schools 1965

Year	1	2	3	4	5
Moat Boys	33.5	29.5	32.5	29.4	22
Moat Girls	27.5	24.5	26.8	26.8	24

Source: Secondary Education Sub-Committee minutes

There are now fourteen immigrant boys and six immigrant girls resident in the Moat area and unplaced in schools. The committee is asked to decide where the children shall attend school. A similar situation exists in respect of admission to Ellis School. There is ample room but the Headmistress declined to take more immigrants. The acting head of Westcoates has also asked that no more immigrant children be admitted to school. The Heads of other schools in the city - when approached to take out of area immigrant pupils - often proved to accept a small number of these children but were unable to provide a mid-day meal for them.[41]

It can be seen here that children were left without places in schools denying them access to education, although it was admitted that there was ample room in the two Moat Schools and in Ellis School. Indeed, it can be seen that class sizes at the Moat Schools were low. But schools were refusing to take black and Asian children.

The Director reminded the committee that a full report on immigrant children was to be submitted to a further meeting of the General Purposes Sub-Committee. In fact the promised full report was deferred on three more occasions and three interim reports were produced instead. The number of immigrants in Moat schools now exceeded 50%. Chairman of Moat School Governors committee Mrs A I Pollard asked that the matter should be discussed before accepting more pupils. The negative views which Mrs Pollard, who was also Vice-Chairman (sic) of the Housing Committee of Leicester City Council, expressed about West Indians were quoted in Chapter Four. The minutes stated that:

She gave details of acute problems at Moat school resulting from a high percentage of immigrants in the school.[42]

In June 1968, the minutes of the General Purposes Sub-Committee record that there were 'frustrations in secondary schools' and 'teachers met problems every hour of the day'. It was 'resolved that the children should be dispersed'.[43]

The third feature of the LEA's response to black and Asian children in Leicester Schools is the approach adopted to cultural differences. The view that the culture of 'immigrant' children was a problem to the educational system at first centred on the issue of language. Non-English speaking children provided a focus for concerns that were actually wider than the technical and administrative difficulties posed for teachers and pupils in classrooms where communication was difficult. Early concern centred on the inability of some children to speak English. The first special group for teaching English to 'immigrant' children was set up at Moat Boys' School in 1957.[44]

The Secondary Education Sub-Committee first discussed the issue of non-English speaking children at the Dale (eleven to fifteen) Intermediate Schools in Leicester in December 1961.[45] An investigation was carried out which was then discussed on 2 January 1962. It was reported that there were fifteen children in the Dale Boys' School who could not speak English. These children received regular daily individual and group teaching. In the Girls' School there were no girls 'incapable of working in a small remove class'. The committee minutes stated:

> It is not thought to be either necessary or desirable to bring these foreign (sic) children together at some central class.[46]

The Committee were assured that the problem was kept constantly under review and that help was being given by the Indian League.[47]

In July 1962 Councillor Smith reported that the Headmistress of Dale Girls' School was concerned at the 'tendency for children of various nationalities to form separate communities'.[48]

The Director of Education stated that consideration was being given to the problem and a report was being prepared. The Governors of Rushey Mead Boys' School were also concerned about non-English speaking children.[49]

The prejudices and ignorance of many LEA committee members officials and indeed teachers can be illustrated by the way in which the issue of language was approached. The imposition of the racialised category 'immigrant' to describe black and Asian migrants impaired the ability to recognise important differences between groups. While some children of Asian origin were non-English speakers, African Caribbean Indian children spoke Creole or Patois but would have been familiar with English. They had been taught in an English education system using English texts and with English speaking teachers. Robinson wrote:

> As the matter of communication is one of some concern to teachers in England generally and one which teachers in Leicester have frequently referred to, some space will be devoted to it here.
>
> English is the vernacular in the West Indies, there are however a multiplicity of dialects and enunciation between the various islands. Added to this is the use of English patois (again varying from island to island) pronunciation, colloquial phrases, special vocabularies, etc all of which often make it difficult or at times

impossible to understand the West Indian. This difficulty is not restricted to the English listener. West Indians also find it difficult to understand other West Indians, much in the same way as some English people may find it difficult to understand some Welsh, Scottish or 'Cockney' people. It takes a trained ear to distinguish for example the speech of Jamaicans and Barbadians or Windward Islanders from Antiguans or Trinidadians. Since immigrants from Dominica and St Lucia are now also coming to Leicester, added difficulties are likely to arise, as they are mainly bilingual, speaking the local French patois as well as English with a most pronounced foreign accent.[50]

Errol Lawrence (1982, p.73) has argued in relation to black children that:

Common sense tends to make a leap from the recognition that English is not their first language to the feeling that they are incapable of speaking English.

Studies, for example that of V K Edwards (1979, p.92) showed that West Indian speech was viewed negatively by groups in the population as a whole and this negative view was shared by teachers. In her research, children speaking with a middle class accent were held to have higher academic potential and white working class boys were viewed more favourably than West Indian. Further Edwards found, in her small sample of twenty student teachers, that West Indian children were judged to be the least desirable as members of a class by teachers. As the Rampton report acknowledged in 1981:

The attitudes of schools and teachers towards a West Indian child's language is of critical importance. If teachers simply reject a West Indian child's language as 'bad English' the child may see the rejection as meaning that he is inadequate and that his family and indeed his ethnic group are not respected by the teacher.[51]

While clearly problems of communication posed difficulties in the classroom, the negative assessment of children's linguistic abilities, and extrapolation of this to abilities in general, can only be seen as based on prejudice. Robinson's comments about bilingual children from Dominica and St Lucia demonstrate that the problem lay in the social position of West Indians as a group. The knowledge of the bilingual West Indian child was defined as ignorance and the ignorance of the white English teacher was defined as knowledge.[52]

The approach and policies of the LEA with respect to African Caribbean and Asian children in Leicester schools are shown most clearly in reports, and in the response of the committees to the reports, prepared by the Director. There were four reports in all. The authority was first required by the Government to count the number of children in 1966. These reports demonstrate the use of a racialised understanding of the category 'immigrant', the focus of 'immigrants' as a problem and the perceived need to keep numbers in each school low. They also illustrate the way in which 'West Indian' culture was viewed as deficient. The first of the Director's reports can be seen as an example of this.

On 27 November 1964 the General Purposes Sub-Committee of the Education Committee considered the first of these reports on immigrant children, prepared by the Director. The managers of Charnwood Infant and Junior Schools had reported problems 'following a large influx of immigrant children'. It was decided that the report would be sent individually to members of the Education Committee in confidence and not reported openly.[53] The report stated that while no record was kept, there were immigrant children in nearly all of the Leicester schools. In two areas there were concentrations. These were in the north, Mellor Infant and Juniors, Ellis Infant and Rushey Mead Secondary School.

Table 6.2   Immigrants in Leicester Schools 1964

School	West Indian	Indians/ Pakistani	Nation- ality (other)	Total Immi- grants	Total	% Immi- grant	Number of Non- English Speakers
Bridge Junior	18	49	14	81	288	28	17
Charnwood Infants	48	23	9	80	172	46.5	16
Charnwood Juniors	36	54	17	107	274	39	38
GreenLane Infants	43	37	15	95	321	29.6	20
Highfields Infants	41	15	14	70	245	28.5	15
Medway Infants	32	30	17	79	234	33.3	25
Moat Infants	22	26	13	61	213	285	13
St Peters Junior	28	21	15	64	207	30.9	8
Moat Boys	31	120		151	637	23.7	40
Moat Girls	44	68		112	654	17.1	25

Source: General Purposes Sub Committee 27 November 1964

The report went on to say that the number of immigrant children led to overcrowding.

Unless there is some change in immigration policy, the situation seems likely to get worse.[54]

The table is interesting in that it was the first occasion when immigrants other than African Caribbeans and Asians were included. It showed quite clearly that there is no relationship between the number of non-English speakers and the percentage of immigrants or with the number of any one particular group. The basis upon which the children were categorised as non-English speakers is not known nor whether consistent criteria were applied in the assessment of the children's abilities. No attempt was made in the table to identify the first language of non-English speakers. It is clear from the table that many black and Asian immigrants could speak English. However, subsequent discussions of the Education Sub Committees continued to focus on the number of 'immigrants' who could not speak English. Although 'immigrants' other than African Caribbean and Asians were included in this able, no comment was made concerning 'nationality other' category and other surveys for example those shown in tables fifteen and sixteen, showing knowledge of English of immigrant children, only West Indian and Indians/Pakistanis were included. It is clear in the minutes of the Committees, that the term 'immigrant' referred to black and Asian people only and did not include, for example, Polish children. Black and Asian children were treated as a problem whether individuals spoke English or not. This continued to be the case with some modification until the 1970s.

The Director's report outlined three aspects of 'the problem'. First a small proportion of 'immigrants' were manageable.[55] The numbers were to be kept small, 15% of the school's roll. Second, as numbers built up, administrative action would be needed in the form of additional or specialist staff, extra books and equipment and advice to teachers. Third when the increasing population of immigrant children reaches a certain level - the Department of Education and Science (DES) put it at 30%:

the situation runs out of hand unless action is taken. Our schools become immigrant schools - purveyors of an immigrant instead of a British culture. Some schools in the Eastern area have now reached this stage.

This is major and long term difficulty. There is no easy answer possible. How are schools to be kept less than 30% and preferably 25% of immigrant children on roll? The DES recommendations, based on Southall, is that immigrants should be dispersed - with each school only having a small percentage. This is sound in as far as it goes, but does not cover the situation in which all schools in an area have over 30%. It is clear that dispersal would present problems - of transport, administration and human relations.[56]

Dispersal would not have been an issue if black and Asian people had not been concentrated residentially in the Highfields district of Leicester. This is something that was attributed to the 'immigrants' own choice. However, African Caribbeans interviewed, suggested otherwise. Many lived in Highfields at least in part because the actions of estate agents and building societies made it difficult for them to move to other areas.[57]

The Government's policy of dispersal was first raised in the House of Commons by Sir Edward Boyle in November 1963, when he stated that schools should have no more than 30% immigrants.[58] Leicester LEA discussed the DES recommended limit of 30% in the General Purposes Sub Committee meeting of 27 November 1964. It was commented that 'that does not cover a situation in which all schools in an area have over 30%'.[59] The Government's circular 7/65 had stated:

Where the [Dispersal] proves impractical simply because the school serves an area which is occupied largely by immigrants, every effort should be made to disperse the immigrant children round a greater number of schools and to meet such problems of transport as they may arise. It is important for the success of such measures that the reasons should be explained beforehand to the parents of both the immigrant and the other children, and their co-operation obtained... It will be helpful if the parents of non-immigrant children can see that all practical means have been taken to deal with the problems in the schools and that the progress of their own children is not being restricted by the undue preoccupation of the teaching staff with the linguistic and other difficulties of immigrant children.[60]

The approach of Leicester LEA echoed that of central government and can be seen to lend support to the views of Hazel Carby who has argued that no attempt was made to meet the needs of 'immigrant' children in the 1960s at national level, rather concerns were about assimilation, numbers and the desires not to antagonise whites. For example in the Second Report of the Commonwealth Immigrants Advisory Council it was stated:

The education of children of unfamiliar backgrounds and cultures presents real difficulties at a time when classes are already overcrowded. There are problems arising from different customs, habits and attitudes to learning and life, which immigrant children bring to school, as well as educational problems in the more academic sense of the word.[61]

Rex and Tomlinson (1976, pp.162-163) wrote:

There was no planning at all for the absorption of immigrant children into the education system... and the way in which the debate was structured fostered racism.

Discussion continued on the issue of future actions to be taken in Leicester. These were, first, that overcrowding was to be tackled by the redrafting of catchment areas and children diverted to less crowded schools. Second, it was admitted that the problem of inability to speak English 'was not so acute as is sometimes thought'. Language difficulties could be overcome given sufficient teachers, and other support.[62]

This report was the first occasion on which the LEA had attempted to make any kind of systematic assessment of the scale of the problem of non-English speakers. The acknowledgement that the problem was 'not so acute as is sometimes thought' is revealing. There was evidence from schools in Leicester that inability to speak English on arrival could not be held responsible for low achievement. The *Leicester Mercury* contained regular reports in the 1960s of examination success by pupils who had arrived in Leicester, speaking no English only a few years before and sitting public examinations at sixteen. For example in a report of prize giving at Mundella School in December 1967, it was reported that boys who had spoken no English at all three years previously had gained distinction at General Certificate of Education 'O' levels.[63] The report also included an appendix showing action already taken and included examples of specific action taken in particular schools, for example two extra half time teachers for non-English speaking pupils at Moat Girls' and the appointment of an Indian language teacher at Medway Junior. St Peter's Junior had a full time 'West Indian' teacher added to the staff.[64] The report also included the results of a sample survey of knowledge of English of immigrant children in two schools. The children were graded on a scale A-E on their ability to speak English. 'A' represented fluency and 'E' no fluency at all.

Table 6.3   **Knowledge of English of Immigrant Children in Two Leicester Schools**

School A

Time in School in Eng	Indian/ Pakistani	West Indian	A	B	C	D	E	Total
Over 5 years		1A2B1D	1	2		1		4
4-5 years	2B2C	1C1D		2	3	1		6
3-4 years	1A8B4C	1A3B4C	2	11	8	1		22
2-3 years	8B1C2D1E	3B3C3D1E	11	4	5	2		22
1-2 years	3B2C2D2E	1A2B1C1D	1	5	3	3	2	14
11 months or under	5D13E	1A2B1C2D		1	2	1	7	13

School B

Time in School in Eng	Indian/ Pakistani	West Indian	A	B	C	D	E	Total
4-5 years	1A1B	14A1C	15	1	1			17
3-4 years	5A2B2C	1A1B	6	3	2			11
2-3 years	3A5B2C	8A3B1C	11	8	2		1	22
1-2 years	4B2C1D	1B		5	2	1		8
11 months or under	5C13D2E	1B	1	5	13		2	21

Source: General Purposes Sub Committee 27 November 1964

In the above tables it can be seen that only five children spoke no English at all whereas 48% were fluent.

The third 'future action' to be considered by the Committee related to 'cultural difficulties'. The definition of 'immigrant' children as a problem and the assimilationist perspective is demonstrated quite clearly in the report. It is hard to see how the statement that:

> schools which have more than 30% immigrant become purveyors of an immigrant culture rather than a British one ...

could be justified in view of the control exercised by the Local Authority, the Head and staff of the school over the curriculum both formal and informal. At Moat a Head of Department with responsibility for less able pupils included responsibility for immigrant pupils, illustrating the perceived link between low ability and immigrant pupils.[65] Government policy was made clear in circular 7/65 which was recorded as being received by the committee on 3 September 1965. It is clear that the Director accepted the government's policy that the dispersal of immigrants was the correct response to the problem of 'cultural difficulties', suggesting only the practical difficulties in implementing this policy.

In June 1967 Dennis Howell, Under Secretary of State for Education and Science, with special responsibility for immigrant children, came to Leicester to discuss the situation with officers of the authority.

> Mr Howell was insistent that forward planning is possible only on the basis of estimated numbers. The officers pointed out the difficulty, that for new arrivals there is no way of estimating these figures in advance.[66]

In February 1968 the General Purposes Sub Committee considered a second report and resolved that the discussion be deferred. The report was circulated to all members of the Education Committee in strict confidence. Only the Chair and Vice Chair were allowed to issue public statements.[67] This control on public discussion was a response to the increasingly hysterical tone of newspaper reports about immigration in general and in relation to education in particular. Chapter Three has shown that the *Leicester Mercury* had been carrying stories highlighting the supposed threat of black immigration to Leicester since the early 1950s. Reports of 'immigrants' bringing leprosy and tuberculosis to Leicester based on the report of the Chief Medical Officer of Health were carried in September 1965.[68] On occasions members of the teaching profession lent support to the anti immigration lobby which had found expression in several organisations.[69] For example on 9 July 1962 the *Leicester Mercury* carried the headline 'City School Overflows As More Immigrants Move In'. The piece continued:

> A Headmistress is reported to have said 'they do tend to have large families and the problem will be with us for a long time'.[70]

Robinson had shown the negative attitudes expressed by white teachers towards West Indian children in schools in Leicester. At a teacher's meeting held at the 'Porkpie Chapel' in May 1964, a teacher spoke of the greater physical maturity of the West Indian girls and of their antagonism to authority. One Head said staff had reached the limits of their endurance. Robinson comments that particular difficulties had been allowed to influence the general conclusion and went on:

> One Primary School Head expressed the view that teachers with large numbers of coloured children had an impossible task...Certain Headteachers did make some comments and suggestions which showed a lack of understanding of the children's background. There was for example the suggestion that West Indian children should before being admitted to school go through a process of becoming better acquainted with white people.

He continued:

> The fact that this was accepted as a good idea means that several teachers thought that the West Indians were a sort of - from another Kingdom. The overall pictures makes it clear, I think that the assessment of attainment by teachers were, possibly apart from school X, substantially lower than they in fact are.[71]

Robinson, with great restraint, reports that he 'offered his services to Headteachers to help'.[72]

Some teachers seemed to support the view of the Authority regarding 'immigrant' children and exerted some pressure upon it. In 1967 the National Association of Schoolmasters put forward a motion at their Eastern Conference supporting a 30% maximum proportion of 'immigrants' in schools. Ronald Jackson, a mathematics teacher at Moat Boys said:

> It is a problem one cannot fully understand until one works in a school with a large number of 'immigrant' children who have no knowledge of English.[73]

An article in Alderman Newton Boys' School magazine, quoted in the *Leicester Mercury* argued that:

> Immigration should be stopped ... I rather fancy that liberal advocates of greater understanding have not lived next door to some coloured immigrants, smelt the stink of cooking or been woken up by raucous music late at night.[74]

This second report on immigrant children which had been written in November 1967 included an extensive discussion based on research in schools in Leicester of immigrant children. It was more moderate in tone than the first and admitted 'not all immigrant children present educational problems'. It also admitted that few immigrant children had been admitted to grammar schools despite evidence of ability. It concluded that the main problem was the 'rate of arrival'.[75] It was also stated in the report that only 2.2% of pupils 'needed special tuition'. This represented 1047 of the 3635 immigrant children in schools in January 1967. The conclusion of the report was that government policy of dispersal 'was suspect'.[76] Official policy was outward movement only of immigrant children. Howell on his visit had made it clear that 'moving (white) children to central schools would be impractical'. The more reasoned assessment in this report was effectively ignored by the committee.

In the period leading up to the passing of the Commonwealth Immigrants Act of 1968 there was increased agitation at national and local level concerning immigration. This was reflected in the local press in Leicester. On 24 February 1968 it was reported on the front page of the *Leicester Mercury*, 'three more planeloads arrive at Heathrow' and 'Asians heading for Leicester.[77] On 1 March 1968 the *Leicester Mercury* reported that:

> the influx of Asians from Kenya had thrown a special report being prepared for the Education Committee on Immigration and difficulties in school places completely out of gear.[78]

Chairman of the Education Committee Alderman Harold Heard said 'We cannot now debate the report until things have settled down.[79] On 29 March, Tom Bradley, the Conservative MP for Leicester North East said 'he had lots of complaints from constituents about the education their children are getting'.[80] On 20 April, Enoch Powell made his 'rivers of blood' speech in Birmingham. This received much attention both nationally and locally and led to his sacking from the Shadow Cabinet (Foot, 1967, p.116), which produced many letters of support for Powell in the pages of the *Mercury*.[81] The paper carried a full page advertisement of the Anti Immigration Society (AIMS) in May 1968 and increasingly lent support to the organisation.[82] In 1968 the *Leicester Schoolmaster*, a publication of the Leicester and Leicestershire Schoolmasters Association, produced a report on immigrant children in Leicester Schools. A full page extract was published in the *Leicester Mercury*[83] and had been discussed at the General Purposes Sub Committee.[84] The report claimed teachers were being forced to resign and described the 'hopelessness' of some language and music lessons. It also claimed 'it is vain to think of anglicising immigrants in a school in which they are the majority'.[85]

The discussions in the Sub Committee and elsewhere, in this period outlined here indicated the continuance of the assimilationist perspective. However, Chris Mullard has argued that, at national level, the second phase of government policy which he describes as integrationist, had begun in 1965. The speech made by Roy Jenkins, Home Secretary to a meeting of Voluntary Liaison Committees in London in 1966 is seen as signalling a significant change in government policy. In it he said that what was required was:

> not a flattening process of assimilation, but equal opportunity accompanied by cultural diversity in an atmosphere of mutual tolerance (Mullard, 1985, p.44).

While such a change was beginning to be evident in Leicester by 1968, the established assimilationist perspective continued alongside it.[86]

By 1973 the number of immigrants of South Asian origin from Kenya (1968) and Uganda (1972) had increased so that whereas the ration of blacks to Asians in Leicester had been two to one, by 1973 the ratio was reversed and Asians to African Caribbeans were now four to one. This was reflected in the changing proportion of immigrant children in Leicester's school from various countries.

Table 6.4   **Country of Origin of Immigrant Children in Leicester Schools 1966-1974 Expressed as a Percentage of All Immigrant Children in Schools**

Year	Kenya	Other African	Indian	Pakistan	West Indian	Other European
1966	0	49	7	27	16	
1967	3	53	7	26	12	
1968	7	56	5	23	9	
1969	18	6	43	4	21	8
1970	22	7	41	4	20	7
1971	25	9	40	4	17	6
1972	30	10	38	4	14	6
1973	29	19	36	3	9	4
1974	31	25	32	3	6	4

Source: Derived from John Mander[87]

There were still 500 'immigrant' children of school age not placed in schools at the time the data was collected,[88] showing that the LEA continued to keep children from school places well into the 1970s.

While 'immigrants' were still regarded as a problem, there was some attempt to see other cultures as positive even if the opinions expressed continued to demonstrate ignorance of African Caribbean culture.

> There is a proud Negro culture. Knowledge of this is curiously limited. I consider it to be important that the West Indian community should have the means to prove an arena to exhibit the best Negro art, music, dancing and craft.[89]

In 1972, a group of African Caribbeans set up the Saturday School for black children. It aimed to help children with basic skills, to foster community awareness and to develop ethnic studies. It received a grant from LCCR and was first housed in Crown Hills Secondary School and later moved to the Highfields Community Centre.[90]

By 1974 Control of Education passed from the City to Leicestershire County Council. The selective school system, which had been supported by the Labour Party in Leicester was then changed to a comprehensive system in line with the policy of Leicester County Council. Black, Asian and white teachers with groups such as the African Caribbean who organised the Saturday School and organisations like the Indian Workers Association began to develop community initiatives in multicultural and antiracist education. A task group on multicultural education, eventually was instrumental in establishing Leicestershire's Centre for Multicultual Education in 1984. But commitment to meeting the needs of minority children and to educating the indigenous majority concerning the background and cultures of minority groups remained patchy and depended heavily on the work of committed teachers.

Conclusion

The memories provided by Caribbean people of their childhood in Leicester schools mirror the policy decisions of Leicester LEA to which the children were subject and are remarkably consistent with these policies as revealed in the deliberations of the various education committees. Those policies were developed within the framework of a racialised construction of the problem of 'immigrants' rather than an attempt to meet the needs of what were diverse groups of new children in schools.

Caribbean, Asian, Polish and other immigrants were arriving in Leicester from 1945. Yet there was little attempt by local government to plan for the inevitable arrival of children from these groups in schools. This is despite the very favourable circumstances of falling rolls of indigenous children due to their migration out of the city. Class sizes in table 6.1 show this. It was not until the early 1960s that the issue was addressed and it was then addressed as a problem in need of containment. African Caribbean parents were powerless at this time to influence policy, while officials had little or no understanding of West Indian parents' concerns or aspirations. Towards the end of the 1970s the beginnings of a minimal recognition of the needs of children was being made. However the racialised framework constructing blacks and Asians as 'immigrants' and as a problem and the view that cultural assimilation needed to be achieved was set. The problems that black parents and children had in responding to this situation was exacerbated by their becoming a decreasing proportion of this 'immigrant' group over the period. As Kenyan and then Ugandan Asians arrived in Leicester policies were increasingly directed towards the perceived problems of dealing with these groups.

By the early 1970s many African Caribbeans in Leicester were aware that English schools were failing to meet their needs. Bernard Coard's (1971) short but devastating piece *How the West Indian Child is Made Educationally Subnormal in the English Education System* was published in 1971. Leicester's African Caribbean community set up the Saturday School for black children in an effort to counter the damaging effects of the system on the achievement of black children. At the same time the LEA, like others in Britain, was beginning to make some moves towards what became known at the 'multi-cultural' approach. However, this developed alongside rather than replaced the one established in the 1960s. The establishment of the Saturday School was one of a range of communally organised attempts to counter the effects of, and to fight against, racism. This is explored in Chapter Seven.

Notes

1   Interview with Clifton Robinson, 6 February 1995.
2   Ibid.
3   House of Commons, sessional papers, 1972-73, Select Committee on Race Relations and Immigration, 24 May 1973, HMSO London.
4   *Who's Who*, A. and C. Black, London 1995, page 1641.
5   Select committee, op cit.
6   Interview with Clifton Robinson, op cit.
7   Satish Chander Kapur, 'Black Ethnic Minorites of Leicester with Special

Reference to Education', Med thesis, University of Nottingham, 1983, page 87. According to Kapur there were no ethnic minority teachers at Deputy Head level or above in Leicestershire in 1983.

8   See Chapter Five.

9   Interview with Editha Drew, 5 May 1994.

10 Ibid.

11 Interview with Oscar Frank, 25 September 1994.

12 Ibid.

13 Interview with June Grey, 31 August 1994. This is a pseudonym.

14 C E B Robinson, 'A General Survey of West Indian Children in the Primary Schools of Leicester', M Ed Thesis, University of Leicester 1964.

15 The book caused some controversy in Leicester and elsewhere. It was felt by some that it would lend support to racist stereotypes of black family life. The novel describes abuse within the family and racism from whites in Leicester.
'They don't like Neaga (sic) here.' Her father's words came unbidden and unwelcome to her ears. She would have liked to blot them out, but in her heart she knew that truth of it', p.46.

16 Robinson, Survey, op cit.

17 Ibid.

18 Ibid.

19 Editha Drew, op cit.

20 Oscar Frank, op cit.

21 Coalville is a small town north west of Leicester.

22 Interview with John Taylor, 25 March 1994.

23 Edwards interviewed twenty white middle class children and twenty white working class children.

24 Robinson, Survey, op cit.

25 Interview with Doris Cope, 19 January 1994.

26 Robinson, Survey, op cit.

27 Ibid.

28 House of Commons, Sessional Papers, 1972-73, Select Committee on Race Relations and Immigration, 'Memorandum Submitted by Leicester LEA', 24 May 1973, HMSO, London.

29 Robinson, Survey, op cit.

30 Ibid.

31 Robinson, Survey, op cit.

32 House of Commons, Sessional Papers, 1972-73, Select Committee on Race Relations and Immigration, 24 May 1973, HMSO, London, para 865. Mr A Hudson is in fact Eric Hudson, who was, at the time the Select Committee took evidence, Chair of the Jamaica Service Group and a pioneer of the Leicester African Caribbean community.

33 Cmnd 2739, Parliamentary Papers, Session 1964-65 Vol 28, page 53.

34   Secondary Education Sub-Committee minutes show it was Secondary Heads who were refusing to take 'immigrant' children. See below.
35   LRO, 19D9VII, 687 Secondary Education Sub-Committee, 28 April 1964.
36   Ibid.
37   LRO, 19D59/VII 681, General Purposes Sub-Committee, 1964.
38   Ibid.
39   Robinson, Survey, op cit.
40   LRO, 19D59/VII, 688, Secondary Education Sub-Committee, 1965.
41   Ibid.
42   The nature of the problems are not stated.
43   LRO, 19D59/VII, 688, op cit.
44   Ibid.
45   LRO, 19D59/VII, 686, Secondary Education Sub-Committee, 1961.
46   LRO, 19D59/VII, 687, , Secondary Education Sub-Committee, 1962.
47   Ibid.
48   LRO, 19D59/VII, 687, Secondary Education Sub-Committee, 1962.
49   Ibid.
50   Robinson, Survey, op cit.
51   Cmnd 8273, 'West Indian Children in Our Schools', Interim Report of the Committee of Inquiry into the Education of Children from Ethnic Minority Groups, page 23.
52   The negative evaluation of what have come to be called 'community languages' (CLS) compared with European languages continues. It has been argued that CLS are associated with the deficit model of education for 'ethnic minority communities' and are second class with lower status compared with European languages. This is enshrined in the Educational (National Curriculum) (Modern Foreign Languages) order 1989 as a division between Schedule 1 languages and Schedule 2. (Bhatt, 1990, pp.88-90).
53   LRO, 19D59/VII, 681, General Purposes Sub-Committee, 27 November 1964.
54   Ibid.
55   Ibid.
56   LRO, General Purposes Sub Committee 27 November 1964, op cit. These words are close to those expressed in government reports. See for example Second Report of the Commonwealth Immigrants Advisory Council, February 1964, Cmnd 2266. It has been argued that dispersal in Leicester was simply a result of overcrowding due to the arrival of Ugandan Asians in 1972. This view is contradicted by evidence here. (Killian, 1979).
57   See Chapter Four.
58   Hansard (Commons), Vol 658, Cols 433-444, 27 November 1963, quoted in Mullard, op cit, page 43.

59   LRO, General Purposes sub committee, 19D59/VII, 27 November 1964.

60   Circular 7/65, DES 14 June 1965, page 5.

61   Second Report of the Commonwealth Immigrants Advisory Council, op cit, page 5.

62   LRO, General Purposes Sub Committee, 27 November 1964, op cit.

63   *Leicester Mercury*, 6 December 1967.

64   This teacher was C E B Robinson.

65   LRO, General Purposes Sub Committee, 1964, op cit.

66   LRO, 19D59/VII/682, 1968, 'Report on Immigrant Children in Leicester', November 1967. This was the second interim report. It was discussed in February 1968.

67   Ibid.

68   *Leicester Mercury*, 24 September 1965.

69   The Anti Immigration Society was formed in March 1968. Members of the British Movement held a meeting to set up a branch in Leicester in February 1969, a Leicester branch of the National Democratic Party was established in April 1969 and the National Front set up its first Leicester branch in August 1969.

70   *Leicester Mercury*, 9 July 1962.

71   C.E.B. Robinson, Survey, op cit.

72   Ibid.

73   *Leicester Mercury*, 14 March 1967.

74   Ibid, 10 April 1965.

75   'Report on Immigrant Children in Leicester', op cit.

76   Ibid.

77   *Leicester Mercury*, 24 February 1968.

78   Ibid, 1 March 1968.

79   Ibid.

80   Ibid, 29 March 1968.

81   *Leicester Mercury*, 11 April 1968, 24 April 1968, 25 April 1968.

82   Ibid, 4 May 1968.

83   Ibid, 16 December 1968.

84   LRO, 19D59/VII/682, General Purposes Sub Committee, 28 November 1968.

85   *Leicester Mercury*, 16 December 1968.

86   LRO, 19D59/VII/682, General Purposes Sub Committee, 1 February 1968.

87   Derived from John Mander, 'Freedom and constraint in a Local Education Authority', PhD Thesis, University of Leicester, page 270. From Leicester Schools on form 7(I), 1975.

88   Ibid.

89   House of Commons, Sessional Papers, 1972-73, Select Committee on Race Relations and Immigration, Memorandum Submitted by Leicester

LEA, 24 May 1973.
90   LCCR Annual Report 1972 1973.

References

Bhatt, Arvind (1990), 'Community Languages in the Curriculum', *Forum*, Vol 23, No 3.

Byron, Margaret (1995), *Post War Caribbean Migration to Britain: The Unfinished Cycle*, Avebury, Aldershot.

Carby, Hazel (1982), 'Schooling in Babylon', in Centre for Contemporary Cultural Studies, *The Empire Strikes Back*, Hutchinson, London.

Chamberlain, Mary (1994), 'Family and Identity, Barbadian Migrants to Britain', *International Year Book of Oral History and Life Stories*, Vol 3, Migration and Identity, Oxford.

Coard, Bernard (1971), *How the West Indian Child is Made Educationally Subnormal in the British Education System*, New Beacon Books, London.

Davison, R B (1962), *The Social and Economic Facts of Migration from the West Indies*, Oxford University Press, London.

Douglas, J W B (1967), *The Home and the School* (2nd ed), Panther, Manchester.

Edwards, V K (1979), *The West Indian Language Issue in British Schools*, Routledge and Kegan Paul, London.

Foot, Paul (1969), *The Rise of Enoch Powell*, Penguin, Harmondsworth.

Grosvenor, Ian (1987), 'A Different Reality: Education and the Racialisation of the Black Child', *History of Education*, Vol 16, No 4.

hooks, bell (1982), *Ain't I a Woman: Black Women and Feminism*, Pluto Press, London.

Jackson, Brian and Marsden, Dennis (1962), *Education and the Working Class*, Penguin, Harmondsworth.

Killian, Lewis M (1979), 'School Bussing in Britain: Policies and Perceptions', *Harvard Educational Review*, Vol 89, No 2, pp.85-206.

Lawrence, Errol (1982), 'Just Plain Common Sense: The Roots of Racism', and Hazel Carby, 'White Women Listen! Black Feminism and the Boundaries of Sisterhood', both in Centre For Contemporary Cultural Studies, *The Empire Strikes Back*, Hutchinson, London.

Mander, John (1980), *Leicester Schools, 1944-74*, Recreation and Arts Department, Leicester City Council, Leicester.

Marett, Valerie (1989), *Immigrants Settling in the City*, Leicester University Press, London.

Mullard, Chris (1985), 'Multiracial Education in Britain: From Assimilation to Cultural Pluralism', and Andrew Dorn, 'Education and the Race Relations Act', both in Madelaine Arnot (ed), *Race and Gender: Equal Opportunities Policies in Education*, Open University, Pergamon Press, Oxford.

Nehaul, Kemala (1996), *The Schooling of Children of Caribbean Heritage*, Trentham, Stoke on Trent.

Reeves, Frank (1989), *Race and Borough Politics*, Avebury, Aldershot, p.79.

Rex, J and Tomlinson, S (1976), *Colonial Immigrants in a British City*, Routledge and Kegan Paul, London.

Riley, Joan (1985), *The Unbelonging*, The Women's Press, London.

Stone, M (1981), *The Education of the Black Child in Britain*, Fontana, Glasgow.

Thomas-Hope, E (1977), 'Population Mobility in the West Indies: The Role of Perceptual and Environmental Differentials', PhD thesis, University of Oxford.

Tomlinson, S (1980), 'The Educational Performance of Ethnic Minority Children', *New Community*, Vol 3, No 3.

Tomlinson, S (1981), *Educational Subnormality*, Routledge and Kegan Paul, London.

Troyna, Barry and Hatcher, Richard (1992), *Racism in Children's Lives: A Study of Mainly White Primary Schools*, Routledge, London.

Troyna, Barry and Williams, Jeny (1986), *Racism, Education and the State: The Racialisation of Educational Policy*, Croom Helm, London.

7 Fighting Back: Anti-Racist Organisations and the Far Right, 1962-1981

Introduction

During the 1950s African Caribbeans were largely ignored in terms of policy by the local authority. The continuing pervasive nature of racism in the national culture of Britain meant that West Indians were subjected to racism on a personal level in their dealings with the general population, officials and the police. Furthermore a racist discourse permeated the local press, but local records show no concern to adopt any measures specifically in relation to the developing immigrant communities. Indeed there is no mention of them.[1] Cyril Osborne's campaign to establish immigration controls had a high profile in local papers from 1955 onwards but it was not until later in the decade, around the time of the 1958 'white riots' that immigration became a political issue at national and local level. This is not to say that there was no opposition to racism among whites. Some campaigns against racism are discussed here. The growing debate on 'coloured immigration' was expressed locally in the growth, in the late 1960s, of the organisations such as the Anti Immigration Society (AIMS), the National Democratic Party (NDP), the National Front (NF) and a variety of anti-racist organisations. African Caribbeans in Leicester responded by developing organisations to protect their interests. However, these groups adopted, as did the largely white anti-racist groups, a variety of approaches to the problems of racism. African Caribbeans also formed different kinds of organisations of a cultural, welfare and sporting kind,[2] as well as organisations to represent their interests in relation to the local state. Twentieth century British politics has been a male dominated affair and political struggles in Leicester are consistent with this. This is not to say there were not women active in politics as the discussion below shows.

Early Organisations

It has become an academically established view that West Indians in Britain have failed to form organisations and an implicitly unfavourable comparison has been made with other migrant groups such as South Asians who have been seen to be very successful in this endeavour. A variety of reasons have been suggested for this apparent failure, including the individualism of West Indians and divided island loyalties (Banton, 1955, p.24; Glass, 1960, p.211; Collin, 1957; Patterson, 1963; Rose, 1969, p.423; Lawrence, 1974; Pryce, 1986). Pearson (1981, p.12) for example argued that:

> South Asian groupings have been far more successful than West Indians in developing self-help associations.

In fact, from the earliest days of their arrival in Leicester African Caribbean people developed organisations. The nature of these organisations reflected needs of the time and fall into six categories. First, early groups were sporting and social in nature. These groups were formed in response to exclusion from existing provision and fulfilled a need to maintain traditional forms of socialising and leisure activities embedded in culture. By the late 1950s immigration was increasingly politicised and public hostility towards black people led to the formation of political organisations which reflected diverse perspectives on how to combat racism and the growth of the far right and to represent the interests of black people. A third group of organisations relate to a continuing relationships with societies 'back home' and the need to assist and support development in the Caribbean. By the 1970s a proliferation of cultural groups had been formed to practice dance music and drama. These social and cultural organisations became increasingly important as public discourse in relation to blacks and Asians evolved from defining these groups of peoples as immigrants to a characterisation based on ethnicity. It is not that the old perspective was forgotten, rather that a new discourse overlaid the old. African Caribbeans also through the period established organisations to secure their material and cultural interests. Nigel Harris (1995, pp.139-140) has described the way in which associations formed by migrants change to reflect the needs of the time:

> Immigrants are often fashioned by the wider society into socially close knit groups with a high degree of internal self-dependence. Associations are set up

to create a community. These may be savings and credit associations. Often the associations are unseen in the wider society until a challenge occurs *which appears to threaten the position of the immigrant group* [my emphasis].

The Leicester Credit Union was set up to provide financial services in a situation where mainstream financial institutions failed to meet needs. In addition some African Caribbeans had seen the need as early as the late 1950s for an organisation which could represent them and protect their interests as a group. Some had worked hard to establish a centre where West Indians could pursue cultural and leisure activities. These were difficult to sustain in a hostile environment which denied access to suitable buildings or facilities. This was finally successful and the Leicester United Caribbean Association (LUCA) was established in 1974. The continuing existence of LUCA has reflected the growing consciousness of identity among some African Caribbeans and a developing sense of community. Its role has evolved as the definition of black people in Leicester has moved away from that of 'immigrant' towards that of 'ethnic minority'. However, racism and the racialised politics of immigration underpin relationships between black and Asian people on the one hand and local whites on the other, in everyday social intercourse as well as in the relationships of black people to the agents of the state. It is the local political organisation established to counter the political movement of the far right in Leicester that is the focus of this chapter. African Caribbeans together with local anti-racist whites saw the need to intervene in public political debate in the early 1950s. The Anglo-Overseas Association was the product in Leicester of this need. Local Quakers played an important role in Leicester as elsewhere in supporting immigrants. They offered the use of the Friends Meeting House to the Anglo-Overseas Association. This organisation included local whites and African Caribbeans. The Chair was George Hythe, a local white Quaker and the vice Chair was C E B (Robby) Robinson who was so important in education in Leicester.[3] Other officers were Councillor H L Millard, and Mr Leslie Smith, Secretary of the Race Relations Committee of the Society of Friends. Also important was Mervin Ishmael.[4] Robby Robinson described the help given by the Quakers.

I got that one going...It would help if we could begin a process on integration without loosing our cultural position... One of the good things about that was that I knew a couple of them [Quakers]. I told them what I was seeking. The vision that I had was that I was expecting to have to pay - for lighting etc but they said no.[5]

The Anglo-Overseas Association was an attempt to counter the prejudice and ignorance of the local white population of Leicester. It can be seen to pre-date the initiative in 1962 of Miss Nadine Peppard who visited Leicester as part of a tour of the country in her capacity as advisory officer of the National Committee for Commonwealth Immigration, a government body set up to direct coordination and liaison work with immigrants (Foot, 1965, pp.221-222). The racist coverage of immigration in the pages of the *Leicester Chronicle* and the *Leicester Mercury* throughout the 1950s, especially in the writings of Cyril Osborne,[6] made the task even more difficult. As early as 1955 Robinson was speaking at meetings in the city.[7] Others like Carlton Sweeney also talked at youth clubs and schools.

> We formed a group and we got this notion... we must make the people realise who we are...This was a Leicester based thing... about 1954. We used to meet at the Friends Meeting Place on Queens Road. They let us have that free and we aimed to encourage the indigenous English to come and meet with us and so on. After a time it just petered out. We didn't like the way it was going ... certain individuals weren't progressive enough in my estimation. I don't believe in wasting time ... What we did as individuals, we used to go around and lecture to youth clubs societies and various clubs. Another chap and another fellow we used to go... I brought over some of my seed work, handicraft stuff from the Caribbean. ... One [of us] was from Antigua and another from Barbados. They [the English] had this notion you see; their geography was very poor in school which surprised us because we were forced to learn about so much of the British Isles and the Commonwealth.[8]

In 1958 the impact of national events on the situation in Leicester became apparent. The white riots in Notting Hill and Nottingham received extensive coverage in the Leicester press. For example the *Leicester Mercury* of 27th August 1958 carried stories of reactions in South Africa to the 'riots', a story of a colour bar operating in Sheffield and of court cases arising from the disturbances in Nottingham as well as an editorial on the 'world wide fight' to save the life a Negro in Alabama sentenced to death for stealing fourteen shillings.[9] Fear was generated that violence could also happen in Leicester and attempts were made in the pages of the *Leicester Mercury* to reassure that it could not. In an editorial on 27 August 1958 headed 'Racial Trouble' the *Mercury* argued:

The racial riots in Nottingham has shaken us all. Nobody in Nottingham thought this kind of thing possible. We can all apply the most level headed and objective verdicts on race problems until they happen on our own doorstep.

And what did happen in Nottingham? The Consultative Committee of the Welfare of Coloured People has already made an investigation. It has condemned a small minority of irresponsible individuals white and black. They blame these people for taking the law into their own hands and doing immeasurable harm to the good relations which have always existed between all races in the city.

The Nottingham committee which has already done much to help the West Indians in housing employment and social activity is wise to add an appeal to all Nottingham people to show a greater degree of tolerance and understanding in their everyday contact with West Indians.

Every city which has a growing coloured population might take that message to heart for what happened in Nottingham could be described under the omnibus title colour problem. In more particular terms it was an explosion of fears, jealousies and grudges turned into vicious hatreds.

It is natural that Leicester people should ask could this happen here? A direct answer might be unwise but it is important to realise that Nottingham has 2000 coloured people in the St Ann's district, a poor quarter where many of the male white inhabitants are of the teddy boy kind. Once a fight starts between black and white and gets to the proportion of a gunfight it is likely that if bystanders are drawn in the whites join in with whites and the blacks with blacks. That is the nub of the colour problem. The solution of it is in the peaceful and useful integration of the West Indians into the society of a community. That can be achieved successfully but there is no hurrying the process.[10]

On 28th August under the Headline 'Race Riots are not Likely in Leicester' the fear and attempts to reassure continued. The long standing myth of Leicester as a city with good race relations has been created in writings such as this.[11]

The ugly scenes of street brawling were echoing through the country. It was in this normally peaceful Midlands town that black fought white in a struggle which later acquired a race riot tag. Since then evidence has come to light which suggests that the incident started as a sordid weekend incident. Hundreds of street brawls flare up every Saturday night. This was different. The antagonists were of different colours...Could it happen here? It would be tempting to say it can never happen in Leicester but it would appear that disorder of last Saturday's nature are far less likely to occur here.[12]

The piece went on to compare Nottingham with Leicester, arguing that Leicester's coloured population was smaller, that it was not confined to a definite coloured quarter and that coloured workers have proved to be good employees. It quoted Canon Eaton as saying that he hadn't 'heard of any ill feeling between white and coloured'.[13] This long editorial claimed that there was no serious overcrowding problem among 'coloureds', that clubs had been set up to cater for their needs and that there was no 'colour bar' in dance halls or other places.[14]

This picture of harmony and happiness was, however, contradicted in news reports throughout its own pages during 1958 and 1959 and in acrimonious exchanges of letters, some of which argued for white supremacy and for immigration to be ended. Letters were published which opposed this view including some from members of the Anglo-Overseas Association. Canon Eaton, who had spent twenty years of his life in South Africa, wrote criticising the West Indian community in Leicester.[15]

The 'good race relations' myth was also contradicted by the experience of African Caribbeans who endured racial harassment and attack which largely went unrecorded in the local press. Every African Caribbean has a story to tell about verbal abuse. The *Mercury* did carry some reports, for example on 8 September 1958, an attack on a 'coloured man' by five whites was described.[16] There was some activity by the extreme right in Leicester as elsewhere during this period, although its extent is hard to establish. The link between racial attacks and the activities of the far right in Notting Hill has been noted (Ramdin, 1987, p.206; Wickenden, 1958, p.41; Pilkington, 1988, p.100). In July 1958 Market Harborough Councillor Noel H Symington published a booklet entitled *Return to Responsibility* in which he expressed his willingness to found a new Fascist movement.[17] He had been a Mosley supporter who had broken with him in 1956. 'Cypriots were attacked in Leicester' and the culprits were fined £50 in August.[18] A planned meeting of Mosley's Union Movement, to be addressed by Mosley himself in November 1958 at the Corn Exchange in Leicester Market, was cancelled by the Market Committee. This was followed by an editorial in September headed 'No Tears for Mosley' which supported the ban.[19] This position is in marked contrast to the position of the *Mercury* in the late 1960s and during the 1970s when the National Front was very active in Leicester. At that time the right of the National Front to hold meetings was defended by the paper.

The increasing level of attacks on blacks and increased activity of the right led to greater activity by members of the Anglo-Overseas Association and other anti racist groups in the city. The Trades' Council held a meeting in September 1958 during which Mervin Ishmael argued against immigration restrictions. A resolution against the colour bar was passed unanimously and the meeting endorsed the making of racial discrimination a punishable offence. A leaflet was produced which urged black and white workers to unite and 'sweep racialists off the streets'.[20]

On 23 September Roy Rowe, described in the Leicester Mercury as a 'coloured bus conductor' was assaulted. A thirty three year old white man, Kenneth Teasdale was told by the judge. 'No matter what his colour is you are not allowed to strike him.' He was fined £3 for assault and beating.[21] Roy Rowe described what happened:

> The bloke was on the bus... you see... and then when we stopped at the clock Tower he got off the bus. I suddenly realised that the bloke had left something on the bus...It's like a case... which looks like an instrument. I said 'is that yours?'... He said 'You black bastard' [and he] hit me in the face...I ran after him. I caught him. The police came... In a sense he got off very light.[22]

In November the *Mercury* reported that a butcher was cleared of assaulting a 'coloured man' in his shop in Upper Conduit Street.[23]

During this time individuals in the African Caribbean community continued to campaign against racism. Robinson wrote to the *Mercury* on 2 October attacking white superiority.[24] At this time a local bus company was advertising coach trips to see 'the terror spots of Nottingham'. The Sheriff of Nottingham was horrified.

> notices were displayed outside the bus garage booking office in Leicester giving full details of the trip. The police were asked to intervene and requested that the trip was withdrawn.[25]

On 2 February 1959 the Anglo Overseas Association held a conference to promote integration. While both white and black argued against immigration control some white members saw the Association as primarily a welfare organisation which also helped West Indians to assimilate culturally. Certainly people were helped to find lodgings and to 'settle in'. But some blacks resented the patronising attitude of 'middle-class do-gooders of Leicester'.[26]

Individual African Caribbeans continued their efforts to counter prejudice.   For example on 19 May the *Mercury* published a letter headlined 'Negro's Plea Why Can't We Be Brothers?'

> I am a Negro and as I face my daily routine I have to face such insults that my skin has grown much blacker. The sheer rot and ignorance talked about the Negro makes us Negroes laugh. We folk from the West Indies are British despite being black. We are law abiding people and are proud of our colour. ...Our education is as good as white people's, our culture is as good as yours our names are as good or better than those of the English and in all my life I have never heard of Teddy Boys until now. ...I work as an orderly at a hospital. I have been insulted. ... White people cheat us and rob us and whip us. Why I ask cannot we be brothers?[27]

On 22 June 1959 the Mercury carried a story of two city coffee bars operating a colour bar.[28] A protest march was organised on 24 June. Some marchers carried banners reading 'No Colour Bar in Leicester' and 'No Notting Hill in Leicester'.[29] This march included both black and white and university students in their gowns. The paper reported that it had received many letters opposing the colour bar, including one from the Anglo-Overseas Centre, but it declined to print any of them. Little is heard of the Anglo Overseas Association after this.

While throughout the 1950s immigration of 'coloured immigrants' received a great deal of coverage in the local press, in many other respects the presence in Leicester of developing immigrant communities was largely ignored. Immigration was not an issue in the city Council elections of May 1961.[30] The local state paid little attention to them. Notwithstanding the existence of widespread discrimination, the operation of the colour bar and racist harassment, African Caribbeans were able to get jobs and accommodation. They also received help and support from some locals; racism was not monolithic. But apart from the census, neither the national nor the local state kept records of people entering the city. No special provision was made and Leicester City council records show almost no recognition of the existence of groups of people who were widely regarded as a 'problem'. It was not until the end of the decade that there was any official response to a developing multicultural society. Arguably the events of 1958 and the clamour for legislation leading to the 1962 Act changed that situation. These events turned immigration into a public political issue at national level.   This politicisation was reflected in Leicester in the growth of both racist and anti-racist organisations during the 1960s.

Politicisation produced a need for greater activity on the part of African

Caribbeans in defending their interests. This development was reflected in debate held within the Sports and Social Club. While some wanted the organisation to retain its original welfare and social character others wanted to become involved in anti-racist activities. Some former members now argue that the consequent split was really about personality differences.[31] Others have suggested that the desire to become more political was sparked off by a clash between the police and some West Indians.[32] Certainly the incident received attention in the *Mercury*[33] and was regarded as significant by the police. An exceptionally long and defensive report on the event was included in the Chief Constables report 1964. Twenty five police officers were called to a party of forty to one hundred 'immigrants'. A policeman was stabbed and another injured. Later one of those arrested alleged assault by a group of police officers while he was being held in custody.[34] The magistrate who presided over the case was George Bromley who achieved fame as the Union official opposed to strikers at Imperial Typewriters.[35] The incident certainly brought anxiety to a member of the African Caribbean population and led Clifford S Hill, a minister of the Congregation Church who was visiting to urge the people of Leicester to keep 'colour' out of the forthcoming general election.[36] But there is no doubt that the heart of the split in the Sports and Social Club was related to politics. Some members began working with the Campaign for Racial Equality, a more militant group. As in the case of the formation of the National Committee Against Racial Discrimination (CARD), which grew from a visit of Martin Luther King to London in 1964, this demonstrates the importance of national and international events, in this case the civil rights movement in the United States, on the consciousness of people in the city. The organisation eventually split in 1966. The Chair and Secretary of the Sports and Social Club both left. The Chair later became Community Relations Officer of the London Borough of Lambeth and the Secretary became Conciliation Officer for the Community Relations Council in Leicester. The Club continued to function solely as a cricket club with a reduced membership (Pearson, 1981, p.72).

The Development of the Right

It was in the second half of the 1960s that anti immigration hysteria mushroomed in Leicester. This was encouraged by the progress of the issue at national level and as Paul Foot (1965, p.195):

Political reactions to the process of immigration have been shaped to a significant extent by pressure groups formed with the main purpose of campaigning against immigration.

This racist political campaigning produced a response in the form of organisations with a variety of political approaches among African Caribbeans Asians and whites opposed to racism in Leicester.

In 1966 Colin Madsen stood for election to the local council as a 'Rhodesia Front' candidate. He later became the Chair of South Leicestershire National Front.[37] The Anti Immigration Society (AIMS) began in Leicester with a coupon reply advertisement setting out its beliefs and calling for support in the *Leicester Mercury*. The advertisement declared:

All immigrants are to become liable to phased repatriation to their countries of origin on generous terms.[38]

The initiator was Dennis Taylor who had led with a letter signed by thirty men from the factory where he worked. AIMS got support from around thirty other such organisations set up round the country.

By 1967 AIMS had become more active in Leicester. Leaflets were given out and some meetings were broken up by local left wing activists and members of the CRE.[39] Much racist campaigning at this time centred on the imminent arrival of Kenyan Asians to Leicester which had begun in 1968. On 24 February the *Leicester Mercury* ran the headline 'Asians heading for Leicester'. In April students at the University led a campaign against the racist coverage of the *Mercury* including a protest march to the *Mercury* office itself.[40] The local Conservative Member of Parliament, John Peel, joined in anti-immigration sentiment.[41] But Enoch Powell's 'rivers of blood' speech of April 20th 1968 marked an increase in both racist and anti racist activity. By June 1968 AIMS claimed to have 13,000 supporters in Leicester and David Ennals, Labour's Minister with responsibility for Immigration visited Leicester in the same month. At this time the controlling conservative group on the City council were calling for a temporary ban on immigration. Ennals met with AIMS and had 'friendly discussions'. The *Leicester Mercury* was lending support to AIMS in its editorials.[42]

In May 1969 there was an anti apartheid demonstration against a South African Trade delegation. The National Front, whose Leicester Branch originated in the drawing office of the local firm of Wolsey and Co, was now the biggest of Leicester's ultra right organisations. The Synagogue in Highfields Street was daubed with National Front slogans. The *Mercury's* coverage which had always been implicitly racist had by now taken a distinctly rightward turn. In 1970 the National Democratic Party published a full page advertisement attacking immigrant workers and calling for support against immigration, while at the same time the *Mercury* refused to print the election address of the Labour Party. In the 1970 general election the National Front, the National Democratic Party and AIMS got 3,000 votes between them.   Public houses used by immigrants such as the Balmoral Hotel in Belgrave Road were threatened and attacked.

One immediate response to AIMS was initiated by Dr Jim Dyos, Dean to the Faculty of Social Science at Leicester University. He sought and got support for a full page advertisement in the *Leicester Mercury* opposing 'racialism' under the heading 'Unity Against Racialism'.   The advertisement stated:

> We believe that Racialism is not only wrong in itself but dangerous to the peace and prosperity of all the people of Leicester.[43]

The advertisement was backed by local worthies such as the Bishop of Leicester, the Reverend Ronald Williams, the Vice Chancellor of Leicester University, several former Mayors, church leaders, lawyers, trade unionists, teachers, busmen and others.   Jim Dyos later became vice president of Leicester's Council for Community Relations established in 1970, many other officers of which were also involved in the unity advertisement.

Opposition to 'racialism' in Leicester was also organised by the East Midlands area Race Relations Board. The Chair was C Forsythe J P and two of the Board's members were from Leicester: G Bromley, District Secretary of the TGWU and C E B Robinson, who was now Deputy Head of Charnwood Junior School.[44]   In 1974 George Bromley was to be a key figure in opposing Asian workers on strike at Imperial Typewriters, an important employer of black and Asian labour who openly discriminated against black and Asian workers in Leicester.   The Board was based in Nottingham.   Leicester's branch of CARD published a newsletter called 'Equality'.[45]   The secretary was Maggie Nandy, one of the few prominent women in the anti racist movement, who some time later became a founder member of the Inter-Racial Solidarity Campaign (Simon, 1983, p.80).

African Caribbeans in Leicester were increasingly concerned about their situation. In the Autumn of 1969 the Jamaican High Commissioner visited Leicester. He agreed to fund a group which became the Jamaican Service

Group (JSG). This organisation has been very important not only to Jamaicans but also to other West Indians, although the identification with Jamaica has caused a certain amount of acrimony among Caribbeans throughout its history. Most, but not all, members have been of Jamaican origin. About one quarter was active and most were men (Pearson, 1981). The JSG was orientated towards community development and the support it offered African Caribbeans was important in such a hostile environment.

The main project of the Group was to establish a Community Centre. Funds were raised through dances, socials and parties where food and drink was sold (Pearson, 1981, p.77). The JSG was the only West Indian organisation represented on the Community Relations Council. A newspaper was produced for a short time (Pearson, 1981, pp.77-78). The executive committee included people with a variety of occupations but was dominated by a small group of, male, pioneers who were thought by those arguing for a more overtly political response to the situation of African Caribbeans to be too deferential to officials and others. The organisation was seen to be 'moderate' in the face of white racism and was prepared to put up with too much. It has been argued that the difference in approach was based on a conflict of generations; the militancy of younger African Caribbeans is juxtaposed against the moderation of the older generation who are said to have held on to deferential attitudes to whites learnt in the Caribbean (Pearson, 1981, pp.72-82). While there may be a relationship between age and political approach it is argued here that this view of political difference is inadequate. Evidence from first generation immigrants suggests that the resistance and opposition to racism from many on an individual level was uncompromising. But the very small size of the community in the early 1950s meant that there was little that could be done about the ignorance and hostility encountered at a wider level. Nor is it the case that racism grew as numbers of immigrants increased, but rather that as the community grew, more organised activity was possible and racism became exposed at a political level encouraging a political response.

Black Peoples Liberation Party

The Black People's Liberation Party (BPLP) was founded in 1969. It can be seen as a response to the 'pressure of society' (*Visions of Bena Balunda: A Documentary History of the Black Power Movement in Leicester*, 1990), which was very much a feature of Leicester life for black people in the late 1960s. However as Bena Balunda, one of the founder members of the

BPLP[46] said in an interview published in the *Leicester Chronicle*, in response to a question of the influence of the Black Panthers in the USA,

> The blacks have always felt the urge to fight, but they haven't realised the advantage of collectiveness until the last few years. I don't think that we are influenced by the Panthers to any extent. The moment here arose simply because the blacks were being pressurised by society. We take certain lessons off the Panthers of course because they have been at it longer than we have, and are highly organised. But it must be remembered that Black-Power is just part of a world revolution, a feeling of brotherhood between oppressed peoples (Vision of Bena Balunda, 1990, p.2).

Despite this disclaimer many details of BPLP organisation were directly modelled on the Panthers including titles of officers. The BPLP began with a dozen or so members (Pearson, 1981, p.84) which grew to around twenty in the early 1970s. It was a male dominated group. Although the Party existed for only two years its importance and influence on Leicester politics belied its nature as a small and short lived organisation. Given the high profile of immigration as a political issue nationally and locally, the increasingly public activity and organisation of racist organisations in Leicester and the inspiration provided by American black civil rights agitating and political organisation, it is hardly surprising that such a party would be formed in Leicester.

Balunda argued in December 1970 that:

> We, the black people of Leicester, must realise that Leicester is the stronghold of fascism in Britain today, and must try and understand what this means as far as black people are concerned (Vision of Bena Belunda, 1990, p.15).

The party, like white political organisations, had more male activists than female. There was some effort to try to get more women into the BPLP. An article headed 'Invitation to Soul Sisters' in *Black Chat*, the party's paper asked sisters to 'come forward as the Black People's Liberation Party needs you. The article claims that:

> You are just as important as me because after every war on revolution we need people and only you can produce them (Vision of Bena Belunda, 1990, p.10).

In a further piece by Sister Orkarlia, women are asked not to:

Judge the black brothers of the BPLP by their morals or immoral outlook, but by their political outlook (Vision of Bena Belunda, 1990, p.29).

Other issues addressed equality for women (Black People's Liberation Party, 1990, pp.42-45). Sister Orkarlia wrote a further article in December 1971 arguing:

sisters get off your asses and move towards the action (Vision of Bena Belunda, 1990, p.49).

What is revealing is the way in which the party oriented its struggle. While the predominantly white anti racist organisations focused on the growing menace of the National Front, and anti immigration right, to many black people particularly black males, in Leicester the police were one of the main vehicles through which racism was experienced. While racism was embodied in the policies of the local state with respect to education and housing, discrimination in these areas was perhaps less immediate and not experienced so obviously and directly on an individual level. In relationships with the police actions and words were overtly racist. Carmel Charles said:

I don't think much about the police. I think they are prejudice. It's heartbreaking.

Carmel's son was mistaken for a man wanted for theft. Although this was later admitted, the aggressive action of the police led to an unpleasant confrontation and a court case.[47]

Lee Morris was one of a group of community leaders who met with police as a result of an initiative by the Leicestershire Constabulary which followed the Report of the Select Committee on Race Relations and Immigration in 1973 in order to establish better relationships with black people. However, Lee himself experienced harassment: Late one night there was a threatening incident in this street so Lee called the police, only to find himself arrested. Later he was asked to give evidence in court. The charges were dropped and there was a letter of apology.

That in a way has done something to me... I'm not resentful. I continued to attend the joint meetings [with the police].[48]

Later Lee Morris became a magistrate.

Problems with the police were acute for young people particularly men and experiences in Leicester are similar to those recorded in other cities. Ramdin (1987, p.461) wrote:

> One major experience of racism is related to confrontation with the police in their day-to-day whereabouts in their communities...Police harassment and brutality were recurring experiences for black youths.

The problematic nature of the relationship between the police and black people was first acknowledged by the police in 1967, when the first Race Liaison Officer was appointed. The Chief Constable's Annual Report included a section for the first time called 'The Police and Coloured Communities'. It declared:

> These various immigrant communities have their different social, cultural and religious background and friction can easily be caused between immigrants and the police because of the lack of knowledge and understanding about each other.[49]

Police initiatives grew in scale through the late 1970s and it was clear that the West Indian community was the target of these initiatives to improve 'rapport'.[50] A regular meeting with members of the Jamaican Service Group and other West Indian Organisations was established. By 1976 policing methods in Highfields were changed to a policy of community policing. Many interviewees had stories to tell of racism by the police. For the BPLP confronting police racism was seen as revolutionary, as going to the heart of the struggle and had priority over 'taking on' the NF and other white racists. Island loyalties were unimportant and the original group comprised of younger people who had attended school in England.

The organisation began in Bena Balunda's front room at 91 Laurel Road, a house which became known as the 'Black House' or the 'Power House'. A member described it:

> We had a flag on it as well with the colours of Africa and some people took offence to it. A lot of black people responded to it in the sense they couldn't understand how a number of black people could be so bold as to occupy an house and fly a flag of Africa in the building you know. To a degree they admired what we were doing. Some were frightened because black people

were the weakest section in society, they feel that they had no protection and here you are doing things like that.[51]

The aims and objectives of the BPLP, which were reprinted in every issue of *Black Chat*, were, however, a moderate set of proposals and embodied the kind of projects that were to become commonplace policies of local authorities in the 1980s.

1 To re-educate black people on politics so that they can see clearly just what politics is doing to them.

2 The organisation will whenever possible give practical and ideological aid to other black people in other parts of the world, fighting for the freedom of black people.

3 To fight for the right of black people in England for economic and social justice, and to defend these rights by the most effective means at its disposal.

4 To raise funds by all legitimate means, to advance the aims and objectives of the party.

5 The demand that African history and culture be added to the educational programmes of all black children so they too can be proud of their ancestry, and also see the reasons for migrations.

6 To establish community Advice Centres.

7 To form community self help organisations.

8 To co-operate with organisations, groups for parties whose aims and objectives are similar to ours.

9 The organisation will insist upon discipline of all members. The disciplinary measures for activities against the organisation will be enforced after discussion.

10 The organisation will have an official party journal to propagate its views and to win other members for the organisation.

11 All major decisions will be made by a simple majority of the members providing at least two thirds are present and all members are required to carry out these decisions.

Balunda summed it up thus:

> Basically what we was saying is justice for black peoples - you know in education in housing and welfare, health and politics and social aspects.[52]

Asked about police response to the existence of the Black House Balunda responded:

> Hysteria. The house was a threat to law and order. Members were constantly harassed daily and nightly. ... They used to have the Babylon outside watching the house twenty four hours you know. One ran up the road and goes to another and he runs down the road. If you go to Bradford we were followed all the way to Derby. Police in Derby take over and follow us up the Motorway. We're Stopped in Bradford. We have reason to believe you have given us permission to search your van.

Balunda says this was accompanied by verbal abuse.

> You bastards, you have to either go back to where you come from or be hanged ...if you were in South Africa they would throw you fuckers away... If someone dropped litter they would say 'pick it up'. These confrontations would lead to arrests and being taken to court... They knocked on the door at 2 o'clock in the morning and say 'is there a blues party here, can I buy some drugs here?'

> We had all sorts of people [sic] coming and asking to buy drugs and can we get women in this building. Those kind of things. Sometimes it was the police themselves and sometimes their agents. They had that kind of mentality. They were sure we were getting some kind of aid from China and Russia because we were too militant. The Headquarters was raided and the media sent a reporter twice so we expressed ourselves on radio and the house was raided. Police came from Nottingham and Northamptonshire and five ambulances. They needed an axe to get in. Men in uniform came round and grabbed us - five to each one. They dragged us out to the police van. While in the van they kicked us. 'Who the fuck do you think you are coming here and talking about black power?'

> We were charged with selling illegal drink without a licence and being in possession of ganga and allowing the premises to be used for the purposes of illegal drugs.

> We was running blues parties selling food and using the money to buy print materials - duplicators and typewriters. We were put on probation and fined.

One of our brethren was sent to prison he was already on a suspended sentence.[53]

The policy of the BPLP had been to put energies into combating the very real and immediate presence of state repression in the way that the police related to black people.

What is the police force for? This is a question black people want to know the answer to - because so far all these pigs represent and protect is fascism. The constant harassment of black people can be seen to be a major role of the pigs. Not so long ago a fascist by the name of Ian Paisley came to Leicester's Melbourne Road 'Free' Church hall, and a lot of people were there who weren't exactly his fans. When the time came for this pig to come out of course there was a thin blue line of racist flat foots formed. And when we'd been there some time this same blue line began their role by singling out black people, arresting them and proceeding to beat them up. A member of the BPLP was one of the targets of this cowardly attack. After these arrests were made a few party members went to the police station, and were again subjected to more harassing by the pigs. Read this statement by Mr R Duberry and see what fascist acts happens when a black person goes to the police station to see about the welfare of his black brothers:

We went down to Charles Street Police station to find out what he was arrested for. We were told it had nothing to do with us, and the officer at the desk walked off. Another officer walked by, I asked him if I could see the night inspector. He came and said that Miller had been arrested. We asked 'on what charge?' He said 'I don't know - but we will find one for all of you if you don't leave'. He then left. We sat on the benches next to a Mr A Acherson, who said that they just arrested two of his friends... The Inspector came out again with two officers and said 'Throw them out'. A police constable grabbed me and started pushing me towards the door. I said 'I am here to try and bail my friend.' The Inspector said 'We will let him out when we feel like it'. I said to the Inspector 'Haven't we got the right to wait?' As soon as I said this I received several kicks in the leg. I said 'Did you see that?' He replied 'Throw these Blacks out', which they did. The police came outside and the Inspector said, 'I would like to put all you black wogs where your friend is behind bars, but he will take what you can't get'. He told two of the policemen to follow the black wogs. A police car came from the station following us. They drove very slowly saying, 'Get on you black bastards. Go back where you came from' and other things of this nature...(Visions of Bena Balunda, 1990, pp.7-8).

The BPLP made a complaint about police behaviour after this event along with other anti racist organisations such as the IRSC.

A great deal of the space in the party's newspaper *Black Chat* was given over to discussing the role of the police in relation to black people. For example an article by T Zampaladus, more usually called Tyrone Carr, whose title was Minister of Information stated:

Having received some publicity in recent months, the Black People's Liberation Party is convinced that blacks in Britain can only relinquish their second class citizenship by uniting... The pigs believe that as we are allowed to come to this place we must be grateful... go to work, and be satisfied with whatever the pigs of the power structure dish out... Recently we, and other groups, called for a public inquiry into pig police harassment and beatings. Members of the BPLP were not surprised when the Department of Public Prosecutions (DPP) said there was not enough evidence to bring anyone to court...But if you want to see institutional racism at its best then go along to the court, our local Town Hall, any black man who goes there is guilty ...(Visions of Bena Belunda, 1990, p.12).

The police response to the existence of the BPLP was a policy of destabilisation. It has been claimed that the organisation was the subject of a state operation to destroy it.[54]   Balunda, in *Black Chat* describes a raid.

In February of this year the Leicestershire and Rutland police force, along with Police from Northampton and Nottingham broke into 91 Laurel Road, Leicester, (the headquarters of the BPLP) at about 2.30 am on Saturday 15th. At the time of the break-in by the pigs, a party was in progress so it wasn't quite clear what the pigs wanted. It wasn't until several hours later and several arrests that it was made clear that they were looking for drugs. Several people were arrested, most of them members of the BPLP.

The interesting aspect of this raid, as the pigs called it, is that as far as 91 Laurel Road is concerned it is not an isolated case. It is the general pattern all over the country for police to break into black people's property on the pretence of looking for drugs. All over the country in areas where black people are organised or trying to organise themselves, it is customary for the police force of that area to carry out so-called raids on the premises of black people, particularly if they are established headquarters. Owing to the frequency of these raids, it is quite clear that there is a conspiracy which is obviously intended to discredit and degrade black people who are in any way politically active. It is quite obvious that the police forces have declared war upon the black organising communities in this country. Whenever black people look like organising themselves, before they can begin to establish themselves as any kind of effective organisation it is normal practice for the police to move with the gestapo tactics, and harass, intimidate and arrest all those whom they consider to be of any importance to the black community, more often than not those arrested are usually on trumped-up charges (Visions of Bena Balunda, 1990, p.24).

According to Mackenzie Frank, the BPLP was:

systematically hounded out of existence by the local police force. By the end of 1972 many of the party's Central Committee were either imprisoned or had fled to such places as Torquay, Southampton, Birmingham or Nottingham.[55]

In an interview with the *Leicester Chronicle* Balunda was asked about the relationship of the BPLP with other left wing and anti-racist groups. He replied:

Of course they can help the struggle. In the final analysis we're both fighting against the same system. And we'll cooperate with the white radicals if we feel that it will benefit us (Visions of Bena Balunda, 1990, p.2).

The BPLP did make an arrangement with members of the Trotskyist led Anti Fascist Committee in Leicester and some printing facilities were shared. They also attended each others' meetings. The BPLP did sometimes go on demonstrations organised by the mainly white Anti Racist Group in the city and they also organised their own demonstrations.

In addition to the BPLP black individuals were also involved with anti racist organisations which involved whites. These had developed in response to the expansion of white racist activity and organisation in Leicester. Many white people saw the desire of African Caribbeans to organise separately as being in some way the same as white imposed segregation of racialised groups. The BPLP was seen as deeply threatening to white society.

When asked about segregation in the *Chronicle* interview Balunda replied:

You use the word segregation, but that's an enforced splitting-up. We are not in favour of this, but we can see the advantage of separation which would be voluntary. Integration has now become a dirty word for deep-thinking blacks. After all, it's been tried, but the whites have fought against it. The trouble is that to integrate, blacks are expected to take on the white man's way. It's nothing more than cultural genocide. We'd have to become white people and were not prepared to do that. However, we do feel that our two races could live peacefully in co-existence (Visions of Bena Balunda, 1990, p.2).

After the demise of the BPLP some activists turned their attention to other projects. Raddle Book Shop was founded in 1979 and a project to help homeless black men developed much later into the Foundation Housing Association. Many maintained their personal commitment to Rastafarianism which was clearly an integral aspect of the ideas of the party.

Black people, particularly men, have continued to suffer from racism at the hands of the police. By the 1980s the Highfields Community Council had been established, with its prime raison détre being a way of communicating with the local police over its treatment of black people particularly young black men. Mothers often found themselves summoned to the police station when their sons had been arrested. Women became very powerful in the Highfields Community Council. It was chaired for many years by Ruby Grant.[56]

White Led Anti Racism

Leicester has been described as a city:

> characterised by traditions of both racism (which is specifically manifest as 'racial exclusionism') and anti-racism which are more deeply rooted than in many other multi-racial areas (Fitzgerald, 1988, p.7).

White anti racist response to the growing menace of the far right through the 1970s was divided between two political approaches. The first approach can best be represented by that of the Inter Racial Solidarity Campaign (IRSC). The Community Relations Council (CRC) and its successor the Campaign for Racial Equality (CRE) adopted a similar approach. Indeed there was an overlapping membership between these bodies. The paper of the CRE, *Equality*, became that of the IRSC.

The IRSC was founded in the summer of 1969 in response to increased right wing activity. It was an initiative of the Young Communist League and the Communist Party (CP) together with the Indian Workers Association and others. Later it was also supported by the Young Liberals and some sections, but not all, of the local Labour party. It also included some Christians, anti racists such as the Quakers and individuals such as the Reverend Middleton. Its policy was to mobilise public opinion and to influence mainstream political organisations. Its aim was to isolate the far right politically. According to Ray Sutton, a leading member of the IRSC:

refusing to exclude liberals and Christians in this movement the Communists from the start attempted to orientate the whole work of the campaign towards the working class, arguing that the major struggle taking place was that between the working class and the forces of monopoly capitalism in which the capitalist class would not hesitate to use the weapon of racialism in order to split and divide the workers.[57]

The second approach to opposing racism can be seen in the Anti Fascist Committee. In 1971 an 'anti fascist' committee was established in Leicester by a group based at Leicester University, although it also had some trade union support. This group tended towards a Trotskyist political affiliation in contrast the CP led IRSC. They worked with the trades unions, the Labour Party and had the support of a branch of the Indian Workers Association and the Asian Youth group, the Red Star. While the IRSC concentrated on a political campaign, the Anti Fascist Committee had a policy of physical response to the growth of the far right in Leicester. The slogan was 'no platform for fascists' and was more activity based. Later when the Trades Council established its own Anti Racist Committee (ARC) the Anti Fascist Committee subsumed itself within this new organisation and later in the decade many supporters joined the Anti-Nazi League (ANL). The two political approaches to opposing fascism represented by the IRSC and the ANL existed in competition with each other throughout the period of the rise and fall of the National Front (NF) in Leicester which spanned the 1970s. In practice there was also a great deal of common activity. For example both groups picketed the NF newspaper sellers in the city centre. But the ideological battles were at times bitter and sectarian. Individual black people such as Herdle White worked within these organisations but both were white led. A degree of cooperation was established between the BPLP and both the predominantly white anti racist groups although all three organisations maintained their independence.

The NF had become increasingly active by 1970 and the *Leicester Mercury* in cooperation with local conservatives launched its own anti immigration campaign. The *Mercury*'s coverage of immigration was so extreme as to attract national attention; it was described as a 'daily diet of thundering editorials' by the *Economist* and the paper was accused of printing letters which 'often contained racialist nonsense of the worst kind'.[58]

The *Leicester Mercury*, described by one African Caribbean as 'never a friend to black people'[59] was widely regarded by anti-racists as being sympathetic to the NF. Troyna (1981) has argued that the *Mercury*'s coverage of race issues in the 1970s used the NF position as a boundary marker in debate (Marett, p.10). The police were also regarded by many as being less than even handed in their dealings with the NF on the one hand and anti-racists on the other. The Chief Constable's description of the 1979 NF march as a 'St George's Day celebration' suggests a benignity which defies the evidence. In 1972 when it became obvious that many Asians expelled from Uganda would want to come to Leicester the City Council reacted with 'astonishment and anxiety' and advised them in an infamous advertisement in the *Ugandan Argus* on the 15th September 1972 to keep away (Marett, 1989, p.10). The advertisement stated that:

In your own interest and that of your family you should accept the advice of the Ugandan Resettlement Board and not come to Leicester.

These actions by the City Council have been seen as:

the abrupt and public abandonment of the laissez faire policies adopted since 1968 towards immigrants by Leicester's elected council and chief officers (Marett, 1989, p.53).

While the Council may not have taken a public stance against immigration, prior to 1972 laissez faire is misleading as a description of its policies. These policies towards black and Asian residents in Leicester in the areas of housing and education had been discriminatory; black people were excluded from public housing and denied places in schools.

The 1972 'Ugandan Asian crisis' brought Leicester into the national news. Conservative councillors were totally against Asians coming to Leicester and the Labour party too joined an all-party delegation to the Home Office on 31st August 1972 to oppose more Asian immigration to Leicester. Increasing hysteria characterised council meetings. Prime Minister Edward Heath visited the city at the end of September. However, nine Labour councillors revolted against the ruling Labour Party policy. The NF, the National Democratic Party and the Immigration Control Association with some members of the British Movement marched through Leicester on 9th September 1972. Colin Jordan of the British Movement said: 'Leicester's decision will set a shining example to the rest of the country'.[60] The *Mercury* produced some pro Enoch Powell editorials and a Support Enoch Powell group was formed in Leicester in October.[61] The *Leicester Mercury*, and local conservatives organised a continuous campaign against immigration. This lent legitimacy to local fascists.

The anti racists were losing the propaganda battle. The Anti Racist Committee had a strategy to leaflet every house in Leicester and the IRSC tried to mobilise public opinion against fascism. It had a bigger base of support than the ARC and a long list of bodies affiliated to it but had powerful forces with which to contend.

In 1974 the strike at Imperial Typewriters led by Asian workers gave occasion for increased right wing activity and anti racists from the IRSC and ARC lent support to the strikers. Technically ARC was a sub committee of the Trades Council but in practice it involved representatives from community organisations as well as trade union delegates. A 500 strong march led by the NF in support of white workers at Imperial was countered by 6,000 people in a march against racialism held on 24 August 1974. The NF increasingly targeted Leicester as the spearhead of their activities. The first regional office of the NF was set up on the corner of Humberstone Road and Spinney Hill Road on the edge of Highfields with a branch organiser: Anthony Reed Herbert a local solicitor.[62] A planned national demonstration was switched from Mansfield to Leicester. The Front wanted to march through Highfields but the plan met local opposition. The Labour group on the Council was asked to ban the march on grounds of racism. But instead both the Front march and the counter demonstration were banned as a threat to public order. Eventually the NF was allowed to march but not past the Imperial factory. Leaflets opposed to the march were distributed to 30,000 households. The Front's electoral support rose steadily through the early 1970s reaching a peak in 1976. Thereafter its electoral support began to decline. The IRSC calculated votes per candidate in various local elections in the area as:

**Table 7.1   Average Votes Per Candidate in Local Elections in the
Leicester Area 1972-1977**

May	1972	399
April	1973	646
June	1973	683
May	1976	911
May	1977	523
November	1977	270

Source: Equality Spring 1978[63]

In the city elections of 1976 the NF polled nearly 18.5% of the total votes (43,000) and came within 61 votes of victory in Abbey ward.[64]

By the time of the county elections of May 1979 the vote had slumped to 13.5%. At a by election in Wigston in November the vote had fallen from 14% to 8.6% within six months. While electoral support was declining, anti racist opposition continued. The NF was unable to sell its paper without continued opposition from the IRSC and ARC. The conflict between racists and their opponents became increasingly physical. The windows of the CRC and the local left wing bookshop were broken regularly and the front doors of known anti fascists were painted with NF slogans. Sikh temples were painted with 'wogs out'. The *National Front News* of February 1977 carried an article headlined, 'Leicester Faces Immigrant Flood For Years to Come' and claimed to have a secret internal memorandum of Leicestershire County Council sent by an employee outlining projected arrivals of immigrant children in Leicester. It carried a picture of a lone white child surrounded by dark skinned children and carried the caption 'outnumbered... surrounded - your child?'[65]

The Leicester branch of the NF produced its own news bulletin edited by Peter Ash of Woodland Road, Leicester.[66] An issue in 1978 attacked multi cultural education, singled out Robby Robinson for criticism and called for help in distributing leaflets to schools.[67] Robby Robinson who by this time was deputy Chair of the CRE in London had long been a target for the local NF. On one occasion while head of Uplands Junior School he found a film crew, supported by a group of racist parents, filming in his playground and interviewing black children. The police were called to remove the crew. Later Mr Robinson wrote to the Chief Constable asking for the film to be confiscated. Robinson experienced harassment from the NF locally until he left Leicester to join the CRE in 1977.[68] In September 1978 another anti racist had his jaw broken by an NF member who was arrested for attacking a member of the IRSC.

The increasingly public political activists of the NF and its opposition through the 1970s brought problems for the police which were reflected in many levels of complaints against the police. For example, between 1974 and 1975 complaints increased by 64%, by the increasing level of arrests for public order offences up between 1975 and 1976 by 45% and in the same year the staffing increase in the number of police officers injured in assaults, a rise of 65%.[69] By 1977 the Chief Constable was reporting a new direction for police methods carrying far greater firmness and protection for officers.

The IRSC continued to promote cultural events aimed at reinforcing racial harmony. For example an event called Unity Against Racialism which included a procession and carnival was held on 12 August 1978. A 'Rock Against Racism' (a London based movement) concert was held on 13 October 1978 at Leicester Polytechnic. The NF had also began a policy of leafleting schools. Wreake Valley College in Syston was daubed with NF slogans and other racist graffiti and the Young NF attempted to leaflet Bosworth College in Desford. Protests were made over the refusal of the local public libraries to remove the NF magazine *Spearhead* from the shelves. But the county Librarian would not change the policy arguing that libraries have a 'responsibility to represent all shades of opinion'. The IRSC also challenged the colour bar operating at the British Legion Club in Syston. Jim Marshall and Greville Janner, both Labour MPs for constituencies in the city, protested in the House of Commons when an NF spokesman spoke on the Radio Leicester 'Crosstalk' programme. Journalists at the radio station had proposed to strike but had dropped their action when threatened with dismissal. On the actual day an unsuccessful attempt was made to jam the 'phone in' programme. A picket called by the Trades Council, was held outside the station headquarters in Epic House. The station manager Owen Bently, who had been one of the signatories of the Unity Against Racialism declaration ten years previously insisted on the programme going ahead and Brian Piper, a prominent member of the IRSC, debated with the NF representative on the programme.[70]

By 1978 a new national anti racist organisation, the Anti Nazi League, an organisation initiated by the Socialist Workers Party, had been set up in London. The political approach of this organisation was similar to that of ARC in Leicester and most of the activists in ARC affiliated to the ANL.[71] However a small group refused and ARC continued to exist until 1980. A new phase of activism began and posters saying 'No Nazis in Leicester' appeared all over the city. The ANL also continued ARC's telephone tree. Whenever an activist got news of NF action such as a meeting, a telephone call would be made to another anti racist, who telephoned another. Through this, people mobilised to physically confront the NF wherever they appeared in Leicester.

Arguably the most important event led by the ANL in Leicester was the counter demonstration against the NF held in Leicester on 21 April 1979. The NF had planned a march through Leicester on that date to mark the start of their 1979 election campaign. The police report on the march described it as a march to promote candidates in the local elections and a St George's Day parade celebration.[72] Their electoral success was already in deep decline in Leicester but the organisation still considered the city to be very important. The Leicester branch sold more copies of *NF News* than anywhere in Britain apart from the West Midlands.[73]

The political differences between the ANL and the IRSC can be seen most clearly in the way in which they opposed the planned NF march. The ANL wanted to stop the fascist march and meeting altogether using physical confrontation, whereas the IRSC, having failed in attempts to get the march banned, planned a counter march along a route away from that of the NF.

On the day the ANL had a well organised plan to confront the NF march along its proposed route. Supporters from the Post Office Workers Union had twelve public telephone kiosks in Leicester with 'Out of Order' notices on them so that ANL members could use them to coordinate activities. However, independently organised groups of anti racists also acted alone. A group of engineers met NF supporters when they arrived at the railway station to harass them and 'make life as difficult as possible'.[74] Another group of building workers and miners from Nottingham and Mansfield attacked the march in Welford Road soon after it set off. The police were forced to re-route the march up Regent Road, taking a shorter route to a planned meeting at Wygeston School. Anti fascists shadowed the march into De Montfort Street and eventually broke through the police cordon. Police dogs were let loose on the demonstrators. One woman had her leg bitten by a dog and fourteen anti-racists were hospitalised. The police operation involved 5,000 police from twenty one different forces. There were eighty seven arrests of anti-racists of whom at least four were jailed. Brian Piper a Justice of the Peace who was also a prominent supporter of the IRSC was involved in fining ANL supporters for offences on the day. Four NF supporters were arrested. The *Leicester Mercury* commented:

> Leicester paid a high price for the doubtful privilege of being the place where the NF had to be allowed to march through the streets.[75]

The new policing methods initiated in 1977 were in place in 1981 when Leicester experienced 'the most serious violence' during the 'riots' of July 1981 which followed the events in Brixton of April that year. Police behind riot shields met large gangs of rioters wielding petrol bombs. Acid was also thrown and there were ninety arrests (Kettle and Hodges, 1982). The police report claims that there were 112 premises attacked, twenty cars damaged and thirty one officers injured, by both black and white youths. Assistance was needed from nineteen other forces. The Chief Constable referred to a 'tension-ridden society'. These events have been seen as highly significant and brought a new seriousness in approach from the national and local state towards what were now called ethnic minorities. The events of 21 April can be seen as marking the end of the NF as a political force in Leicester. Indeed soon afterwards, the NF split. Anthony Reed Herbert, the Leicester organiser left to form the British Democratic Party.[76]

Conclusion

African Caribbeans were active in the political life of Leicester from the time of their arrival. The organisations they found or were involved in reflect a range of political perspectives of the left from the moderate integrationist members of the Anglo-Overseas Association to the more radical Black Peoples Liberation Party. The politics of the BPLP were a result of different influences. The nature of their experiences with the police in Leicester was one important pressure. It was in the day to day interaction with police that many black people experienced racism. But clearly the model provided by the American Black Power movement was important in shaping the nature of the politics of the BPLP. Opposition to the State was important and to many people the power of the state was most heavily felt through interaction with the police. The threat from the far right NF was less a focus of attention for the BPLP than for the white led anti-racist organisation.   With some notable exceptions most of the organised political groups were male led.   However some African Caribbean women became powerful leaders of other kinds of organisations discussed below.   During the 1970s some African Caribbeans who had been active politically consolidated their commitment to Rastafarianism. During this decade African Caribbeans also became more conscious of an identity as a 'community' and the establishment of Leicester United Caribbean Association (LUCA) can be seen to reflect this.   These aspects of African Caribbean life are raised in Chapter Eight.

Notes

1   There were no references to African Caribbeans in Housing Committee Minutes through the period, LRO, DE 32 77, or in Chief Constable's Annual Reports, LRO, L352.2, or in Education Committee Minutes before 1964. The General Purposes Sub Committee of the Education Committee does not mention 'Immigrant Children' before November 1964, LRO, 19D59/VII/681.   The Secondary Education Sub Committee makes no mention of 'Immigrant Children' before December 1961, LRO, 1959/VII/686 and the Primary Education Sub Committee before September 1967, LRO, 19D59/VII/683.

2   See Chapter Eight.

3   See Chapter Six for a brief biography of Robinson.

4   Also one of the 'Pioneers' see Chapter Five.

5   Interview with C E B Robinson, 6 February 1995.

6   See Chapter Three.

7   *Leicester Mercury*, 31 January 1955.

8   Interview with Carlton Sweeney, 4 August 1994.

9   *Leicester Mercury*, 27 August 1958.

10   Ibid.

11   Edward Heath on a visit to Leicester during the General Election Campaign of 1979 said that 'the people of Leicester provide the rest of Britain with a shining example of how successful a multiracial society can be. The rest of Britain will continue to look to you here in Leicester as a model of how to build and maintain race relations.' Leicester's reputation for good race relations also referred to in Government Committees. See House of Commons, Session 1980-81, Fifth Report from Home Affairs Committee, HMSO, London.   The *Leicester Mercury* also made such claims. See for example, *Leicester Mercury*, 15 December 1961 and 5 April 1965 (Troyna, 1981, p.58).

12   *Leicester Mercury*, 28 August 1958.
13   Ibid.
14   Ibid.
15   See Chapter Eight.
16   *Leicester Mercury*, 8 September 1958.
17   *Leicester Mercury*, 12 July 1958.
18   Ibid, 8 August 1958.
19   Ibid, 12 September 1958.
20   Ibid, 17 September 1958.
21   Ibid, 23 September 1958.
22   Interview with Roy Rowe, 6 September 1994.
23   *Leicester Mercury* 12 November 1958.
24   Ibid, 2 October 1958.
25   Institute of Race Relations   Transcript of a film, *A Common History*, Director, Colin Prescod.
26   Ibid.
27   *Leicester Mercury*, 19 May 1959.
28   Ibid, 22 June 1959.
29   Ibid, 24 June 1959.
30   Ibid, 9 May 1961.
31   Interview with Lee Morris, former member of the Sports and Social Club, 5 September 1994.
32   See Dwight S. Browne, 'A Comparative Study of West Indian Social and Political Associations in Leicester', MA Dissertation, University of Leicester 1973.
33   *Leicester Mercury*, 5 April 1964.
34   LRO, 2.352.2, City Police Report 1964.
35   *Leicester Mercury*, 5 April 1964.
36   Ibid, 6 April 1964.
37   Ray Sutton, 'The Struggle Against Racism', IRSC, leaflet, undated.
38   *Observer*, 2 June 1968.
39   Institute of Race Relations, op cit.
40   *Leicester Mercury*, 26 April 1968.
41   Ibid, 3 March 1968.
42   Ibid, 8 June 1968.
43   Advertisement, undated.
44   See Chapter Six.
45   *Equality* May/June 1967.
46   A room in the Highfields Community Centre is dedicated to Bena Balunda who died in 1984.
47   Interview with Carmel Charles, 13 July 1994.
48   Interview with Lee Morris, 5 September 1994.
49   LRO, L352.2, Leicester Constabulary Report, 1967.

50   LRO, L352.2, Leicester Constabulary Report 1972.
51   Institute of Race Relations, op cit.
52   Ibid.
53   Ibid.
54   Interview with Paul Winstone, 25 September 1995.
55   *Black Chat*, February 1971.
56   Interview with Ruby Grant, 13 December 1996.
57   Sutton, op cit.
58   *Economist*, 16 December 1972.
59   Interview with Linda Herbert, 9 September 1994.
60   *Leicester Mercury*, 11 September 1972.
61   Ibid, 12 September 1972 and 19 October 1972.
62   *National Front News*, No 7, February 1977.
63   *Equality*, Spring 1978.
64   Ibid.
65   *National Front News*, 7 February 1977.
66   Ibid, August 1979 issue 18.
67   National Front News Bulletin, Leicester Branch, undated.
68   Interview with C. E. B. Robinson, 6 February 1995.
69   LRO, L 352.2, Leicester Constabulary Annual Report, 1976.
70   Interview with Paul Winstone, 25 September 1995.
71   Ibid.
72   LRO, L.352.2, Leicester Constabulary Annual Report, 1978.
73   *National Front News*, August 1979.
74   Interview with Terry Allcott, Anti Nazi League activist 14 November
        1995.
75   *Leicester Mercury*, 23 April 1979.
76   *Equality*, Autumn 1979.

References

Banton, Michael (1955), *The Coloured Quarter*, Allen and Unwin, Jonathan Cape,
    London.
Collin, Sydney (1957), *Coloured Minorities in Britain*, Lutterworth, London.
Fitzgerald, Marian (1988), 'Racial Harassment in Leicester', *Federation of Black
    Housing Organisations*, Vol 14, No.3.
Foot, Paul (1965), *Immigration and Race in British Politics*, Penguin,
    Harmondsworth.
Glass, Ruth (1960), *The Newcomers*, Allen and Unwin, London.
Harris, Nigel (1995), *The New Untouchables*, Penguin, London.

Kettle, Martin and Hodges, Lucy (1982), *The Police, The People and the Riots in Britain's Cities*, Pan, London.

Lawrence, Daniel (1974), *Black Migrants: White Natives*, Cambridge University Press, London.

Marett, Valerie (1989), *Immigrants Settling in the City*, Leicester University Press, London.

Patterson, Sheila (1963), *Dark Strangers*, Tavistock Publications, London.

Pearson, David (1981), *Race, Class and Political Activism: A Study of West Indians in Britain*, Gower, Aldershot.

Pilkington, Edward (1988), *Beyond the Mother Country: West Indians and the Notting Hill White Riots*, I B Tauris, London.

Pryce, Ken (1986), *Endless Pressure*, Bristol Classical Press, Bristol.

Ramdin, Rom (1987), *The Making of the Black Working Class in Britain*, Gower, Aldershot.

Rose, E J B, et al (1969), *Colour and Citizenship*, Oxford University Press, London.

Simon, Brian (ed) (1983), *Margaret Gracie; A Teacher For Our Time*, no place of publication given.

Troyna, Barry (1981), *Public Awareness and the Media. A Study of Reporting on Race*, Commission for Racial Equality, London.

Troyna, Barry (1981), *Public Awareness and the Media: A Study of Reporting on Race*, Commission for Racial Equality, London.

Visions of Bena Balunda: A Documentary History of the Black Power Movement in Leicester 1970-72, Raddle Publications, Leicester, 1990.

Wickenden, James (1958), *Colour In Britain*, Oxford University Press, London.

8 Leisure and Religion, 1945-1981

Introduction

There exists immense confusion surrounding issues of ethnicity and culture both in academic and popular discourse. In everyday understanding 'ethnicity', at least in Great Britain, is applied only to minority groups. The ethnic identity of the majority is taken as given. Indeed, in popular discourse in Britain, 'ethnic minority' commonly is defined in a racialised way to apply only to people with dark skins. Like 'migrant' before it the use of this term represents the persistence of emphasis on 'race' with the division between black and white being paramount (Barker, 1981).[1]

Ethnicity refers to culture and in the academy too there is no consensus regarding the approach to the study of culture. For sociologists culture includes every aspect of life that is constructed by human beings and includes not just beliefs, values and aesthetics but also the institutions of society, its social structures and material environment. In this definition we are all part of a culture and we all have ethnicity. However, academics tend to turn their gaze downwards and unlike the subcultures of disadvantaged groups and minorities which are studied, those of the rich and powerful are rarely problematised.

Minority groups have been subjected to a certain amount of cultural tourism from academics (Rex and Moore, 1957, p.156). Aspects of the culture of subordinate groups have been used to explain the disadvantages which they face, for example, aspects of the culture of blacks have been used to explain educational performance.[2] The culture of working class people has been similarly pathologised. Alternatively, aspects of culture have been seen as an expression of oppression (Cashmore and Troyna, 1990, pp.144-162). The subcultures of dominant groups tend to remain either covert and unacknowledged or seen as the highest form of human endeavour and achievement. Aspects of the culture of the rich and powerful is sometimes taken as knowledge itself.

The study of 'ethnicity' is a developing area of research and in contrast to 'everyday understanding' the ethnicities of all kinds of minorities, black and white, have become the focus of research. Very recently the ethnicity of majority groups has also received attention although this area is very much in its infancy (Roediger, 1990). However, many academics are content to apply the concept of 'ethnicity' to minority groups and also to define the concept to include an element of racialisation.

Black immigrants to Leicester shared many aspects of culture with the white society which they joined; religion and language being the most notable. There were many differences and the cultures of all groups are flexible and fluid, ragged round the edges and influenced by the culture of other groups both near and far. African Caribbeans were ready to adapt to the society into which they had moved and over time, aspects of their culture have also influenced the white majority; for example in youth subculture (Sewell, 1997). Rex and Moore (1967, p.158) in their study of Sparkbrook have written about West Indians:

Respondents protested that they are no different from anyone else. They want homes for their families. They want acceptance into local organisations and have little time for exotic cultural exercises.

The conditions under which assimilation takes place are not explored here (Panayi, 1994, pp.76-101). The focus here is racialisation. The way in which the identity of African Caribbeans has moved from 'immigrant' to 'ethnic minority' masks the continued salience of racialisation as a means whereby dominant groups ignore their perspective as minorities. This is not to endorse Castle's (1987, p.96) view in its entirety, which seems to deny the existence of the migrants' culture prior to migration.

Becoming a minority is a process whereby dominant groups in society ascribe certain (real or imagined) characteristics to the newcomers, and use these to justify the assignment of specific economic, social and political roles. In response to their experiences migrants and their descendants develop their own culture and institutions and perceive themselves as distinct groups within society.

It is shown how the 'normal' leisure and cultural activities of African Caribbeans in Leicester have been practised and developed within a changing context. In the first two decades African Caribbeans turned first to join in with the majority while also maintaining their traditional leisure and cultural pursuits. By the end of the period cultural activities were beginning to be encouraged by the local authority as the ethnic identity of black people was fostered in response to the acknowledgement of Leicester as a multicultural city.

It is argued here that many centres of public entertainment, sporting and social life in Leicester in the 1950s and the early 1960s were closed to West Indians. Either an overt 'colour bar' operated or more commonly West Indians were made to feel unwelcome. Both informal and organised social life for Caribbeans developed within this context. By the 1970s overt discrimination in public places had been made illegal[3] and although exclusion still operated it was less widespread. However, this period was also one of growing influence of far right organisations in Leicester which lent legitimacy to a more public expression of racist attitudes and views. This had the effect of increasing the discomfort of some black people in public places where they anticipated meeting, and indeed met, racial abuse. The by now established black community in Leicester, defined now as a cultural ethnic group, developed more cultural and social organisations during this period expanding into a wider range of activities.   This facilitated both the development of social life in a more comfortable environment and the expression of different aspects of culture, artistic and recreational.

During the 1950s and 1960s no provision was made by Leicester City Council for the cultural, leisure, sporting and social life of African Caribbeans. The exception to this was in the area of social provision for young people, more specifically young men who were perceived to be a problem in relation to the majority community. Youth clubs were set up. During the 1970s the voluntary organisations were beginning to be given some financial support from the Local Authority. The fostering, through financial support, of cultural groups by the City Council reached its peak after, and was a response to, the uprisings of 1981.

More personal aspects of relationships with white people have not been explored. However, it is worth noting that throughout the period there was a great deal of personal interaction with white people including intimate relationships of various kinds. Almost all the people interviewed for this study had some white relatives in the immediate or wider family.

Culture Shock and Ignorance

Caribbean migrants experienced culture shock when they arrived in Britain. This was particularly acute for the earliest arrivals; those who came in the late 1940s and early 1950s. Aspects of this have been documented elsewhere (Richmond, 1954; Banton, 1955; Patterson, 1963; Richmond, 1973; Foner, 1979; Highfields Rangers, 1993). There are striking similarities in the accounts given by West Indians concerning their initial reactions to life in Great Britain. Many have described the assumption that rows of terraced houses with smoke bellowing from chimneys were in fact factories and the surprise at learning that these were in fact homes 'joined together'.[4] Reuben Nelson who arrived from Jamaica in 1961, already in his forties said:

We learn in school about England so much, when we come here I could fly back home. Everything completely different from what I had heard about. ... I went into the country - the shock of me seeing the house with smoke coming from the chimneys. I believe it's a factory. I thought I'll get a job soon. I saw a house with a fire inside! But then I enjoyed the fire because I was cold. ... I never see a white man ride a push bike before. I never see a white man do any work.[5] I never see a woman drive a bus. I never see a white lady cut her own hedge. I was shocked.[6]

Carlton Sweeney (1978, p.10) wrote:

Have you ever had the feeling of being watched? ... I had such feelings as I walked through the streets. I noticed the blue, grey and brown peepers eyeing my person...One of the tasks from the outset was to overthrow the misconception held by many British ... that a dark pigmentation of the skin was synonymous with unintelligence.

and he added:

Those arriving in England in the late 1960s and the visitors of the 1970s have not the slightest idea of what the early migrants had to suffer (p.21).

Elvy Moreton also came in 1961 from St Kitts.

It was dull and grim and cold. It looked very dirty. I had never seen an escalator before.[7]

Elvy Moreton put her bags and parcels on the first step of the escalator but because it was a new experience it took rather a long time to get on herself. 'My things went sailing off and I never saw them again.' Linda Herbert thought:

> Snow was ashes from the sky...horrible English weather. The weather was just like the people. Today they say hello and the next couple of hours they don't want to know you. They change just as often as the weather.[8]

Cultural differences made many aspects of life rather a struggle. West Indians were unable to obtain the kind of food to which they were accustomed. Green bananas or sweet potatoes and many other foods were unheard of in Leicester of the early 1950s. However, some small corner shops made an effort to get West Indian foods when requested.[9] Carlton Sweeney said:

> We had a healthy diet in the West Indies. We ate guava, cashew nuts and all kinds of Caribbean fruits. We couldn't get the right rice [in Leicester]. We also used to doctor ourselves [with natural remedies]. The abundance of different kinds of fruit in the West Indies is something missed by many West Indians in England. West Indians had to adapt themselves. Later they obtained rice and there was always Irish potatoes.[10]

Carlton Sweeney provided his Leicester landlady with sugar, butter and cheese brought with him and later sent from Antigua, when there was rationing in Britain in the early 1950s.

Migrants were also shocked by the levels of ignorance and prejudice of local whites. West Indians who came to Leicester in the 1950s and early 1960s can recall embarrassing or hurtful incidents resulting from attitudes of local people. Reuban Nelson was asked 'Do you people have houses in Jamaica?'[11] June Grey said:

> When I came to Leicester I hated it. I cried. I sat on a bus next to a lady who said couldn't you sit somewhere else? You are taking our jobs away'.[12]

Caribbeans were hurt and embarrassed by an apparent belief among some of the indigenous population that black people had tails. Carmel Charles came into conflict at work because another employee at the hospital where she worked was trying to see if this was true.

He used to look at me every time I bend over. He thought I had a tail. It's very embarrassing. They are ignorant. They think we were monkeys.[13]

West Indians were also asked if they lived in trees. Ignorance was expressed about the geographical location of the West Indies and some people were asked in what part of Africa was the West Indies? Another assumption was that the West Indies was synonymous with Jamaica. Carmel Charles had a typical response to these views:

My reaction was that the people was ignorant. I didn't realise they didn't know anything about black people. When I had my daughter they used to touch her.[14]

These ideas were not confined to the generally uneducated. Eldridge, in a study of Race Relations at the University of Leicester carried out in 1959, remarked that:

[white] students held many of the popular stereotypes with regard to non-Europeans and that this was linked with a considerable ignorance of the countries from which non-European students came, which in some cases was total.[15]

Such opinions were based on a measure of genuine ignorance conflated with racism. Black people continued to hear these ideas as conscious and overt expressions of racism long after the time when genuine ignorance dissipated. The ignorance of the histories and cultures of Britain's former colonies has been raised elsewhere in this thesis.[16] However, at all levels of society it was the culture and perceptions of Caribbean people that were seen as problematic. This widely held view was expressed in the *Leicester Mercury*. For example an editorial in September 1958, after the Nottingham and Notting Hill 'riots', proclaimed:

The government should insist that all coloured people intending to settle should be given talks on the British outlooks and customs... whenever in Britain do as the British.[17]

Nonetheless not all interactions with white people were unhappy and new arrivals also obtained help. Monroe Thomas travelled to Leicester Square on the Underground believing he was going to Leicester. He sat on the station waiting to be met by his relations until 1am. Eventually a ...

...fellow from the big island [Jamaica] put us on a train to St Pancras but when we arrived in Leicester there was nobody there to receive us.[18]

A white taxi driver drove Monroe and his young companion round to various West Indians he had met in Leicester until they had found Monroe's relatives.[19]

Those who lived in Leicester in the early 1950s were conscious of their minority status. Eric Hudson said:

There was a very small community in 1955...In town if you saw a black person you stopped and talked... There was hardly any social life. Christmas could be particularly difficult.[20]

Social life centred on visits to each others' houses. Christmas was mentioned as a lonely time by others too. Lee Morris said:

The Christmas I was used to at home was very exciting...going to church then out in a motor boat. I wasn't expecting exactly that sort of thing but I was expecting a bit more public activities. But over the years we adapted ourselves...A lot of us when we came we had no outlet...we used to make our own entertainment ... parties and things in our houses.[21]

Roy Rowe who came in 1956 confirms this experience.

It was so dull...no life at all in them days. No TV. I can remember two weeks after I came to this country I went to an electrical place and bought a record player. I paid a lot for it. The only place you could go and see one of your own colour was a pub down by Conduit Street.[22]

Ronald Rochester who came to Leicester in 1949, had been the subject of a full page *Leicester Mercury* article on him and his family. The piece clearly had the intention of dispelling some myths about Black people in Leicester and attempted to be sympathetic. But the article led to criticism and hostility from white people living near him. Reflecting on the impact of the article Ronald Rochester said:

I started to say too much. It made things harder for me. I didn't care. I could take care of myself.[23]

West Indians found themselves excluded or made to feel unwelcome in public places of entertainment and social life. Leicester had been a centre of temperance in the nineteenth century (Simmons, 1974, p.41). Parts of the city have few public houses and most excluded West Indians. The Burlington in Highfields at first tried to bar black people[24] but by the late 1960s the Burlington and the Imperial Hotel were among the few pubs in Leicester where black people could meet others on a basis of equality.[25] There were campaigns by black people and white anti racists against the 'colour bar' in public places during the late 1950s and 1960s. Mrs Olga Pepper who owned two coffee bars, the Casabollero and the Temple Garden in Rutland Street barred 'coloured' people. A protest march was organised in June 1959.[26] In the summer of 1964 the colour bar operated at the Admiral Nelson pub was opposed by local left wing activists. The pub was leafleted and picketed. A group of black and white people had a 'sit-in' in the pub where black people demanded to be served.[27] The licensee defended the bar by arguing that it was not unfair to ban 'coloureds' from one room which is only open at the weekends.[28] Everards Brewery refused to intervene. A march in protest at the 'colour bar' was organised.[29] In many places black people were not formally excluded but made to feel unwelcome. Many black people took the view that while they were prepared to argue against employers and landlords who were discriminating against them, social life was different.

> At the Palais if you asked a woman for a dance you were just refused so many people began to shy away from those places so as not to be offended.[30]

> Blacks were pushed around and whites would drop their trousers and show us their arses in Leicester...you just have to look after yourself... I didn't go in pubs. I wouldn't stay long enough to be insulted. In them days a person got called nigger and abused ...it used to be horrible. They used black people to scare kids.[31]

Cricket

The small community of the early 1950s soon began organising its own social and leisure activities.

> [Cricket] teams developed in Leicester. Some West Indians played for factory teams. As the population grew teams with names appeared to compete, going as far as London to play teams there. Cricket kept West Indians together. The women gave good support. Some played given the chance.[32]

Roy Rowe described the social life that grew around cricket:

> We started to organise dances and things - children's parties. When in 1955 the West Indian cricket team came we invited them to Leicester and celebrated with a cricket dance.[33]

After this first 'cricket dance', Carlton Sweeney suggested:

> It became the practice to provide a function for visiting cricketing teams, and we gave what advice we could as to how to beat England.[34]

The activities organised by West Indians took various forms. The first formal organisations in Leicester were sporting and social in nature with cricket providing the focus. The Sports and Social Club was founded in 1948[35] by two Jamaicans and an Antiguan: all ex-servicemen. This group organised dances, film evenings and outings. Big dances have been an important form of entertainment and socialising for West Indians and it was often difficult to find suitable venues to hold these events. Another early organisation was the Leicester Caribbean Cricket Club and like the Sports and Social Club this was founded by ex-servicemen. These two cricket teams came together in matches during the July holiday fortnight, Leicester's traditional two week period of factory closure and annual holidays. Their reputation was such that members of the teams were offered jobs by local firms who wanted to acquire their skills for works teams. One such team had nine Caribbean players but was led by a white captain and white vice-captain.[36] In 1957 the West Indian Sports and Social Club was founded from the two cricket clubs and it remained in existence until 1966.

For me men, playing cricket helped white people to see them more as fellow human beings. Carlton Sweeney played cricket for a team based at Imperial Typewriters.

> The first game we played I gained some acceptance and respect - because from my department I went in last. We had fourteen runs more to make and I knocked them off. Next time they sent me higher up the order. We always won. I played until I had to wear glasses. Working in artificial light all the time my eyes went. My father was a first class cricketer. We used to play a lot of English teams.[37]

Eric Hudson helped organise the Cricket Club. Its importance as a social organisation for both men and women was clear. The club organised dances once a year and always when the West Indian team came to England to play.

> They always visited Leicester and there was a celebration dance. At first these were held in the Roman Catholic church hall on Wellington Street.[38]

The Sports and Social Club split in 1966 as some members wanted the organisation to take a more political role.[39] However it remained in existence with its original function after 1966 but with a reduced membership.

Football

'Cricket was king' (Highfields Rangers, 1993, p.3) in the Caribbean and many male migrants had not played football until they arrived in Leicester. Many boys quickly developed their talents at schools, at youth clubs and informally on Spinney Hill Park. The park played a particularly important role in the lives of some young black people particularly boys growing up in Leicester in the 1960s and 1970s.

> We used to spend a lot of time on the park in the summer evenings, playing football. Guys were down from Highfields gambling and things like that... We had lots of fun... There was always a game of football on weekends - it was good.[40]

The park was an important open space for black people living in Highfields, where most of the houses had no gardens.

> Many adults also found the park a useful place to meet with their young children to play games or run about. Their back yards were small and restricted areas especially if renting rooms.[41]

Antigua 'versus the Caribbean' teams played matches on Victoria Park in the Early 1970s (Highfields Rangers, 1993, p.51) and matches were also played regularly on Spinney Hill Park. Highfields Rangers Club was formed in the early 1970s.

> Highfields in those days was where the black people and them lived, Highfields was recognised for the black people. We wanted to be Highfields Rangers, well that's how we felt (Highfields Rangers, 1993, p.53).

The Club became important not only to many black youths in Leicester but other African Caribbeans who lived in Highfields. The history of the club has been told in a recently published oral account (Highfields Rangers, 1993). It was the first really successful black football club, although it also included white players. The team faced prejudice and abuse when playing.

> We seemed to get racial abuse all the time. It's funny because we found it more when we went out to the country teams (Highfields Rangers, 1993, p.51).

> We were called niggers, coons, we had some nasty physical challenges. We had jeering from people at the side. We were like what women's football is about now, that is the nearest could compare it to. We were seen as 'Hey black people can't play football, what are they doing on a football pitch?

As Carlton Sweeney commented:

> Many African Caribbeans found it sad that they could not have fun without useless racial abuse, especially if the opposition was receiving a beating.[42]

The club also faced great difficulties in securing a club house and a permanent home. It was excluded from the Leicester Senior League and later joined the Central Midlands League.[43] It was only after the uprisings of 1981 that the Local Authority helped Highfield Rangers to secure a new ground and a new home.

The Blues

As well as more formal social events West Indians organised semi public 'blues' parties where food and drink could be bought. Although these kinds of parties have their origins in the culture of the Caribbean, exclusion from pubs in Leicester meant that such parties were the only kind of semi public venues where West Indians were able to meet together to consume alcohol in a social setting. The selling of alcohol in unlicensed premises made this illegal and together with noise that sometimes disturbed neighbours, often resulted in conflict with the police. A party held on 5 April 1964 received press attention as there were arrests and complaints about police conduct by party goers.[44]

These kind of events have attracted some academic attention as part of the life style of Caribbeans and can be seen as an example of the approach to cultural minorities described above. The best known study is that of Ken Pryce (1986) carried out in Bristol. Pryce's thesis is that West Indian communities in Britain have adopted two responses to the pressure of 'poverty and race in their background of hardship under British Colonial rule' (Pryce, 1986, p.27). The first he calls 'expressive - disreputable' and the second the 'law-abiding'. 'Blues dances' are seen as part of the disreputable response. Ken Pryce's ethnographic study has lent support to a perspective which pathologises aspects of West Indian culture. This is in part because, as is acknowledged by Robin Cohen, (Pryce, 1986, p.xvii) the 'hustlers' are more fully drawn than the other groups in the model. Another, but less well developed, ethnographic study providing a broadly similar view to that of Pryce was conducted some years earlier in Leicester. K O'Brien's comparison of Leicester and an area of North London presents a division between what he calls 'insiders' who are comparable to Pryce's 'disreputable orientation', and 'outsiders' or 'law-abiding' group, which is not as clear cut as the division in Pryce. The law-abiding outsiders, sometimes would attend blues parties because, as O'Brien acknowledged, the parties are the 'only places where West Indians can mix socially'.[45] This was compared to London where there were legitimate clubs attended by West Indians in which gambling was legal. People came from all around the country to blues parties in Leicester. They have been described:

> ...basically it was illegal but... it gave people somewhere to go. It'd probably run from twelve o'clock till whatever time people decided to go away... And it wouldn't just be black people, white people, you'd get Asian people, the odd Asian person, not so many of them not so many... There's gambling houses that used to run twenty four hour...illegal so-called gambling dens, where people just sit round and just gamble (Highfields Remembered, 1996, p.58).

Another form of social gathering revolved around politics. These exclusively male groups would meet over a weekend to drink and discuss the political issues of 'back home' and in Leicester.

Sometimes my Dad would go out on a Friday night and my mum wouldn't know where the hell he was until Sunday afternoon.[46]

By the 1960s West Indians were setting up other formal organisations to meet their leisure interests. The Leicester Invaders Domino Club was established in 1964 (Leicester Carribean Directory, undated, p.24) and many other organisations which included a social dimension were set up.[47] As children became established in Leicester schools from the late 1950s football became important too.

Women

Football, like cricket and other major sporting interests are male dominated. So too are other organised recreational games such as dominoes. Such leisure pursuits were not so easily available to women, although women often joined when they could. Women followed as spectators both cricket and football and the cricket dances were important social activities for women but many were heavily involved with caring for families. African Caribbean women were more likely than white women to be working in full time paid employment as well as being responsible for domestic work in the home. For women work and leisure are less likely to be discreet and separate activities than they are for men. Unpaid domestic labour and social life are sometimes more integrated.

I didn't have much of a social life. I visited friends at weekends. We had a drink, played music. We congregated that way. If there was a dance we got to that way left my husband ... I left with six children and we were living in one room... You give up everything...A woman has to be careful. A man can do his own thing. A woman can't have the friends men do. Men can go to a party, women have to have good friends...I put family first. That was all I did for nine years. I left friends behind and felt lonely.[48]

But women were very active in some kinds of organisation. One such, was the Anglo-Caribbean Association also called the British West Indian Club. This was a kind of self help and lobbying group (Pearson, 1981, p.82), which was founded by a small group of women in 1970. Cecelia, Gweneth, Monica, Grace, Beatrice and Elvy got together. At first they met at the top of a little cafe in King Street and then Cecelia opened a hairdressing salon in Evington Road where the group met.[49]   They organised concerns which were very successful. They wanted a building for West Indians to meet.

> We went around speaking in Highfields, knocking on doors. It was snowing, asking what would they think of a community centre... Also our children were not doing well in school and we thought about setting up a Saturday School.[50]

This organisation was the only female led group and was also unusual in that it had members from many islands. It was not dominated quite so much by the 'big island/small island' rivalry which is reported to have plagued the Jamaica Service Group. Graham Brown was the only man and also the only white English person in the Club.

> The Anglo-Caribbean Club was a group of women and me. I was the Anglo. We used to meet on the Tuesday night in Cecelia's hairdressers. We got chairs round. There was about a dozen of us. We got together a load of groceries for elderly people, not just West Indians. It was very informal. Everything was informal in those days.[51]

Women had other less important problems, but which contributed to a feeling of being 'outside'.

> The English people didn't know a thing about black people's hair. Our hair is different, it needs to be treated differently. Getting it styled [was a problem].[52]

> There was no make up for black women. I went to Boots to ask why they didn't produce it in the 1970s.[53]

Back Home

Many, although not all, West Indians have maintained a close relationship with families back in the Caribbean. Many have always sent money and/or gifts to family members. This aspect of the relationship with islands of origin has been well established in studies of migration where it has generally been regarded as an aspect of the economic relationship between sending and receiving societies. Women have played a particularly important role in organisations set up to help islands of origin. These organisations have not only provided valuable material support but have also served an important social function for West Indians in Leicester.

They can be seen as an example of the way in which the unpaid labour of women is often integrated with social activities.

Organisations set up to help islands of origin such as the Barbuda Association formed in 1960, the Nevis Development Society, established in 1969 and the Antiguan and Barbuda Association, set up in 1980, have played an important role in supporting people 'back home'. The Nevis Development Association has branches in Leicester and Leeds where the main communities of Nevisians live. Founded and chaired by Linda Herbert it has helped to buy equipment for the hospital on Nevis.[54] Many people have kept cultural links with their home islands, have continued to read Caribbean Newspapers such as the *Jamaican Gleaner* and the *Antiguan Observer* and have followed Caribbean politics. As might have been expected British born black people have not shown such an interest in the Caribbean even though they may continue to refer to their parents' island of origin as 'back home'.

The migrants of the 1950s, often could not afford to visit their families and friends in the Caribbean. But most people interviewed for this study have visited the Caribbean once or twice and some have visited many times. It has been very important for some people to visit regularly and even those on very low incomes have saved to enable them to go home. Veronica Williams saved so that she could return to Barbuda every year for four weeks.[55] These visits are holidays or visits to attend family occasions such as funerals. For some people it has been important to take children or grandchildren so that they can experience life in the Caribbean.

West Indians have also participated in the cultural changes in British society in relation to leisure pursuits. Like other working class people, African Caribbeans began to take package holidays in Spain and France during the 1960s. However, the expense of visits to the Caribbean has meant that some West Indians who would have liked to have travelled more to Europe have had to forgo those kinds of holidays. Some West Indians have also visited the Caribbean, at least in part, to maintain claims to land and property in preparation for a return at some future date. Return migration has been raised as a possible future for many black British people (Byron, 1994).

Youth Clubs

The first generation migrants, both men and women, often sent for their children as they became established in Leicester in the 1960s. This generation joined Leicester schools. Having spent some or much of their early lives in the Caribbean, many were lonely and unhappy at first.[56] For some of these young people as teenagers in Leicester in the 1970s, the youth club established in Highfields was very important in their lives. Novelette Mackoy's father came to Leicester in 1961 with his eldest son. Novelette, her mother and other brothers and sisters joined him in 1970.

> I was depressed when I got here. ... I used to sit at the front door. I didn't know about prostitution and a man approached me and my dad dragged me in. After that I felt shut in.[57]

While the issue of immigration and race has been highly politicised in Great Britain since the Second World War, these matters had a particularly high profile in the press and debate at national and local level at the time Novelette came to Leicester. The far right in Leicester was becoming very active and immigration and race were charged with emotion in public discussion.

> Local whites in Leicester were very racist. If you travelled through the centre, we got a lot of racism. We were verbally abused for no reason. It hurt. I ignored it. ... The elderly were very racist. I never saw a middle aged white woman smile at us.[58]

Young people like Novelette Mackoy found a haven from racism in the Highfields Youth Club in the early 1970s.

> We all got together, we could relax, race didn't have anything to do with it. It was so nice. No whites watching over our shoulders. I was about fourteen when I started.[59]

The youth club that was so important to Novelette Mackoy and other young black people in Leicester had been established in 1967. In 1965 a committee of the Youth Service Development Council, chaired by Lord Hunt, was appointed by the government 'to consider the needs of young immigrants in England and Wales and to make recommendations'.[60] Immigrant here was defined as black and Asian and local discussions arising from the Hunt Report largely ignored the white immigrant population of Leicester. The view of 'immigrants' as a social problem in national public debate about immigration was reflected in this report. 'Immigrants' were defined in a racialised way as a problem and the focus was on the culture of newcomers and numbers.   This paralleled the approach taken at national and local level to the education of immigrants outlined in Chapter Six.   The aim was to form bridges with the host community and to foster integration. Separate provision, the report argued, should not be made for immigrants except in exceptional circumstances.

> The problems of adjustment and adaptation are nowadays intensified by attitudes about colour and race, and by the sheer size of the latest wave of immigration.[61]

It was argued that local authorities should inform the Secretary of State by the end of 1968 of the action taken to further the integration of young coloured immigrants and grants under section eleven of the Local Government Act of 1966 were available for this. Both official and voluntary youth organisations should be involved.

The City of Leicester Youth Committee discussed the situation in Leicester.   Two city centre youth clubs, the Avalon Club and the Moat Club both had substantial numbers of 'immigrant people' attending and 'immigrants' have also joined church and other voluntary organisations. The committee wanted to appoint a full-time youth leader in September 1967 to be based at the Moat club but this proved difficult and eventually John Harris, a white student from the University, was appointed.[62]   It was clear that the club was to cater mainly but not exclusively for 'immigrants' in Highfields where there had been no facilities for young people.   A need had been clearly identified in that some classes organised by the Melbourne Further Education Centre based at Moat Boys' School were attended almost entirely by young people.   But whereas Asian young people attended formal classes, West Indian youth attended a social club held on Wednesdays. These were mostly boys but included eight girls.

The report by the Senior Youth Officer in January 1968 which proposed the appointment of John Harris, described him as a former youth officer from Essex who had experience of 'immigrants'. In a revealing comment the report claimed Mr Harris had previously worked in New York with Negro residents.[63]   A West Indian assistant youth leader, Earle Robinson, was also appointed for two nights per week along with a female volunteer who had experience of voluntary service overseas. Activities were mainly sports, and this catered for the interests of young men such as cricket, table tennis and basket ball.

In June 1968 a report on the progress of the Club during its first year was considered by the Youth Committee.   Particular concern was expressed over young West Indian men. Football matches had been arranged particularly with the Avalon Club. This report contained a similar perspective to that adopted at national and local level towards the presence of black people in Britain.   The problem is seen to lie with the culture, attitudes and behaviour of 'immigrants' rather than in the racism of British society.

> It has been possible to help young people with employment problems and to help them understand aspects of British life with which they have difficulty... On the other hand there have been more serious difficulties such as the need to give lengthy explanations of the implications of the Race Relations Bill to a group of aggressive West Indian youngsters.[64]

The report acknowledged the importance of the assistant leader, Mr Earle Robinson.

> It would not be unfair to say that most of the success achieved is due to Mr Robinson's deep understanding of the pattern of West Indian life in Britain.[65]

A further report of the senior youth and community officer, concerning the Moat club, produced in 1969, also adopted this perspective. The Moat club had become the largest of any club in the city. The popularity of the club could be shown by the fact that black people came from outside the area, sometimes making long journeys to attend.   In a comment which again reveals the way in which black people were seen first and foremost through a racialised gaze, the report stated:

> During this time one of the problems the worker [the youth leader] found most difficult to overcome was the identification of the West Indian boys, every face looked the same.[66]

The pervasive 'deficit' model was also revealed in attitudes to language.

> West Indians had to understand, apart from the handicap of having a different linguistic background, West Indians also appeared to suffer from an overall deprivation of language experience.[67]

John Harris was succeeded as leader by Philip Parkinson, who was another white man and Earle Robinson whose crucial role in the success of the club was acknowledged, remained an assistant. Earle later became an influential and important community leader of African Caribbeans in Leicester. He had been a late arrival compared with other leaders most of whom had arrived during or soon after the war. Earle came to Leicester in 1958.

> With a colleague of mine we were sitting in a newspaper office in Kingston. We were sat in the office talking about the riots. I saw a picture of a woman with an axe in her hand and we said 'look at what's going on down there'. Three weeks later we were here, five of us came on the boat.[68]

Earle had a brother and an aunt in Leicester. He was sent as a delegate from the cricket club to a seminar organised by the Leicester Youth Service in 1966 to discuss the Hunt Report. The Senior Youth Officer, Roy Fisher, was keen to involve Earle. Earle recalled Roy Fisher. 'He was a Quaker. Quakers always support immigrants'.[69] When he arrived Earle had in fact been helped to find accommodation by the Anglo-Overseas Association, the organisation led by pioneers and Quakers.[70] Earle had a rather different perspective on youth in Leicester. He saw the problems facing young black people, rather than seeing them as the problem.

Earle's first involvement with young people had been at the Avalon Club, where he had been a part-time member of staff.

> They didn't like black people in the club, but if they were good at football that was fine but you were not made welcome. They thought they were taking away white girls.[71]

Earle thought that a club oriented towards the needs of young black people was 'the only way to deal with this'.[72] The new Moat Club attracted 200-300 people a week and they came from all over the city.

> Then we had girls coming ... the club caused a stink in the city. The usual problem; the club was accused of going down the road of separatism. But it wasn't exclusive to blacks. There were Asians, blacks and whites including Polish people.[73]

However, there were few girls, so the club started to use a female drama teacher. She taught English and Drama and knew a bit of dance. Her work eventually developed into the Grassroots Dance Club. Premises was a problem. The club used a building in Spinney Hill Park later to become the Highfields Adventure Playground. This building was also used by Highfields Rangers. The next stage was therefore to acquire premises. Eventually Highfields Community Centre was built. Earle was active in supporting young people in opposing racism. He led a party of young people to the Palais, where at one period the management had been refusing entry to black people. Earle took the whole youth club down.

A later popular and successful youth club leader was Lee Morris. Like Earle Robinson, he also became an important community leader. He had moved to Leicester in 1955 when he was twenty-five years old to join his father who had come in the 1940s. He had become leader of the youth club in the early 1970s and was an important figure to young black people who used the club.[74]

The Leicester United Caribbean Association

It has been shown that from the 1950s African Caribbeans had seen the need for an organisation to represent their interests in the city. The visit of the Jamaican High Commissioner in 1969 gave a spur to the campaign to establish a Community Centre pioneered by the Anglo-Caribbean Club, the Jamaican Service Group and others. It was to be 1974 before the Leicester United Caribbean Association (LUCA) was established. In its evidence to the government's Select Committee on Race Relations and Immigration in 1975 representatives of LUCA gave its aims as:

- to facilitate community relations in the area by encouraging West Indian community activities on a self help basis
- to act as an enabler to community care in the area
- to encourage the development of existing organisations
- to improve the social, recreational and educational facilities in the neighbourhood.[75]

This group can be seen as marking an evolving view of African Caribbeans as an 'ethnic group' with a need for an organisation to represent the community. There were four founder groups and later other groups affiliated. In their evidence to the Select Committee representatives of LUCA attempted to demonstrate the need for an information and advice centre including counselling services. It was argued that members of the Caribbean community were reluctant to approach formal agencies, statutory or voluntary, for help and advice. Young people were even more reluctant. Existing agencies, it was argued, were effectively rationing their services through poor advertising, off putting reception and waiting areas and filtering out applicants at reception where junior staff exercised arbitrary discretion. Staff also had a detached professional attitude which was bewildering to deprived people and finally business hours were inconvenient to people from the Caribbean.[76]

LUCA proposed that they might be able to set up an information and advice centre which would be able to establish the needs and aspirations of Caribbean people to discuss needs unmet by existing agencies and to devise ways of meeting these needs. It would also provide a referral point for official bodies. However, LUCA also needed an administrative headquarters with staff and clerical support. A centre could also provide facilities for the proliferation of leisure, cultural and artistic groups which had sprung up in the early 1970s, those such as the Grassroots Dance group, the West Indian Drama, and many other sporting and recreational groups.

LUCA was to be an umbrella organisation for many different kinds of organisations including island development organisations and the Leicester Credit Union. Eventually, some fifteen groups representing 600 West Indians supported the work of LUCA. It became increasingly involved in developing a varied programme of activities and supported many projects such as the Saturday School set up to help young black people with their education, the Highfields Adventure Playground, the Youth Club and a literacy programme. It offered advice on a wide range of issues such as education, housing, immigration and legal matters, employment and welfare. It organised socials, dances and sports such as netball, table tennis and basketball. It also ran sport exchanges, summer play schemes and various youth projects. There was support and counselling for young black people and LUCA also produced a newsletter.

The LUCA steering committee consisted of Eric Hudson, while the General Secretary was Earle Robinson and the Treasurer Rupert Francis. The Public Relations Officer was Linda Herbert and the Social Secretary was Elvy Moreton. These people were among those who had worked for many years to establish organisations for African Caribbeans in Leicester and represented a coherent group of people identified as 'Community Leaders'. The struggle of LUCA and indeed earlier organisations to establish a Community Centre was long and hard. The attitude of the local state was that it would not be fair to give financial aid to such a project to meet the need of what was seen as one section of the population. In a view which was characteristic of the approach of the local authority up to and throughout the 1970s, the Town Clerk said:

that if other immigrant groups have provided their own facilities, West Indians should be able to do the same.[77]

The difficulties for African Caribbeans in Leicester who were largely a working class and relatively poor group of people of funding such a project was not recognised. The unfavourable comparison with Asian groups was representative of the approach of the local council. This has been a continuing feature of the council's relationship to African Caribbeans. It was argued to the Select Committee:

There are lots of cultural reasons why West Indians are a special case - they don't have many business men or professionals among them to give money. Their community is poor and made up of mainly working class people.[78]

In 1975 LUCA applied for a grant from the CRC to support the information and opinion centre to cover staffing advice, equipment, running costs and sessional tutors fees.[79] The grant was approved in 1976 and staff were appointed in February 1977, when they were able to find suitable space for them. However, the organisation still had major problems. The first premises for LUCA had been a terraced house in Highfields. There were only two rooms.

Expectations were high and some of the community needs were becoming identifiable. Limited financial resources, along with inadequate accommodation, made it unrealistic to embark on any significant community programme, particularly those which needed a large space.[80]

Despite this, around eleven projects were initiated including a radio programme, community newsheet, youth exchanges and an exhibition.[81]

In 1978 LUCA managed to find premises for a permanent base. This was a building owned by Leicester City Council near to the centre of the city. African Caribbeans have a strong traditional identification with Highfields and some expressed concern that the LUCA Centre was not in

Highfields,[82] but the city centre site did at least prevent opposition from local residents to the noises and disturbances of dances being held in a densely populated residential area which had occurred previously when dances had been held in Highfields Community Centre.[83]   Leicester City Council provided a grant which assisted with the cost of renovating the building and later some of the running costs and by 1980 they had funded the salary of a full time administrator.   The initial renovation was problematic.   The Manpower Services Commission provided money to pay young people to carry out the renovation.

> Some thirty to thirty five young people, a majority from the Caribbean community, participated in the project, along with up to eight skilled adult supervisors, again mainly from the community.[84]

The Centre opened in October 1979.   However this building was far from ideal and some people were unhappy with its location.   LUCA continued to create some controversy from within the community and had problems in its relations with Leicester City Council.[85]   Once established LUCA was seen as the representative organisation for African Caribbeans in Leicester.   While dogged by problems of political infighting it had defended and promoted the interests of African Caribbeans.

The experience of the BPLP shows that the state would not tolerate overtly political separatist black organisations fighting for the rights of black people in an uncompromising way.   LUCA was never a political party and can be seen as an expression of the developing consciousness of the identity of Caribbean migrants as African Caribbeans in Leicester and of a growing definition of Caribbean people as a community.

Religion

The ostracism of black people in public places of entertainment and social life was replicated in the churches.   Religion is an area of life where West Indians have felt particularly affronted by being allocated an identity as 'black' people.   White people were not constructed as 'white', except where they were forced to defend their prejudices, but black people were made conscious of their racialised identity.   This was felt to be particularly inappropriate in religious life where it was felt that people should be equal as Christians (Hill, 1963, p.78).   Black people set up their own churches from the early 1960s.   These churches had different forms of worship from those in the Church of England.[86] The churches also had an important social dimension for religious people.

Caribbeans who were practising churchgoers found a cold reception in local churches as they did in other public organisations in Leicester. There were two aspects of the problem. First the passive and 'stuffed shirt'[87] style of worship was unfamiliar and they had been used to seeking advice from their local vicars on many everyday problems of life, a practice which they tried to continue in Highfields. Second, they met a degree of hostility from some white churchgoers.

One of the 'pioneers' of Leicester's African Caribbean community, Eric Hudson, tried to attend St Phillips Anglican Church on Evington Lane when he settled in Leicester soon after the war.

> No one would welcome you and no one spoke to you. I'm an Antiguan. I went to St Phillips Church but it was very cold. The vicar might shake your hand but that is all.[88]

Dorothy Henry confirmed this: 'We weren't welcome, we stuck out like sore thumbs.'[89] Carmel Charles was upset that churchgoers did not carry their religious beliefs outside the church.

> I used to go to church every Sunday. My children is confirmed. Where we were living, everywhere you go it's different, some people said the congregation didn't approve [of us]. There's one God, he made us. We didn't make ourselves. I don't know why I'm black. The children went to Sunday School. What annoyed me was, you go to church, you kneel down next to them, nobody knows your name. The hypocrisy of it. The curate preached about colour. When the service is over everybody is nice. But it don't last.[90]

Carlton Sweeney (1978, p.42) wrote:

> There is a number of churches in Britain with majority of coloured worshippers not of their choosing. West Indians are church going people and when they arrive in Britain they find the church of their following. As West Indians made a habit of attending the Church of England it was noticed that in time, many of the white people kept away altogether leaving the church to the coloured people. There are churches in Leicester that I know of and have seen.

These kinds of experiences were noted as typical in a study of West Indians (Hill, 1963, p.29):

The West Indian wants to feel wanted, especially when he goes to church. What he does want is to feel accepted in the same way as any other member of the congregation.

In this study the view was expressed that:

The patronising attitude of so many English Christians towards West Indians has done more damage to the cause of racial integration than all the sneers and blasphemies of their English work mates in factory and workshop.

The study noted the development of Pentecostal Churches in London in the early 1960s.

The Anglican Church, through its link with the state has held a special place in British society for hundreds of years. Increasing secularisation has decreased its influence since the Second World War but in the early post war period the Church of England was still accorded special respect and it representatives regarded as leaders of the community. The Anglican St Peter's Church is situated in the heart of Highfields, the area to which most African Caribbeans who arrived in Leicester through the 1950s moved. The Vicar of St Peter's during this period was Canon A W Eaton. Having become a Canon in 1953, he had spent the years between 1926 and 1946 living in South Africa from where he moved to Leicester. He remained at St Peter's until 1960. He then moved to a post in 'central Africa'. He was a founder member of Leicester Council of Churches and the Leicester Christian Industrial Council. He also edited the Leicester Diocesan Leaflet.[91]

The Notting Hill and Nottingham 'white riots' of 1958 led to a great deal of anxiety in Leicester, especially as Nottingham was so close to Leicester and a city with which Leicester has often been compared. In August 1958, the *Leicester Mercury* carried a long editorial headed 'Race Riots are not Likely in Leicester', subheaded 'Coloured people are accepted here'. Canon Eaton was asked to express an opinion. He said,

I haven't heard of any ill feeling between white and coloured here. Normally relationships are quite good and the coloured people are working hard and fitting in.[92]

The *Mercury* continued:

He [Canon Eaton] had forty to fifty coloured people in the congregation. On another aspect of the problem he said he knew of only three mixed marriages that worked out. On the other hand there have been a few instances of white people moving out as the coloured population has grown.[93]

The following year at a meeting of the Anglo- Overseas Association,[94] one West Indian remarked on how he did not feel welcome in the churches. 'The Churches are half empty and the service dull'.[95] Canon Eaton replied:

The West Indians are not being assimilated into the community because they have nothing in common with the community. They have to learn they have to give to the community if they want to get anything out of it... West Indians came here to make money and when they have made it they will undoubtedly go back.[96]

The Mercury continued that ' He described his efforts to welcome West Indians'.[97] When Canon Eaton left St Peters in 1960 he was replaced by the Reverend EW Carlisle who argued a very different position. In the September 1961 issue of the Parish magazine he wrote:

Don't blame coloured people for the changes in Highfields. The changes were well underway before they arrived...We have got to make amends for the terrible evil [of slavery] inflicted by our forebears.[98]

The Reverend Carlisle was also given space in the *Leicester Mercury* during the 1960s to write about black people and Highfields. He used that space to defend West Indians against attacks on their behaviour and way of life and for being the cause of slums in Highfields.[99] On 26 June 1965, following a particularly racist report from the Medical Officer of Health for Barrow on Soar, the Reverend Carlisle replied in writing:

One agrees with him that if immigration goes on at the present rate a change is bound to occur in the constitution of the English people...the few mixed marriages I know are working out extremely happily.[100]

The Reverend A H Kirkby was Vicar of Victoria Road Church, which is situated just outside the Highfields area in Leicester, in the early 1950s. He had a regular column in the *Illustrated Leicester Chronicle*, through which he argued against the 'colour prejudice' of Cyril Osborne MP who was regularly given space to campaign against 'coloured immigration'.[101]

The Reverend Kirkby argued that 'the immigrants constitute something of a problem' but that Osborne 'exaggerates the problem'.[102] He accused Osborne of being ignorant of history and continued:

> It seems to have escaped him that many difficulties in Jamaica are of our creating. Has he forgotten the slave trade and the shameless exploitation of the slaves in Jamaica?[103]

However, while it is clear that the Reverend Kirkby took an important stand against aspects of Osborne's arguments, he did enable others to present racist views in his church. On February 19th 1955 the *Illustrated Leicester Chronicle* reported:

> On a short visit to Leicester this week a Professor of Theology, who has recently been in South Africa and has strong views on Apartheid, Dr Horton Davies, came to see his friend the Reverend AH Kirkby and gave an address at Victoria Road Church.

> 'The Negroes are not ready no matter how eager they might be to vote in general elections. ...When we see coloured students in Leicester we think of them as representative of their peoples but this is a mistake. The Africans we see in England are the most westernised of their race - those they have left at home are often 2000 years behind us in social development and education.'[104]

One Church of England vicar who was particularly active in the movement to oppose racism in Leicester during the 1960s was the Reverend Derek Sawyer, of St Michael's Church, Knighton. However, despite this commitment from some Christians it is clear that white Christians in Leicester were divided in their response to black people and many saw no conflict between their religious beliefs and adopting a racist response to the arrival of black people in Leicester. The pages of the *Leicester Mercury* not only gave space to prominent members of the Church of England locally, but also provided ordinary Christians with an opportunity to present their views. It is clear from these views that although white identity was defined in various ways, it was always presented in opposition to black. For example, on 19 February 1955 in a letter it was claimed that 'Jesus was white'.[105] The pages of the *Mercury* reported at regular intervals, white missionaries going to Africa and other parts of the world [106] suggesting that Christianity was something 'whites' were bringing to 'blacks'. A decade later on 15 August 1967 one reader wrote in a letter headed 'Christian Example', 'It is not wrong for British people to want to remain a European nation'.[107] He went on to suggest biblical support for this notion.

One group of Christians in Leicester who took a more positive attitude towards black people was the Quakers. They were involved in establishing the Anglo Overseas Association together with black people. This aimed to counter prejudice and ignorance among local whites, even if at times some expressed well meaning but patronising attitudes towards black people.[108] They also helped immigrants find accommodation in Leicester.

Some West Indians persevered and remained loyal to the church of their initial choice. Veronica Williams, for example has worshipped at St Peter's Church since the day she arrived in Leicester in 1959.[109] She said: 'My social life revolved around the Church. I've always gone. It's all right'. She went on to say:

> I don't think much about white people. They get away with a lot of things, more than I get away with. I've nothing against white people but I don't mix with them.[110]

Others left and joined churches where they felt more welcome and yet others began to set up churches of their own. Black people who belonged to the Roman Catholic church also sometimes felt alienated and this has led to a loss of faith in some cases.[111]

Carlton Sweeney, who came to Leicester in 1953, joined the Seventh Day Adventists. This church, like many to which black people owed allegiance, had begun in the United States in 1863 and spread to the Caribbean and to Great Britain. It was a church that maintained a mixed black and white congregation. The Pastor of the church in Leicester was Carlton Sweeney's best man when he got married.

> The pastor was a great help. Later on, the West Indians and friends started coming in. The local people, it wasn't so hard, but the people from the top started [suggesting] that we [black people] were coming in to take over... We gained a reputation in Leicester because when visiting ministers came they were taken up with the singing. It was more vibrant than they had expected. Every time we had a bible quiz, we always answered a lot. We [West Indians in Leicester] had no reservations about meeting Europeans. ... We had two churches, one was in Bodnant Avenue. We sold it to the Wesleyans because it was too small. We resent it, being called a black church. We were able to overcome [racism], behind the scenes. We made a fuss, a big noise.

In the late 1950s we began to enter the leadership locally. I became a youth leader. We got on well and were able to overcome...if people showed an inclination to racism they got sorted out. ... We tackled it. The church officially frowns on that sort of thing. We've had black pastors. West Indians were brought over from the Caribbean. We had a youth department, activities department, charities ...

We collected for charities, but they used to give the impression that only black people needed help. It's like 'white helps black'. That's no good as if the only people who can be sick are black. We pointed that out and they changed it. We threatened not to collect. They had to do it. That was a better way than giving up. All this was kept under wraps because we needed a dignified profile. We've managed to overcome that now. All we needed was fairness.[112]

This view of blacks needing help reflects an aspect of the construction of the relationship between black and white from the age of imperialism when colonisation was justified by the civilising mission of whites. The idea that blacks were people in need of help was still strong during the decades after the war. It was described by June Grey:

If they think you're down and out they're your friend. If you better yourself they can't cope. If they think you live in a home with a bright red front door and cook salt fish all day, they're fine but they think, why should she be better than I am?...They expect all blacks to be down there.[113]

In contrast to the 'stuffed shirt' Anglican churches many West Indians were used to a 'clap hands'[114] or 'hot belly'[115] church.

The New Testament Church of God, a black church, was established in Leicester in the early 1960s. Dorothy Henry recalled that ministers came to proselytise at peoples' doors. Her parents who had been members of this church in Jamaica were pleased. Soon prayer meetings were established in peoples' houses and then Moat School hall was rented for Sunday Worship. In 1963 the group which at that time was quite small, about sixteen people, bought the Church on Melbourne Road.[116] This Church has clearly been very important to some black people in Leicester. It has been argued that the Churches and the illegal 'blues clubs' were the only public places that West Indians could meet socially.[117] Eric Hudson stressed the importance of the church to the social life of many West Indians.[118] Reuban Nelson said:

Church people don't drink, we don't smoke, we only play religious music at home. I would have no social life if I didn't belong to the church... we meet all the people after the service.[119]

The New Testament Church of God organised a variety of social activities including a Senior Citizens Club. These churches were attended by a relatively small group of African Caribbeans and it is hard to determine the extent to which the rejection by white churches contributed to their establishment.

Michael Roberts started the Wesleyan Holiness Church only about six weeks after he arrived in Leicester from Barbuda in 1960. This church is one of seven churches in Leicester whose origins lie in the Caribbean and which have worshipped regularly together.[120] These churches have always been small with only two, the Wesleyan Holiness Church and the Shiloah Pentecostal Church having their own premises. Each of the black churches tends to be associated with black people from different Caribbean islands. For example, the New Testament Church of God has a congregation which is mainly Jamaican, whereas the Wesleyan Church is made up of people from Antigua /Barbuda. Interestingly however the link between islands of origin and churches is not consistent in different towns and cities in Britain. The Wesleyan Church's congregation in Birmingham included many Jamaicans.[121]

The Wesleyan Church like other black churches originated in North America. It was called the Pilgrim Holiness Church until 1968 when it merged with the Wesleyan Methodists. But 'we didn't want to get rid of "Holiness",[122] so we are Wesleyan Holiness'. The church was established in Britain in 1958.

Michael Roberts came to Leicester from Antigua/Barbuda in 1960. He had always been a member of the Wesleyan Holiness Church.

When I came I visited the Melbourne Road Free Church for approximately six weeks. My brother-in-law came from Antigua/Barbuda and he suggested we start something because there were other members of the Church around... A lot of our people were coming over so we started our own church in the home. We were seven, all from Antigua/Barbuda. Then we grew to about twenty and found the room wasn't large enough. We enquired about a school hall so we moved from Dorothy Road to Medway Junior School in St Stephen's Road. They let us have the hall there about three weeks later. The church was officially established and membership went up to about fifty. We stayed at Medway for about ten years. We made some arrangements with the Methodist

Church on Humberstone Road and we stayed there until 1981. We thought we'd be able to get that place because their congregation was dwindling away, but it went to the highest bidder and we couldn't afford it. We had to move. It was a bit of a crisis. We had to share with an Anglican Church - St Hilda's. But we didn't have to stay long. This place came on the market [in Bodnant Avenue]. We bought it from the Seventh Day Adventists.

The church's membership has stayed at about fifty, but around eighty people had attended services. The differences in doctrine between the free churches are small. We do not believe in speaking in tongues or in the washing of feet.

When we came to Leicester, going to the white led churches, we didn't feel right. In the West Indies you could express yourself. If the preacher is preaching you can say 'halleluya' or 'praise the lord'... You have to hold yourself in... That was one of the things. People look at you. They didn't welcome you.[123]

The church has maintained various community projects.

Our church caters for the whole man [sic], body, soul and spirit. We have other African Caribbean centres around but some of the people feel concerned because people smoke and do all kinds of things. So we felt as a church we should create that atmosphere for the elderly. We have a department of youth and a department of evangelism.[124]

Some young people in Leicester embraced Rastafarianism. The link between this religion and politics has been explored elsewhere (Cashmore and Troyna, 1990; Pearson, 1981; Ramdin, 1987, p.392). In Leicester the BPLP was associated with this religion.[125] The attraction of this religion to a younger generation of blacks, born in the Caribbean, but brought up in Britain has been noted. One Rastafarian in Leicester said:

there was... a little colony of us. And we used to have various events and dances, we started putting our own kinds of functions on them. So called blues dances, we used to keep our own, cause we used to have contention with the older generation.. because we'd embrace Rastafarianism and religion. A lot of the older generation, well,... it was opposite to what they would deal with (Highfields Remembered, p.23).

Ramdin (1987, p.462) has suggested that the lifestyle of Rastas is comparable to the lifestyles of members of the Pentecostal or Holiness Churches.

Conclusion

African Caribbeans met rejection from local whites when they tried to participate in organised social, leisure and cultural pursuits including the institutions of religious life. They responded in two ways, some by continuing their involvement in organisations established by the majority society and others by developing their own institutional frameworks for these important aspects of life.

The local state made no provision for the needs of African Caribbeans in these areas except in so far as there was felt to be a problem for the white community, at least until the 1970s. The provision of a youth club in Leicester aimed at young black men was an example of such an exception to the dominant policy.

The establishment of LUCA as an umbrella organisation for African Caribbeans in Leicester marks a stage in the development of black people as an ethnic minority community in Leicester. This organisation received a grant from Leicester City Council and began a relationship with the local state, whereby African Caribbeans came to be seen as a group existing in relation to Asians and white groups. This relationship was consolidated after the 1981 street uprisings which saw the local authority channel funds, provided by central government into community projects, defined by its ethnicity. The apex of these developments can perhaps be seen in the Leicester Caribbean Carnival begun in 1984.

Notes

1   Martin Barker, *The New Racism*, Junction Books, London 1981. This is not true in the USA where the study of ethnicity includes white groups.
2   See Chapter Six.
3   The Race Relations act of 1965 established the Race Relations Board and outlawed discrimination in public places. The 1968 Act extended the provisions of the earlier act to cover employment and a further act in 1976 created the Commission for Racial Equality with greater powers than its predecessor, the Race Relations Board.
4   Interview with Veronica Williams, 8 May 1994.
     Interview with Linda Herbert, 9 September 1994.
5   This provides an interesting contrast to the stereotype, widely held at the time of the lazy workshy black.
6   Interview with Reuban Nelson, 12 December 1993.

7   Interview with Elvy Moreton, 12 December 1994.
8   Linda Herbert, op cit.
9   Interview with Carlton Sweeney, 4 August 1994.
10   Ibid.
11   Reuban Nelson, op cit.
12   Interview with June Grey, 31 August 1994.
13   Interview with Carmel Charles, 13 January 1994. This has also been documented elsewhere. See for example R Murray, *Lest we Forget: The Experiences of World War II West Indian Ex-Service Personnel*, Nottingham West Indian Combined Ex-Service Association, in Association with Hansib Publishing, Nottingham 1996 (Murray, 1996; Highfields Rangers, 1993, p.51).
14   Carmel Charles, op cit.
15   J E Eldridge, 'Race Relations in Leicester University', MA Thesis, University of Leicester, 1972.
16   See Chapter Three.
17   *Leicester Mercury*, 22 September 1958.
18   Interview with Monroe Thomas, 4 October 1994.
19   Ibid.
20   Interview with Eric Hudson, 24 April 1994.
21   Interview with Lee Morris, 5 September 1994.
22   Interview with Roy Rowe, 6 September 1994.
23   Interview with Ronald Rochester, 10 August 1994.
24   Monroe Thomas, op cit.
25   K O'Brien, 'Patterns of Deviance in Two West Indian Settlements', MA Thesis, University of Leicester, 1968, page 40.
26   See Chapter Seven.
27   Letter from Peter Miller, a participant in the picketing to the author, 23 January 1995. The 'sit-in' tactic was undoubtedly borrowed from the civil rights movement in the USA.
28   *Leicester Mercury*, 14 July 1964.
29   Ibid, 24 August 1964.
30   Eric Hudson, op cit.
31   Ronald Rochester, op cit.
32   Interview with Carlton Sweeney, 1 February 1997.
33   Roy Rowe, op cit.
34   Carlton Sweeney, op cit, 1 September 97.
35   Institute of Race Relations, Transcript of *A Common History*, Film, Director, Colin Prescod.
36   Ibid.
37   Carlton Sweeney, op cit, 4 August 1994.
38   Eric Hudson, op cit.

39   See Chapter Seven.

40   Interview with Nick Frank, 28 September 1994.

41   Carlton Sweeney, op cit, 1 February 1997.

42   Carlton Sweeney, op cit, 1 February 1997.

43   The club was finally accepted into the Leicester Senior League in 1992, *Highfields Rangers*, (193, p.89).

44   LRO, L352.2, Chief Constables Annual Report, 1964, page 20.

45   O'Brien, op cit, page 11.

46   Interview with Nick Frank, 28 September 1994.

47   See Chapter Seven.

48   Carmel Charles, op cit.

49   Cecelia herself now lives in Jamaica but the hairdressers called 'Cecelias' still exists, (1999).

50   Interview with Elvy Moreton, op cit. Elvy Moreton founded the Caribbean Carnival in 1984, arguably one of the most important events in the year for African Caribbeans and for the people of Leicester.

51   Interview with Graham Brown, 8 December 1995.

52   Linda Herbert, op cit.

53   Linda Herbert, op cit.

54   Ibid.

55   Veronica Williams, op cit.

56   See Chapter Six.

57   Interview with Novelette Mackoy, 7 August 1994.

58   Ibid.

59   Ibid.

60   LRO, 19D/59VII 694, 'Immigrants and the Youth Service: Report of the Committee of the Youth Service Development Council', City of Leicester Education Committee.

61   Ibid.

62   Ibid.

63   Ibid.

64   Ibid.

65   Ibid.

66   Ibid.

67   LRO, 19D59/VII 694, 'Moat Youth Club, Report on Progress During the First Year', 13 June 1968.

68   Interview with Earle Robinson, 1 December 1995.

69   Ibid.

70   See Chapter Seven.

71   Earle Robinson, op cit.

72   Ibid.

73   Ibid.

74   Novelette Mackoy, op cit.
75   House of Commons, Sessional Papers, 1975-76, Select Committee on Race Relations and Immigration, Memorandum Submitted by Leicester United Caribbean Association, 4 December 1975, HMSO, London.
76   Ibid.
77   Ibid.
78   Ibid.
79   Ibid.
80   LUCA, 'Submission to Director of Recreation and Arts Department, Leicester City Council', undated.
81   Ibid.
82   Interview with Percy Harding, 30 November 1995.
83   Select Committee on Race Relations op cit.
84   'Submission to Director', op cit.
85   Ibid.
86   These forms of worship date back to the last years of slavery, (Walvin, 1993, pages 193-197).
87   Description adopted by Carlton Sweeney in an interview, 9 March 1997.
88   Interview with Eric Hudson, op cit.
89   Interview with Dorothy Henry, 9 September 1996.
90   Carmel Charles, op cit.
91   *Leicester Mercury*, 6 January 1960.
92   Ibid, 28 August 1958.
93   Ibid.
94   See Chapter Seven for a discussion of this organisation.
95   *Leicester Mercury*, 2 February 1959.
96   Ibid.
97   Ibid.
98   Ibid, 30 August 1961.
99   See for example the *Leicester Mercury*, 15 March 1963, 19 December 1963.
100   *Leicester Mercury*, 26 June 1965.
101   See Chapter Three.
102   *Illustrated Leicester Chronicle*, 15 January 1955.
103   Ibid.
104   Ibid, 19 February 1955.
105   *Leicester Mercury*, 19 February 1955.
106   See Chapter Three for a discussion of these articles.
107   *Leicester Mercury*, 15 August 1967.
108   See comments of BPLP in Chapter Seven.
109   Veronica Williams, op cit.
110   Ibid.

111 This was reported by Editha Drew and June Grey in interviews, op cit.
112 Carlton Sweeney, op cit, 9 March 1997.
113 June Grey, op cit.
114 Expression used by Graham Brown in interview, op cit.
115 Expression used by Monroe Thomas in interview, op cit.
116 Dorothy Henry, op cit.
117 O' Brien, op cit, page 39.
118 Eric Hudson, op cit.
119 Reuban Nelson, op cit.
120 By 1997 these had been reduced to five: the Shiloah Pentecostal Church, the New Testament Assembly, the Mount Zion Church of God, the Latter Rain Out Pouring Revival and the Wesleyan Holiness Church.
121 Interview with Pastor Michael Roberts, 18 March 1997.
122 Ibid.
123 Ibid.
124 Ibid.
125 See Chapter Eight.

References

Banton, Michael (1955), *The Coloured Quarter: Negro Immigrants in an English City*, Jonathan Cape, London.

Barker, Martin (1981), *The New Racism*, Junction Books, London.

Byron, Margaret (1994), *Post War Caribbean Migration to Britain: The Unfinished Cycle*, Avebury, Aldershot.

Cashmore, Ellis and Troyna, Barry (1990), *Introduction to Race Relations* (2nd ed), Falmer Press, London, pp.144-162.

Foner, Nancy (1979), *Jamaica Farewell, Jamaican Migrants in London*, Routledge and Kegan Paul, London.

Highfields Rangers: An Oral History (1993), Leicester City Council, Leicester.

Highfields Remembered (1996), Leicestershire County Council, Leicester.

Hill, Clifford S (1963), *West Indian Migrants and the London Churches*, Institute of Race Relations, Oxford University Press, London, p.78.

Leicester Caribbean Directory, Leicester City Council, Leicester undated, p.24.

Murray, R (1996), *Lest we Forget: The Experiences of World War II West Indian Ex-Service Personnel*, Nottingham West Indian Combined Ex-Service Association, in Association with Hansib Publishing, Nottingham.

Panayi, Panikos (1994), *Immigration, Ethnicity and Racism in Britain, 1815-1945*, Manchester University Press, Manchester.

Patterson, Sheila (1963), *Dark Strangers*, Tavistock Publications, London.

Pearson, David (1981), *Race, Class and Political Activism: A Study of West Indians in Britain*, Gower, Aldershot.

Pryce, Ken (1986), *Endless Pressure: A Study of West Indian Life-Styles in Bristol* (2nd ed), University of Bristol, Bristol, p.271.

Ramdin, Ron (1987), *The Making of the Black Working Class in Britain*, Gower, Aldershot.

Rex, John and Moore, Robert (1967), *Race Community and Conflict, a Study of Sparkbrook*, Oxford University Press, London, p.156.

Richmond, Anthony (1954), *Colour Prejudice in Britain: A Study of West Indian Workers in Liverpool, 1941-1953*, Routledge and Kegan Paul, London.

Richmond, Anthony (1973), *Migration and Race Relations in an English City*, Oxford University Press, London.

Roediger, David R (1990), *The Wages of Whiteness: Race and the Making of the American Working Class*, Verso, London.

Sewell, Tony (1997), *Black Masculinities and Schooling*, Trentham Books, Stoke on Trent.

Simmons, Jack (1974), *Leicester Past and Present: Modern City, 1860-1974*, Eyre Methuen, London.

Sweeney, Carlton (1978), *Flight: West Indians Sojourning in Britain*, Eureka Press, Leicester, p.10.

Walvin, James (1993), *Black Ivory*, Harper Collins, London, pp.193-197.

9 Conclusion: From Immigrants to Ethnic Minority and the Emergence of a Community, 1945-1981

The introduction to this book raised the issue of how the lack of documentary sources posed particular challenges for historians of post war black communities in Britain. While the resulting practical problems have been noted by others, less attention has been paid to the significance of this. The nature of the sources available is particularly important in this case. It is not just that the use of oral evidence is important to fill a gap left by the lack of documentary sources. Nor is it simply that the sources chosen by the historian reveal something about the approach to the study of history and the perceptions adopted about what is important in society. Rather it is that the nature of sources available, concerning African Caribbean people in Leicester from 1945, in itself reveals something of the relationship between local government policy and the presence of black, and to some extent Asian immigrants to Leicester.

It is clear from what we know of government policy, outlined in Chapter Two, that black immigration to Britain was discussed from the time of the origins of the immigration in the Second World War, and that successive governments up to 1962 had broadly negative, but contradictory, approaches to that immigration.

Government policy has been seen, sometimes, as being the product of rational decisions aimed at managing events in society. Discussions of policy in relation to black and Asian immigration are an example of this. The legislation enacted in 1962 to limit immigration of parts of the Commonwealth has been seen as a response to public opinion including that expressed through the events in Notting Hill and Nottingham in 1958. Such a perspective assumed a benign neutrality in matters of race on the part of the Government. Examination of recently released documents has shown the need to revise this view. All through the 1950s the Government was considering legislation aimed at excluding black and Asian people

265

from entering Britain. As Ian Spencer (1997) has argued, the question should be, not why was legislation passed in 1962, but rather, why was there no legislation earlier? It is clear that policy makers held views that were similar to other members of society and concurred with racialised and indeed racist views in a similar way to others. They were not immune from the pervasive racialised construction of groups that was a integral component of national culture. This is not to suggest that the views of individual members of the Government were the sole determinants of policy. This is always the product of a complex interaction between internal and external pressures, conflicting ideologies and interests, although of course, some of these pressures have more influence in determining outcomes than others. Indeed the case of immigration provides an example of how opinions can be modfed by economic demands which can produce counter pressures: ideology was tempered by material considerations. In this case the shortage of labour in post war Britain, which at times was desperate, influenced policy on black and Asian people. Government policy is a powerful determinant of peoples' lives but this policy is not created outside of, and separate from, the culture of society. The relevant aspect of culture in this case being pervasive racialisation and racism.

While workers were needed, the hegemonic, racialised construction which underpinned government policy towards immigration and emigration informed an attempt to prevent the development of a multiracial Britain. Consequently, policy was to leave migrants to fend for themselves, to do nothing to challenge the prejudice and ignorance of the indigenous population about the new people arriving into the urban communities, nor to foster integration and harmony. This is in stark contrast to immigration policy aimed at white people. At the same time Members of Parliament participated in the public debate concerning immigration. This debate centred on the question of whether Britain should become a multiracial society, with South Africa and the United States as comparitors. The question raised was, do we want them here? The sometimes implied, but often overt, answer was negative. The debate did not focus on the advantages to society brought by migration, the responsibilities of Britain's Imperial past nor was the debate properly informed by an understanding of numbers of white immigrants and emigrants. Evidence here illustrates, and replicates, this argument at local level.

This is seen in Leicester in two ways. First, in the period up to 1962 there was no mention of black and Asian people in the records of the local authority. This is particularly significant when consideration is given to the fact that there was an hysterical debate taking place in the local press about black and Asian people, but particularly black, in Leicester throughout the period. The black and Asian presence was ignored in policy making locally, in areas of life where local government had direct influence, for example in housing, in education and in the provision of public services. In areas left to the 'free market' employers, building societies and estate agents and in public places the 'colour bar' was allowed free reign.

Second the presence of documentary sources after 1962 appear only in areas where the local authority had direct and major responsibility. After 1962, the arrival of children in Leicester schools meant that policy decisions with respect to black and Asian children had to be made. Children were presenting themselves in schools, heads were refusing to accept them and the LEA was forced to act. The evidence shows that policy makers and officials shared the dominant racialised perspective concerning black and Asian people. Blacks and Asians were regarded as a problem caused by what was seen as characteristics inherent in their nature and culture. The local authority also did not intervene in areas such as housing. The private sector was able to discriminate legally until 1976 and the local Authority operated a residence rule in the allocation of the housing stock under its control which made it hard for immigrants to get council housing. When African Caribbeans were able to qualify for council housing they were channelled, by an unofficial and covert policy, into certain areas of the city. This enabled the operation of the colour bar to be simultaneously supported and yet denied.

The experiences of African Caribbeans, which are central to this study, show that they had a very good understanding of the operation of the colour bar by employers and the local authority in housing, from the time of arrival. While in education this was less obvious to them. Parents, at least initially, were not able to realise that the reasons why their children were left without school places was not because of overcrowding, but because heads were refusing to take 'immigrants'. Nor were parents fully aware of what was happening to their children when they did go to school. By the 1970s understanding of educational practice was becoming clearer and some black parents tried to act. Testimonies here show that children, however, were more aware of the way they were regarded but were not in a position to do anything about this.

African Caribbeans, then, knew full well of the situation which was revealed in successive sociological studies of discrimination that began to appear during the 1960s. The example of Grattons in Leicester shows that discrimination was neither inevitable nor unavoidable. However there is still no comprehensive, history of the operation of the 'colour bar' in Britain and oral evidence from black people remains the important source of information on this: their stories are crucial. It is argued that the 'colour bar' is important not only for what it reveals about the nature of British society, but also because it had a lasting effect on the social class position of African Caribbeans in Britain.

While it is important to avoid arguing a reductionist relationship between the economy and racialised discourse, nevertheless the two are locked in a complex interrelationship. Racist views and practice confined black people to a narrow range of working class jobs. Evidence suggests that African Caribbeans arrived in Leicester in larger numbers than Asians through the 1950s, possessing skills and qualifications which were disregarded by employers and they were consequently directed into manual jobs. This had long term consequences both for individuals and for the group identity of African Caribbeans. The educational policy of the local authority reinforced this through an approach to black children which tended to obstruct achievement. Later this social class profile was then used a evidence for the lack of success of black people in comparison with others, particularly Asians, in Leicester. This in turn has lent support to a racialised comparison between ethnic groups.

While racism was widespread, many people were not racist and indeed many white people in Leicester, as elsewhere, actively opposed racism. In the early post war period anti racist arguments, for example those expressed in the local press, often lacked the support of good quality information. Facts about numbers of immigrants and emigrants, both white and black, and other relevant historical and social facts, were rarely if ever presented as part of the debate leaving anti racists to argue in terms of basic principles of common humanity.   Neither the national government nor local politicians, provided such information. For example at no time did the Leicester Education Authority make any public statements about falling roles in Leicester schools which might have countered the hysterical debate about damage being done to white children by the presence of 'immigrants' in schools.

By the late 1960s public debate about immigration, the terms of which were set, created more political activity by both racists and anti racists. The debate ostensibly about immigration, but actually about race, was intense in Leicester. The BPLP had virtually collapsed as a political group by 1972, although the organisation did leave a legacy of community projects which continued, while AIMS and the NF met opposition from the IRSC, the Anti Fascist Committee and later the Anti Nazi League. The NF gained more votes in some parts of Leicester than anywhere else in the country. Activity levels were high, demonstration and counter demonstration were part of a battle to establish competing views about immigration and race.

By the end of the decade, the NF had been defeated as a political force. However this did not involve the end of racist discourse. Rather is marked the beginning of a reformation. Like notions of gender, racialised difference has the ability to reform and restructure while structures of inequality were maintained. The electoral defeat of the NF in 1979 and the arrival of the new Conservative government has been seen to mark the beginning of a new discourse on race which focused on ethnicity (Barker, 1981). This new discourse, however, did not entirely replace the old but added a new, more respectable and acceptable framework within which to argue racial difference.

In Leicester, organisations which had begun to enable African Caribbeans to pursue their own cultural activities started to take on a new significance. Through the 1970s African Caribbeans developed more of these cultural organizations and LUCA was formed as an umbrella organisation to represent what was beginning to be seen as a community. While it was clear that overtly political groups which claimed to represent black people such as the BPLP, were not to be tolerated, others which were seen to represent the community in terms of culture were developing a relationship with the local state.

LUCA's relationship with Leicester City Council was difficult. African Caribbeans were compared to Asian groups who funded their own cultural organisations. However LUCA did receive a grant from the City Council and began a relationship with the local state whereby African Caribbeans were seen as a group existing in relationship to Asian and white groups. Racialised identities continued to be important but these were rationalised in terms of ethnicity. African Caribbeans now had opportunities to join in leisure and artistic activities. Increasingly they were becoming an 'ethnic minority' rather than a group of immigrants. The collectivity implied in the new description, was also significant. The definition of black people as an ethnic group which was already becoming evident in the early 1970s, was now more pronounced. Thus the definition of groups in terms of ethnicity was not confined to racists, as argued by Martin Barker. Anti racists embraced multi-culturalism but gave it a progressive inflection.

The flowering of ethnic and cultural expression was not achieved however, until after 1981. In Leicester the Caribbean Carnival, began in 1985, can be seen perhaps as the epitome of African Caribbeans as an ethnic community. The nationwide 'disturbances' or 'uprisings' of 1981 had a catalytic impact on Government policy both nationally and locally. There were serious disturbances in Leicester. In response to this the local authority intervened in a different way to develop and foster ethnicity. 'Money poured into the voluntary sector'.[1] Exploration of this 'progressive multiculturalism' is beyond the scope of this study but it is clear that after 1981, the relationship between African Caribbeans as an ethnic groups and LCC was consolidated.

The evolution of government policy in matters of race and immigration and the experiences of African Caribbeans can be set in the context of this changing discourse concerning racialised identities in Britain. But there are other factors, more specific to Leicester, which have contributed to a tripartite division between groups which has evolved in public discourse. This concerns the growth of Leicester's Asian community. By the late 1960s the Asian community in Leicester had grown. The most widely recognized distinguishing feature of the pattern of migration to Leicester from Britain's former colonies lies in what has been called the 'East African Connection'. In 1960 the African Caribbean community was estimated to be twice as big as the Asian community. Ten years later it was one quarter as big. The arrival of Asians from Kenya and later Uganda have had a profound effect on the political and cultural life of the city and all its inhabitants including African Caribbeans. Despite the existence of a variety of white minority groups in Leicester 'immigrants' were defined in both popular and academic discourse to mean people with black or brown skins. Later as the term immigrant was replaced by the term ethnic minority, the purely physical characteristics of dark skin continued to be the defining characteristic of this group. From this perspective, the much smaller groups of African Caribbeans in Leicester became a minority within an (ethnic) minority. This has contributed to the marginalisation of African Caribbeans.

Asian immigrants many of whom were actualy refugees, had a different social class profile. At the time of the Kenyan migration to Leicester in 1968, the Secretary of the committee set up by the Sikh 'Khalsa Dall' to help settle the newcomers placed special value on the middle-class status and English speaking characteristics of the migrants. By 1973 Leicester had two branches of the Bank of India and Asians in Leicester owned factories, mostly in textiles. Although it has been argued that the wealth brought to Leicester by Asians from both Kenya and Uganda may have been exaggerated (Marett, 1989) and many people from East Africa, like African Caribbeans, were forced to take jobs in factories, it is clear that a new middle class Asian group was establishing itself in the city.

African Caribbeans have been since the 1960s both a smaller and predominantly working class group compared to Asians who by 1980s were six times as great numerically and contained a much larger middle class. These comparative features have had consequences for the way in which African Caribbeans have been seen within the body politic in Leicester. The main problem for black people was a lack of material resources. This was due to their position as a relatively poor community located within the working class. Asian organisations were often based on the need to support and maintain aspects of culture such as religion and language. Early West Indian migrants on the other hand, spoke English as their first language and were Christian. Initially, they attempted to join existing local churches and other local groups and to gain access to existing premises to hold cultural and leisure activities. They were often rejected by local whites and excluded from organising their own events using existing facilities. In order to maintain their culture West Indians needed basic amenities such as halls for dances and cultural events and these were difficult for them to gain access to.

While the fostering of community projects from the mid 1970s became a channel for a few African Caribbeans to develop professional status most have remained in the manual working class. This class profile has then been used to compare African Caribbeans unfavourably as a group with the more economically and politically powerful Asians.

A further problem with the development of African Caribbeans (and others) as an ethnic community is that communities are represented by leaders who are much more likely to be men. While there are a few eminent female African Caribbean 'leaders' in Leicester, the notion of 'community' can mask internal differences and impose an artificial homogeneity on a group of people with diverse interests and needs. Communities came to be defined by culture, a concept which in practice is conflated with race. Issues of equality and justice between groups can become submerged as people relate to each other as members of 'ethnic communites'.

The relative importance of race and class in creating life chances and identity has been an important debate within sociology. The development of a group of black immigrants to Leicester and their growth and construction as an ethnic community sheds light on this debate. Powerful notions of 'race' have ensured that African Caribbeans maintained a class identity which was then used in turn to justify a racialised identity as an ethnic minority. These notions of 'class' and 'race;' have lent support to each other. This can be understood only when the position of African Caribbeans is examined over time and through an historical perspective.

Note

1   Interview with Paul Winstone, 25 September 1995.

References

Barker, Martin (1981), *The New Racism*, Junction Books, London.
Marett, Valerie (1984), *Immigrants Settling in the City*, Leicester University Press, London.
Spencer, Ian R G (1997), *British Immigration Policy Since 1939: The Making of Multi-Racial Britain*, Routledge, London.

Bibliography

Primary Sources

1   Interviews

1.1   Interviews (personal experiences)

Carmel Charles	Date of Interview: 13 July 1994
Doris Cope	Date of Interview: 19 January 1994
Edith Drew	Date of Interview: 5 May 1994
Nick Frank	Date of Interview: 28 September 1994
Oscar Frank	Date of Interview: 25 September 1994
June Grey	Date of Interview: 31 August 1994
Percy Harding	Date of Interview: 30 November 1994
Linda Herbert	Date of Interview: 9 September 1994
Eric Hudson	Date of Interview: 28 April 1994
Novelette Mackoy	Date of Interview: 17 August 1994
Elvy Moreton	Date of Interview: 12 December 1994
Lee Morris	Date of Interview: 5 September 1994
Reuban Nelson	Date of Interview: 6 July 1994
Elevina Prince	Date of Interview: 15 August 1994
Pastor Michael Roberts	Date of Interview: 18 March 1997
Clifton Robby Robinson	Date of Interview: 8 February 1995
Ronald Rochester	Date of Interview: 10 August 1994
Roy Rowe	Date of Interview: 6 September 1994
Carlton Sweeney	Date of Interview: 4 August 1994, 1 February 1997 and 9 March 1997
Monroe Thomas	Date of Interview: 4 October 1994
Herdle White	Date of Interview: 28 September 1994
Veronica Williams	Date of Interview: 8 May 1994

1.2   Interviews (members of organisations)

Terry Allcott former officer, Anti Nazi League	Date of Interview: 13 December

Joe Allen, Leicester City Council	Date of Interview: 14 December 1995
Nasser Belamy, Centre Manager, Leicester United Caribbean Association	Date of Interview: 24 November 1994
Cynthia Brown, Leicester City Council	Date of Interview: 19 January 1994 & 1 November 1995
Graham Brown, Manager, Grattons	Date of Interview: 8 February 1995
Nelista Cuffy, Teacher Saturday School	Date of Interview: 21 April 1995
Ruby Grant, former Chair of Highfields Community Council	Date of Interview: 28 November 1994 & 13 December 1994
Dorothy Henry, member of the New Church of God	Date of Interview: 6 June 1996
Satish Kapur, Organisation of Ethnic Minority Teachers in Leicestershire	Date of Interview: 3 April 1995
Mike Keene, Committee Secretariat Leicester City Council	Date of Interview: 13 January 1994
Valerie Marett, former Chair of the Housing Sub Committee of Leicester Council for Community Relations	Date of Interview: 16 June 1997
Robert Murray Nottingham West Indian Combined Ex-Service Association	Date of Interview: 27 January 1994
Ned Newitt, Councillor Leicester City Council	Date of Interview: 11 January 1995 & 14 March 1997
John Perry, former Team Leader Renewal Programme Leicester City Council 1976-1990	Date of Interview: 18 May 1997
David Purdy, Director Race Equality Council	Date of Interview: 12 August 1994
Donovan René Complaints Officer	Date of Interview: 27 September 1994
East Midlands Regional Office Council for Racial Equality	Date of Interview: 10 September 1994
Earle Robinson	Date of Interview: 10 December 1995

John Taylor, former pupil at   Date of Interview: 25 March 1994
Moat School
Paul Winstone   Date of Interview: 5 November
Senior Policy Officer   1993 & 25 September 1995
Equality Unit Leicester City Council

2   Archives

2.1   National

2.1.1 Black Cultural Archive

'The Caribbean at War: British West Indians in World War II'.
North Kensington County Series No 5.

Gloria Locke, *Caribbeans in Wandsworth*, Wandsworth Borough
Council, Wandsworth 1992.

2.1.2 Institute of Race Relations

Transcript and Research notes of <u>A Common History</u> A
Documentary Film, Directed by Colin Prescott.

2.1.3 Public Record Office

LAB 9/202 Conference of Regional Controllers 20 January 1949.
LAB 8/1898 Midlands Region 22 August 1953.
LAB 8/1519 Coloured People in the UK.
LAB 8/968 Memo on Training of Colonial Students (Nurses).
LAB 26/218.
CAB 128/25/337.
CAB 129/81/167-71.
CAB 128/17 (50) 13.7 Coloured People from British colonial
territories.
CAB 128/17 (50) 13.7 Coloured people from British colonial
territories.

CAB 128/17 (50) 37.2 Coloured people from British colonial territories.

CAB128/19 (51) 15.4 Coloured people from British colonial territories.

CAB 128/25 (52) 100.8 GPO Employment of coloured workers.

CAB 128/25 (52) 106.7 General Post Office: Employment of coloured workers.

CAB 128/27 (54) 7.4 Coloured workers.

CAB 128/27 (54) 17.6 Coloured workers.

CAB 128/27 (54) 65.2 Coloured workers.

CAB 128/27 (54) 78.4 Colonial immigrants.

CAB 128/27 (54) 82.7 Colonial immigrants.

CAB 128/28 (55) 3.6 Colonial immigrants.

CAB 128/28 (55) 5.2 Colonial immigrants.

CAB 128/28 (55) 6.1 Colonial immigrants.

CAB 128/28 (55) 8.9 Colonial immigrants.

CAB 128/28 (55) 15.1 Colonial Empire. Indian Communities.

CAB 128/28 (55) 15.4 Colonial immigrants.

CAB 128/28 (55) 25.3 Colonial immigrants.

CAB 128/29 (55) 9.6 Colonial immigrants.

CAB 128/29 (55) 14.4 Colonial immigrants.

CAB 128/29 (55) 16.1 Colonial immigrants.

CAB 128/29 (55) 31.4 Colonial immigrants.

CAB 128/29 (55) 39.7 Colonial immigrants.

CAB 128/30 (56) 48/10 Colonial immigrants.

CAB 128/30 (56) 85.5 Colonial immigrants.

CAB 128/31 (57) 57.5 Colonial immigrants.

CAB 128/32 (58) 51.6 Commonwealth immigrants.

CAB 128/32 (58) 69.3 Racial disturbances.

CAB 128/32 (58) 71.1 Racial disturbances.

CAB 128/33 (59) 11.8 Commonwealth immigrants.

CAB 128/34 (60) 46.2 Commonwealth immigrants.

CAB 128/34 (60) 59.8 Commonwealth immigrants.

CAB 128/35 (61) 7.2 Commonwealth immigrants.

CAB 128/35 (61) 29.7 Commonwealth immigrants.

CAB 128/35 (61) 55.3 Commonwealth immigrants.

CAB 128/35 (61) 61.5 Commonwealth immigrants.

CAB 128/35 (61) 63.2 Commonwealth immigrants.

CAB 128/35 (61) 67.5 Commonwealth immigrants.

2.1.4 **University of Warwick**

2.1.4.1 *Modern Records Centre*

MSS 237/9/2/1-11/6, Engineering Employers Federation Agreements with Trade Unions.

MSS 237/1/13/1-205/88, Engineering Employers Federation, Conference Minutes 1950-1963.

MSS 237/1/13/98-117, Minutes of Special Conferences, December 1953- December 1960.

Subject files

MSS237/3/1/1-3/25, Bond v Ashwell and Nesbitt, Leicester.

MSS 237/3/1/54 and 58-60, Dilution of Labour.

Individual Firms

MSS101/DA/1/7/3602, 3603, 2336,2337, Tubes Ltd March 1966.

MSS101/DA/1/7/318, 319,320,321, Bentley Group, 1966.

MSS101/DA/1/7/1127,1152, Dunlop, 1963.

2.1.4.2 *Research Centre in Ethnic and Racial Studies Resources Centre*

Marian Fitzgerald, 'Racial Harassment in Leicester', *Black Housing* Federation of Black Housing Organisation, Vol 4, No 3, 1988.

Janet Ford, 'Homelessness among Africa Caribbean Women', Loughborough University 1990.

362.925 FOR., 'Caribbean Women', Loughborough University 1990.

362.1.JEW., Nick Jewson, *Health Authority Membership and the Representation of Community Interests: The Case of Ethnicity*, Discussion paper in Sociology, University of Leicester, 1993.

379.157 RAN, Chris Ranger, Ethnic Minority School Teacher (Leicester) CRE 1988, Press cuttings on Leicester.

A Question of Merit - Report of Formal Investigation into Leicester Appointment in Leicestershire, CRE 1991.

362.WES, Sally Westwood, Leicester Black Mental Health Group, 1989.

'Race Attacks', *Search Light*, Part 249, March 1996, page 8-9.

2.2   Local

2.2.1   Leicester City Council

Ethnicity and the 1991 Census.

Minutes of the Meeting of the African Caribbean Working Group, 21 April 1995.

Leicester City Council Renewal Strategy Programme Report 1976.

Leicester Key Facts: Profiles 1991 Census.

K B Duffy and   I C Lincoln, *Earnings and Ethnicity*, Principal Report on Research Conducted by LCC, 1990.

Survey of Leicester, 1983.

Leicester Caribbean Directory.

Official Industrial Handbook, Leicester Corporation, E J Burrow and Co Ltd, undated.

Highfields Review: A consultative document by the Economic Development Branch Leicester City Council. Presented by Kishor Tailor and Rekha Modi, 1992.

2.2.2 The *Leicester Mercury*

The *Leicester Mercury* 'Blue' book (Official in-house history).

2.2.3 Leicester Record Office

Census 1951	Leicester and Leicestershire
Census 1961	Leicester and Leicestershire
Census 1966	Sample census, Leicester and Leicestershire
Census 1971	Leicester and Leicestershire
Census 1981	Leicester and Leicestershire
Census 1991	Leicester and Leicestershire

Illustrated Leicester Chronicle 1950-1962

Leicester Mercury 1941-1981

19D59, Minute Book. General Purposes Sub Committee, City of Leicester Education Committee. 1 January 1955 - May 1972.

19D59, Minute Book. Primary Education Sub Committee, January 1959 - April 1971.

19D59, Dale Secondary School Governors Minutes, July 1962 - February 1963.

19D59, Moat School Governors Minutes, November 1948 - February 1962.

DE 1701/1, Press cuttings on Education in Leicester 1956-1974.

D59/VII., Youth Committee Minutes 1965-1969.

AD59, Youth Employment Committee.

DE 3277, Housing Committee Minutes, 1959-1974.

L.641, The Health of the City of Leicester (Annual Reports) 1946-1972.

L.352.2, Chief Constables Annual Report 1930-1981.

Q 59, Recorders Notebooks Quarter Sessions 1958.

L.381, Leicester and District Trades Council Year Books 1958-1970.

L658, Agreement Imperial Typewriters Co Ltd.   Leicester and Imperial Typewriters Branch (5/221) of the Transport and General Workers Union 10 May 1970.

L658, Imperial Typewriter Directors Reports and Accounts 1959-1965.

L301.451, Imperial Typewriters Co Ltd. Race Today Collection.

L658, Why Imperial Typewriters Must Not Close - A Preliminary Social Account by the Union Action Committee.   Institute of Workers Control Pamphlet No 46. 1975.

L658, Folder of Company Information.

L658, *Polymer Engineering Division of Dunlop Ltd Leicester Report of a Formal Investigation*, Commission for Racial Equality, April 1984.

L650, *Frederick Parker Ltd, Report No 8*, Commission for Racial Equality, 1970.

L620, *Skilled Engineering: Shortages in a High Demand Area. Department of Employment*, Manpower Papers No 3: An Inquiry into the Leicester Area May/June 1970, HMSO.

L.677, Stanislauw Pullé, 'Employment Policies in the Hosiery Industry with Particular Reference to the Position of Minority Workers', Runnymede Industrial Unit, December 1972.

L.301.451, *Ethnic Minorities in Britain, Statistical Information on the Pattern of Settlement*, Commission for Racial Equality, 1981.

88/28, 'Ethnic Minority Businessmen in Leicester', 1987.

L.301.451, J. M. Cooper, 'Elderly West Indians in Leicester', 1976.

L.362.6, Frank Glendenning (ed), 'The Elders in Ethnic Minorities', 1979.

L.301.54, A report of a seminar arranged by the Department of Adult Education, University of Leicester: The Beth Johnson Foundation'. Commission for Racial Equality, 20-22 April 1979.

L301.451, 'Distribution of Ethnic Minorities in Leicester': Information extracted from the electoral register, 1978-1979.

L.027.63, C. T. Clements, 'The West Indian Community in Britain and the Relevance of the Library Service to their Needs with Particular Reference being made to the East Midlands', July 1980.

L362.6, Marian Farrah, 'Black Elders in Leicester', *Public Service*, Vol 51, No 8, June 1977, City Council Directors of Personnel and Management.

Oral History Archive

048/2, 135/1, 201/1/1/2, 273/2, 276/1, 277/2, 277/3, 278/1, 284/1/2, 286/1/2, 286/2/2, 293/2, 395/2/1, 451/1, 451/2/2, 478/2/1.

2.2.4 University of Leicester - Scarman Centre

2.2.4.1 *The Valerie Marett Archive*
(The material in this archive is not catalogued)

Shelter Reports

Housing Conditions in Leicester 1961-1971.

Council Housing in Leicester 1975.

Wasted Assets: Shelter Housing Aid and Research Project 1976.

A Jansari (Research Officer), 'Coloured Households and Owner Occupation: A Study Of The Patterns Of House Purchase Among Ethnic Minorities In Leicester', undated.

Leicester Council for Community Relations

LCCR Constitution (undated).

Housing Investment Programme Strategy Statement 1979-1980.

Access to Council Housing 1980.

Annual Reports 1965-1977.

National Conference of Community Relations, Council Conference Report 1977.

Selected Minutes of Housing Sub Committee 1970-1981.

Selected issues of LCCR News 1970-1981.

Other Documents

Local Authorities and the Housing Implication of Section 71 of the Race Relations Act 1976.

Letter from Chief Executive and Town Clerk   LCC - Street Disturbances July 1981, 24 August 1981.

Selected issues of *Highfields Voice*, 1977-1981.

Response of Chief Executive to LCCR Urban Deprivation - Special Needs of Ethnic Minorities.

2.2.4.2 *University of Leicester - Scarman Centre*

Afrikan Caribbean Research Group Project

'African Caribbean People in Leicestershire' *First Interim Report*, January 1993.

'African Caribbean People in Leicestershire, Comments on Community Experience and Opinion', June 1994.

Afrikan Caribbean Newsletter, August 1992 - April 1993.

2.2.5 Other Local Sources (accessed through private individuals)

National Front News Bulletin - Leicester Branch, 'What is Happening in our Schools', (undated).

Selected issues of *Equality* - Newsletter of Leicester Campaign for Racial Equality and later of Inter Racial Solidarity Campaign (RSC) 1967-1978.

IRSC Members Bulletins 1978.

IRSC Report on its formation, its activities and its projected strategy.

IRSC Selected publicity material.

Leicester United Caribbean Association - Constitution and other documents.

Support the Leicester 87 - Anti Nazi League April 21 Defence Committee.

Selected Issues of *Ripple* Newspaper Leicester University Students Union 1970-1974.

BPLP Statement about the present situation in Uganda 1972, (undated).

National Association for Multi-racial Education - Policy Paper March 1980.

The Struggle Against Racialism in Leicester (undated).

Uhuru - Black People Freedom Movement (Nottingham) Vol 1 No 3 (undated).

Black Workers Action Committee Weekly, Review No 1.

Rasta Voice No 86 and 87.

Charlie Husband, Immigration in Leicester, undated.

Kapur S, 'Section 11 Posts: Review or More of the Same?' Indian Workers Association, Leicester Branch, 1984.

3   Parliamentary Papers

1946 Report on Jamaica, Colonial Office, HMSO 1947.

Cmnd 2266, Second Report of the Commonwealth Advisory Council, 1964.

Cmnd 2739, Parliamentary Papers, Session 1964-65.

House of Commons, Sessional Papers 1972-73, Select Committee on Race Relations and Immigration, HMSO, London.

House of Commons, Sessional Papers, 1975-76, Select Committee on Race Relations and Immigration, HMSO, London.

House of Commons, Sessional Papers, 1976-77, Select Committee on Race Relations and Immigration, HMSO, London.

House of Commons, Session 1980-81, Fifth Report from the Home Affairs Committee, Racial Disadvantage, HMSO, London.

Cmnd 8273, Interim Report of the Committee of Inquiry into the Education of Children from Ethnic Minority Groups, 1981.

Cmnd 6845, Policies for the Inner City.

Hansard (Commons), 5th Series, Vol 610, 1959.

Hansard (Commons), Vol 658, 1963.

4   Newspapers

Black Chat
Daily Mail
Economist
Equality (Newspaper of the Leicester Racial Equality council and later of the Inter Racial Solidarity Campaign)
Guardian
Highfields Voice (Community Newpaper)
Illustrated Leicester Chronicle
Leicester Mercury
National Front News
Rasta Voice
Ripple (Newspaper of Leicester University Students' Union)
Observer
Searchlight
Spectator

Secondary Sources

1   Unpublished Theses and Dissertations

1.1   **PhD Theses**

Deakin Nicholas, 'The Immigration Issue in British Politics (1948-1964)' University of Sussex, 1972.
Diez Ross, 'Loss and Longing - Caribbean Writers in the Metropolis', University of Barcelona, 1995.

Mander J, 'Freedom and Constraints in a Local Education Authority', PhD Thesis, University of Leicester, 1975.

Thomas-Hope, 'Elizabeth Population Mobility in the West Indies: Role of Perceptual and Environmental Differentials', University of Oxford, 1977.

1.2   **MA and MEd Dissertations**

Barker A & O, Pare-Abetta, 'Coloured Workers in Leicester', University of Leicester, 1962.

Beasley M, 'Racial Integration: A Comparative Study University of Leicester', 1969.

Browne D S, 'A Comparative Study of West Indian Socio/Political Associations in Leicester', University of Leicester, 1973.

Coan M J, 'Aspirations and Achievements with Two Coloured Immigrant Groups in Britain', University of Leicester, 1971.

Cross D, 'A Sociological Account of the Rise of Enoch Powell', University of Leicester, 1970.

Cutting D C, 'A Study of Race Relations Amongst Primary School Children', University of Leicester, 1970.

Duncan R & Varcoe I M, 'Social Residential Distance and Ethnic Attitudes in Leicester', University of Leicester, 1965.

Eldridge J E T, 'Race Relations in Leicester University', University of Leicester, 1959.

Fielding R S F, 'An Investigation into the Subject Vocabularies of Native and Immigrant Pupils on Leaving Junior School', Med Thesis, University of Leicester, 1972.

Gibson J A, 'Friendships Between English and Immigrant Children in an Urban School', University of Leicester, 1970.

Gillings H S, 'Problems Faced by First Generation West Indian Immigrants and their Children as Seen Through a Social Work Agency', University of Leicester, 1972.

Hewett J R, 'Race and Work - An Investigation in Race Relations in a Bus Garage', University of Leicester, 1971.

Howarth V, 'A Sociological Study of West Indian Unmarried Mothers in Britain Today', University of Leicester, 1974.

Jacoby A D, 'The Family and a Children's Department - With Particular Reference to use of the Department by West Indian Immigrants', University of Leicester, 1971.

Kapur S, 'Black Ethnic Minorities of Leicester with Special Reference to Education', MEd dissertation, University of Nottingham, 1983.

Mans P, 'Immigrant in Britain: Media Definitions and Educational Functions', University of Leicester, 1973.

Manwell M, 'Children at Work and Play - A Study of Integration at a Leicester School', University of Leicester, 1966.

Marvell J, 'Religions, Beliefs and Moral Values of Immigrant Children', MEd Thesis University of Leicester, 1973.

Middleton J, 'Immigration and Some of the Problems it Poses for Education', University of Leicester, 1972.

Mitchell L E, 'Accommodation Pattern of West Indians in Leicester', University of Leicester, 1967.

Morris F A, 'Britain and the Immigrant Doctor', MA Dissertation, University of Leicester, 1970.

Muir A, 'Immigrant Students in a College of Further Education in Leicester', University of Leicester, 1975.

Neale J A, 'The West Indian in Britain - An Enquiry into the Effects of Immigration Upon West Indian Church Going', MEd Dissertation, University of Leicester, 1965.

Newton S, 'West Indian Children and E S N Schools - A Case Study', University of Leicester, 1974.

Norris S, 'Race Awareness in Young Children', University of Leicester, 1966.

O'Brien K, 'Deviance in Two West Indian Settlements', University of Leicester, 1968.

Rees J, 'Some Educational Problems for the Immigrant in Leicester', University of Leicester, 1974.

Reynolds M H, 'The Press and Race Relations University of Leicester', 1970.

Richardson M J, 'A Sociological Study of Highfields Adventure Playground and its Importance in the Community', University of Leicester, 1973.

Robinson C E B, 'A General Survey of West Indian Children in the Primary Schools of Leicester', DipEd Special Study, University of Leicester 1964.

Ross A, 'Problems of West Indian Integration and the Role of Education and the Youth Service', Moray House, College of Ed, School of Community Studies, 1971.

Sidhu P J, 'Immigrants in England and in the English Educational System', MA Dissertation, University of Leicester, 1974.

Small W, 'Coloured School Leavers in Leicester', MEd dissertation,University of Leicester, 1968.

Sutcliffe J R, 'Asian and West Indian Children in Leicester Primary Schools: Evaluation of their Pedagogical Characteristics', University of Leicester, 1975.

Yates S D, 'Spinney Hills - Housing Satisfaction and Opportunity Among Native and Immigrant Residents', University of Leicester, 1969.

Young M A, 'Socio-Linguistic Approach to the Problems of Educability of West Indian Children', University of Leicester, 1974.

2   **Journal Articles and Research Papers**

Akgunduz A, 'Labour Migration from Turkey to Western Europe (1960-1974)', *Capital Class*, Vol 51, 1993.

Back L & John S, 'Black Politics and Social Change in Birmingham, UK: An Analysis of Recent Trends', *Ethnic and Racial Studies*, Vol 15, No 3, 1992.

Ballard R, 'New Clothes for the Emperor? The Conceptual Nakedness of the Race Relations Industry in Britain', *New Community* Vol 18, No 3, 1992.

Banton M, 'The Economic and Social Position of Negro Immigrants in Britain', *Sociological Review*, New Series, Vol 1, No 2, 1952.

Beckles H, 'Black Men in White Skins: The Formation of a White Proletariat in West Indian Slave Society', *Journal of Imperial and Commonwealth History*, Vol 15, No 1, 1987.

Beckles H, 'White Women and Slavery in the Caribbean', *History Workshop*, No 36, 1993.

Bhatt A, 'Community Languages in the Curriculum', *Forum*, Vol 32, No 3 1990.

Bornat J, Burdell J, Groom B & Thompson P, 'Oral History and Black History Conference Report', *Oral History*, Vol 8, No 1.

Bourne J, 'Cheerleaders and Ombudsmen: The Sociology of Race Relations in Britain', *Race and Class*, Vol 21, 1980.

Bush J, 'Moving On - and Looking Back', *History Workshop*, Vol 36,1993.

Byron M 'The Housing Question: Caribbean Migrants and the British Housing Market', *Research Paper*, 49, Oxford School of Geography.

CARF UK: 'Fighting our Fundamentalism: An Interview with A Sivanandan', *Race and Class*, Vol 36, No 3, 1995.

Carter, B, The Construction of National Identities in the USA and Britain', Greenard M & Halpern R, *Immigration Policy and the Racialisation of Migrant Labour Ethnic and Racial Studies*, Vol 19, No 1, 1996.

Casely-Hayford, 'Black Oral History and Methodology: The Possibilities of Conducting Black Local History', *The Local Historian*, Vol 20, No 2, 1990.

Chamberlain M, 'Families and Identity - Barbadian Migrants to Britain', *International Year Book of Oral History and Life Stories*, Vol 3, 1994.

Chessum L, *The Part - Time Nobody: Part Time Women Teachers in West Yorkshire*, West Yorkshire Centre for Research on Women, University of Bradford, Bradford, 1989.

Comer J P, 'Research and the Black Backlash', *American Journal of Ortho Psychiatry*, Vol 40, Part 1, 1970.

Cousens S H, 'Emigration and Demographic Change in Ireland 185-1861', *Economic History Review*, Vol 14, 1961, Utrecht, NVA Oosthoek's, 1961.

Davison R B, 'West Indian Migration to Britain 1952-1961', *The West Indian Economist*, Vol 4 1-4, 1961.

Dean D W, 'Coping with Colonial Immigration, the Cold War and Colonial Policy: The Labour Government and Black Communities in Great Britain 1945-1951', *Immigrants and Minorities*, Vol 6, Part 3, 1987.

Dean S W, 'Conservative Governments and the Restriction of Commonwealth Immigration in the 1950s: The Problems of Constraint', *Historical Journal*, 1992.

Driver G, 'How West Indians Do Better At School (especially the girls)', *New Society*, 17 January, 1980.

The Economist, 'Leicester - Prejudice Before Pride', anon 16 December, 1972.

Elliott J, 'Validating Case Studies', *Westminster Studies in Education*, Vol 13, 1990.

Farrah Marian, 'Homelessness Among African Caribbean Women in Leicester', *Black Housing*, Vol 4, No 3 (undated).

Fitzgerald M, 'Racial Harassment in Leicester', *Federation of Black Housing Organisation*, London, Vol 14, No 3, 1988.

Fitzpatrick D, 'Irish Emigration in the Late Nineteenth Century', *Irish Historical Studies*, Vol 22, 1980-81.

Goulbourne H, 'Oral History and Black Labour in Britain: An Overview', page 24, *Oral History*, Vol 8, No 1, 1980.

Gretton , 'The Race Industry', *New Society*, 11 March, 1971.

Grosvenor I D, 'A Different Reality: Education and the Racialisation of the Black Child', *History of Education*, Vol 16, No 4, 1987.

Jenkins R, 'Rethinking Ethnicity: Identity, Categorisation and Power', *Ethnic and Racial Studies*, Vol 17, No 2, 1994.

Jones P, 'British Unemployment and Migration: Two Case Studies', *New Community*, Vol 9, Part 1, 1981.

Joshi S & Carter B, 'The Role of Labour in the Creation of a Racist Britain', *Race and Class*, Vol 15, 1984.

Killian, L M, 'School Bussing in Britain: Policies and Perceptions', *Harvard Educational Review*, Vol 49, No 2, 1979.

Killingray D, 'Africans in the United Kingdom: An Introduction', *Immigrants and Minorities* ,Vol 12, No 3, 1993.

Kirk N, 'History, Language, Idea and Post Modernism : A Materialistic View', *Social History*, Vol 19, No 2, 1994.

Malik K, 'Universalism and Difference: Race and the Post Modernists', *Race and Class*, Vol 37, No 3, 1996.

Mason D, 'Some Problems with the Concepts of Race and Racism Discussion Papers in Sociology', No S92/5, University of Leicester 1992.

Miles R & Phizacklea A, 'The TUC and Black Workers 1974-1976: Discrimination and Disadvantage in Employment', *British Journal of Industrial Relations*, vol 16, No 2, 1978.

Panayi P, 'Anti-German Riots in London during the First World War', *German History*, Vol 1, No 2, 1989.

Panayi P, 'Middlesborough 1961: A British Race Riot of the 1960s?', *Social History*, Vol 16, No 2, 1991.

Parker J & Dunginon K, ' Race and The Allocation of Public Housing - a GLC Survey', *New Community*, Vol 6, Part 1-2, 1977.

Paul K, 'British Subjects and British Stock', *Journal of British Studies*, Vol 34, No 2, 1995.

Peach C, 'West Indian Migration to Britain: The Economic Factors', *Race*, Vol 71, 1965.

Peach C, 'Factors Affecting the Distribution of West Indians' in Great Britain', *Transactions of the Institute of British Geographers*, Vol 38, Peach C, 'West Indians as a Replacement Population in England and Wales' *Social and Economic Studies*, Vol 16, Part 3, 1967.

Peach G C K & Winchester S W C, 'Birthplace, Ethnicity and the Under enumeration of West Indians, Indians and Pakistanis in the Censuses of 1966 and 1971', *New Community*, Vol 3, Part 4, 1974.

Peach C, 'Ins and Outs of Home Office and IPS Migration Data', *New Community*, Vol 1, 1981.

Peach C, *The Caribbean in Europe: Contrasting Patterns of Migration and Settlement in Britain, France and the Netherlands*, Research Paper in Ethnic Relations No 15, ESRC Centre for Research in Ethnic Relations, 1991.

Race Today, 'The Strike at Imperial Typewriters', July 1974.

Race Today, 'Imperial Typewriters Strike: The Continuing Story', August 1974.

Race Today, 'Black Women and Nursing: A Job Like Any Other', August 1974.

Rattansi A, 'Race, Class and the State: From Marxism to Post Modernism' *Labour History Review*, Vol 60, Part No 3, 1995.

Ravenstein, D, 'The Laws of Migration', *Journal of the Royal Statistical Society*, Vol 42, June, 1985.

Roberts A, 'Winston Replied that He Didn't Like Blackamoors', *The Spectator*, 9 April, 1994.

Roberts C W, 'Review of West Indian Migration', *Race and Class*, Vol 12, 1970.

Roberts G W & Mils D O, 'Study of External Migration Affecting Jamaica 1953-55', *Social and Economic Studies*, Vol 7, No 2, 1958.

Robinson V, 'Correlates of Asian Migration 1959-1974', *New Community*, Vol 7, 1 and 2, 1980.

Russell R J & McIntine W G, *Barbuda Reconnaissance*, Louisiana State University Studies, Central Studies Series No 16, 1966.

Samuel R, 'The People with Stars in their Eyes', *The Guardian*, 23 September, 1995.

Sivanandan A, 'From Resistance to Rebellion: Asian and African Caribbean Struggles in Britain', *Race and Class*, Vol 23, No 2/3, 1981.

Solomos J & Singh G, *Housing, Racial Equality and Local Politics: Policy Making in a Changing Context*, Policy Paper in Ethnic Relation No 19, 1990.

Spencer I R G, 'The Open Door, Labour Needs and British Immigration Policy 1945-1955', *Immigrants and Minorities*, Vol 15, No 1, March, 1996.

Tannenbaum P H, 'The Effect of Headlines on the Interpretation of News Stories', *Journalism Quarterly*, Vol 30, 1953.

Thomas-Hope E, 'Hopes and Reality in the West Indian Migration to Britain', *Oral History*, Vol 8, No 1, 1980.

Thomas-Hope E, 'Transients and Settlers: Varieties of Caribbean Migrants and their Socio-Economic Implications of their Return', *International*, Vol 24, Part 3, 1986.

Tomlinson S, 'The Educational Performance of Ethnic Minority Children', *New Community*, Vol 3, No 3, Winter 1980.

Troyna B, 'Beyond Reasonable Doubt? Researching Race in Educational Settings', *Oxford Review of Education*, Vol 21, No 4, 1995.

Vernon J, 'Who's Afraid of the Linguistic Turn? The Politics of Social History and It's Disconduct', *Social History*, Vol 19, No 1, 1994.

Waters C, 'Dark Strangers in our Midst: Discourses of Race and Nation in Britain.

Winston J, 'The African Caribbean Presence', *New Left Review*, 193, May/June, 1992.

3   Books

Allen S, Bentley S & Borna J, *Work, Race and Immigration*, University of Bradford, School of Studies in Social Sciences, Bradford, 1997.

Anthias F, *Ethnicity, Class, Gender and Migration: Greek Cypriots in Britain*, Avebury, Aldershot, 1992.

Anthias F & Yuval-Davis S F, *Racialised Boundaries: Race, Nation, Gender, Colour and Class and the Antiracist Struggle*, Routledge, London.

Arnot M (ed), *Race and Gender: Equal Opportunities Policy in Education*, Open University, Pergammon Press, Oxford, 1985.

Baines D, *Migration in a Mature Economy: Emigration and Internal Migration in England and Wales 1861-1900*, Cambridge University Press, Cambridge, 1985.

Baines D, *Emigration From Europe 1815-1930*, Macmillan, London, 1991.

Banton M, *The Coloured Quarter: Negro Immigrants in an English City*, Jonathan Cape, London, 1955.

Banton M, *Racial Minorities*, Fontana, Suffolk, 1972.

Barker M, *The New Racism*, Junction Books, London, 1981.

Baron A, *Work Engendered: Towards a New History of American Labour*,

Cornell University Press, New York, 1991.

Beckles H, *A History of Barbados*, Cambridge University Press, Cambridge, 1990.

Bhat A, Carr-Hill R & Sushel O (eds), *Britain's Black Population: The Radical Statistics Race Group*, (2nd ed), Gower, Aldershot, 1988.

Billig M, *Fascists: A Social Psychological View of the National Front*, Harcourt, Brace, Jovanovich, London, 1978.

Bosquet B & Douglas C, *West Indian Women At War. British Racism in World War II*, Lawrence and Wishart, London, 1991.

Braham P, Rattansi A & Skellington R, *Racism and Anti Racism: Immigration Opportunities and Policies*, Sage and OUP, London, 1992.

Braham P, Rhodes E & Dearn M (eds), *Discrimination and Disadvantage in Employment: The Experience of Black Workers*, Harper and Row, Open University Press, London, 1981.

Brooke S, *The Conservative Party, Immigration and National Identity 1948-1968*, The Conservative Party and British Society 1880-1990, University of Wales, 1996.

Buggings J, *West Indians in Britain during the Second World War: A Short History Drawing on Colonial Office Papers*, National Black Cultural Archive.

Burke G, *Housing and Social Justice*, Longman, London, 1981.

Burney E, *Housing on Trial*, Institute of Race Relations, Open University Press, London, 1967.

Byron Margaret, *Post-War Caribbean Migration to Britain: The Unfinished Cycle*, Avebury, Aldershot, 1994.

Cunningham W, *Alien Immigration to England*, (2nd ed), Frank Cass, London, 1969.

Carter T, *Shattering Illusions: West Indians in British Politics*, Lawrence and Wishart, London, 1986.

Cashmore Ellis and Troyna B, *Introduction to Race Relations*, (2nd ed), Falmer Press, London, 1990.

Castles S & Kosack G, *Immigrant Workers and the Class Structure in Western Europe*, Open University Press, London, 1973.

Castles S, *Here for Good: Western Europe's New Ethnic Minorities*, Pluto, London, 1984.

Centre for Contemporary Cultural Studies, *The Empire Strikes Back: Race and Racism in 70s Britain*, Hutchinson, London, 1982.

Cesarani D, *Justice Delayed: How Britain Becomes a Refuge for Nazi War Criminals*, Heinemann, London, 1992.

Cesarani D and Fulbrook M (eds), *Citizenship, Nationality and Migration in Europe*, Routledge, London, 1996.

Clarke C G (ed), *Caribbean Consciousness: Perspectives on Caribbean Regional Identity*, 1984.

Clarke C, Peach C & Vertovec S, *South Asians Overseas: Migration and Ethnicity*, Cambridge University Press, Cambridge, 1990.

Coard B, *How the West Indian Child is Made Educationally Subnormal in the British School System*, Caribbean Education Community Worker's Association, New Beacon Books, London, 1971.

Cohen S & Young J, *The Manufacture of News: Deviance, Social Problems and the Mass Media*, Constable, London, 1980.

Collin S, *Coloured Minorities in Britain*, Lutterworth, London, 1952.

Collins W, *Jamaican Migrant*, Routledge and Kegan Paul, London, 1965.

Constantine L, *Colour Bar*, Stanley Paul, London, 1954.

Cooke P, Sadler D & Zurbrugg N (eds), *Location Identity: Essays on National, Community and the Self*, De Montfort University, Leicester, 1996.

Cottle T J, *Black Testimony: Voices of Britain's West Indies*, Wildinood House, London, 1978.

Critcher C, Parker M & Sondhi R, *Race in the Provincial Press: A Case Study of Five West Midlands Papers*, UNESCO, Paris, 1975.

Davison R B, *West Indian Migrants: Social and Economic Facts of Migration from the West Indies*, Open University Press, London, 1962.

Donald J & Rattansi A, *Race, Culture and Difference*, Sage, London, 1992.

Douglas J W B, *The Home and the School*, (2nd ed) Panther, Manchester, 1967.

Duffield M, *Black Radicalism and the Politics of De-Industrialisation: The Hidden History of Indian Foundry Workers*, Avebury, Aldershot, 1988.

Edwards V K, *The West Indian Language Issue in British Schools*, Routledge and Kegan Paul, London, 1979.

Evans M, *The Woman Question*, Sage, London, 1994.

Everseley D & Sukdeo F, *The Dependants of the Coloured Commonwealth Population of England and Wales*, Oxford University Press, London, 1969.

Eysenck J H S & Nias D K B, *Sex, Violence and the Media*, Paladin,

London, 1980.

Farrah Marion, *Black Elders in Leicester*, Leicester City Council, Social Services Department, Leicester, November, 1986.

File N & Power C, *Black Settlers in Britain 1855-1958*, Heinemann, London, 1981.

Finegan F, *Poverty and Prejudice: A Study of Irish Immigrants in York 1840-1875*, Cork University Press, Cork, 1982.

Five Views of Multiracial Britain: Talks on Race Relations Broadcasting BBC TV, CRE, London, 1978.

Foner N, *Jamaica Farewell: Jamaican Migrants in London*, Routledge & Kegan Paul, London, 1979.

Foot P, *Immigration and Race in British Politics*, Penguin, Harmondsworth, 1965.

Foot P, *The Rise of Enoch Powell*, Penguin, Harmondsworth, 1969.

Fryer P, *Staying Power: The History of Black People in Britain*, Humanities Press, Atlantic Highlands, NJ, 1984.

Fryer P, *Black People in the British Empire: An Introduction*, Pluto Press, London, 1988.

Gaine C, *No Problem Here*, Hutchinson, London, 1987.

Gilroy P, *There Ain't No Black in the Union Jack*, Hutchinson, London, 1987.

Glass R, *Newcomers*, Allen & Unwin, London, 1960.

Gordon P & Rosenberg D, *Daily Racism: The Press and Black People in Britain*, Runnymede Trust, London, 1989.

Grant J, *Women, Migration and Empire*, Trentham, Stoke on Trent, 1996.

Grigg M, *The White Question,* Secker and Warburg, London, 1967.

Gundara J S & Duffield I, (eds), *Essays on the History of Blacks in Britain: From Roman Times to the Mid-Twentieth Century*, Ashgate, Aldershot, 1992.

Harris N, *The New Untouchables: Immigration and the New World Worker*, I. B. Tannis, London, 1995.

Hartmann P & Husband C, *Racism and the Media*, Davis Poynter, London, 1974.

Heidensohn F, *Women and Crime*, Macmillan, London, 1985.

Helweg A, *Sikhs in England: The Development of a Migrant Community*, Oxford University Press, Oxford, 1979.

Herbert R & Reuss C (eds), *The Impact of the Mass Media*, British Film Institute, London, 1986.

Highfield Rangers: An Oral History, Highfield Ranges Oral History Group
    and Sir Norma Chester Centre for Football Research, University of
    Leicester, Leicester City Council, Living History Unit, Leicester,
    1993.
Highfields Remembered, Leicestershire County Council, Leicester, 1996.
Hill C S, *West Indian Migrants and the London Churches*, Institute of Race
    Relations, Oxford University Press, London, 1963.
Hiro D, *Black British, White British*, Grafton Books, London, 1991.
Hollen Lees L, *Exiles of Erin: Irish Migrants in Victorian*, London,
    Manchester University Press, Manchester, 1979.
Holmes C, *John Bull's Island: Immigration and British Society 1871-1971*,
    Macmillan, London, 1988.
Holt T C, *The Problem of Freedom: Race, Labour and Politics in Jamaica
    and Britain 1832-1938*, Johns Hopkins University Press, Maryland,
    1992.
hooks bell, *Ain't I a Woman: Black Women and Feminism*, Pluto Press,
    London, 1982.
Husband C, *White Media and Black Britain*, Arrow Books, London 1975.
Husband C, *Racial Exclusionism and the City: The Urban Support of the
    National Front*, Allen & Unwin, London, 1983.
Hyman R (ed), *The Labour Government and the End of the Empire 1945-
    1951*, HMSO, London, 1992.
Ionie B, *The Black Press in Britain*, Trentham Books, Stoke on Trent,
    1995.
Jackson B & Marsden D, *Education and the Working Class*, Penguin,
    Harmondsworth, 1962.
Jackson P & Penrone J (eds), *Constructions of Race, Place and Nation*,
    University College London, London, 1993.
James W & Harris C, *Inside Babylon*, Verso, London, 1993.
James C, *Immigration and Social Policy in Britain*, Tavistock Publications,
    London, 1977.
Kasinitz P, *Caribbean New York: Black Immigrants and The Politics of
    Race*, Cornel University Press, London, 1992.
Katz E & Lazarsfeld P, *Personal Influence*, The Free Press, New York,
    1955.
Kettle M and Hodges L, *The Police, The People and the Riots in Britian's
    Cities*, Pan, London, 1982.
Kushner T & Lunn K (eds), *The Politics of Marginality*, Frank Cass,
    London, 1990.

Lawrence D, *Black Immigrants, White Natives: A Study of Race Relations in Nottingham*, Cambridge University Press, London, 1974.

Layton-Henry Z, *The Politics of Race in Britain*, Allen & Unwin, London, 1984.

Layton-Henry Z (ed), *Race, Government and Politics in Britain*, Macmillan, Basingstoke, 1986.

Layton-Henry Z, *The Politics of Immigration*, Blackwell, Oxford, 1992.

Little K, *Negroes in Britain*, Kegan Paul, London, 1947.

Lee T R, *Race and Residence: The Concentration and Dispersal of Immigrants in London*, Clarendon Press, Oxford, 1977.

Mackenzie J (ed), *Imperialism and Popular Culture*, Manchester University Press, Manchester, 1986.

Mackenzie J M, *Propaganda & Empire (The Manipulation of British Public Opinion 1880-1960)*, Manchester University Press, Manchester, 1984.

Mander J, *Leicester Schools 1944-1974*, Recreation and Arts Dept, Leicester City Council, Leicester, 1980.

Marett Valerie, *Immigrants Settling in the City*, Leicester University Press, London, 1989.

Mark Sir R, *In the Office of Constable*, Collins, London, 1978.

Miles R, *Racism*, Routledge, London, 1989.

Miles R & Phizacklea A (eds), *Racism and Political Action in Britain*, Routledge & Kegan Paul, London, 1979.

Miles R & Phizacklea A, *White Man's Country: Racism in British Politics*, Pluto, London, 1984.

Mirza H S, *Young Female and Black*, Routledge, London, 1992.

Moore R, *Racism and Black Resistance in Britain*, Pluto Press, London, 1975.

Moore R & Wallace T, *Slamming the Door: The Administration of Immigration Control*, Martin Robertson, London, 1975.

Morley D, *The Nationwide Audience*, British Film Institute, London, 1980.

Moynihan D, *The Negro Family: The Case for National Action*, Office of Planning and Research, US Dept of Labour, 1965.

Murray R N, *Lest We Forget: The Experiences of World War II West Indian Ex-Service Personnel*, West Indian Combined Ex-Services Association, Nottingham, 1996.

Nash D & Reeder D (eds), *Leicester in the Twentieth Century*, Alan Sutton, Stroud, 1993.

Nehaul K, *The Schooling of Children of Caribbean Heritage*, Trentham, Stoke on Trent, 1996.

Palmer C & Poulton K, *Sex and Race Discrimination in Employment*, Legal Action Group, Keny Press, Luton, 1987.

Panayi P (ed), *Racial Violence in Britain 1840-1950*, Leicester University Press, Leicester, 1993.

Panayi P, *Immigration, Ethnicity and Racism in Britain 1815-1945*, Manchester University Press, Manchester, 1994.

Patterson S, *Dark Strangers*, Tavistock Publications, London, 1963.

Patterson S, *Immigration and Race Relations in Britain 1960-1967*, Oxford University Press, Oxford, 1969.

Peach C, *West Indian Migration to Britain: A Social Geography*, Institute of Race Relation, Oxford University Press, London, 1968.

Peach C (ed), *Urban Social Segregation*, Longman, London, 1975.

Peach C, Robinson V & Smith S, *Ethnic Segregation in Cities*, Croom Helm, London, 1981.

Pearson D G, *Race, Class and Political Activism: A Study of West Indians in Britain*, Gower, Farnborough, 1981.

Philpott S, *West Indian Migration: The Montserrat Case*, University of London, London, 1973.

Phizacklea A & Miles R, *Labour and Racism*, Routledge & Kegan Paul, London, 1980.

Phizacklea A, *One Way Ticket: Migration and Female Labour*, Routledge & Kegan Paul, London, 1983.

Pilkington A, *Race Relations in Britain*, University Tutorial Press, Slough 1984.

Pilkington E, *Beyond the Mother Country: West Indians and the Notting Hill White Riots*, Tauris, London 1988.

Porter B, *The Lion's Share: A Short History of British Imperialism 1850-1983* (2nd ed), Longman, London 1983.

Potts L, *The World Labour Market: A History of Migration*, Zed Books, London 1990.

Prior J, *A Balance of Power*, Hamish Hamilton, London 1986.

Pritchard R M, *Housing and the Spatial Structure of the City*, Cambridge University Press, London, 1976.

Pryce K, *Endless Pressure: A Study of West Indian Life Styles in Bristol*, Bristol Classical Press, Bristol, 1986.

Ramdin R, *The Making of the Black Working Class in Britain*, Gower, Aldershot, 1987.

Ratcliffe P, *Racism and Reaction: A Profile of Handsworth*, Routledge & Kegan Paul, London, 1981.

Reeves F, *Race and Borough Politics*, Avebury, Aldershot, 1989.

Rex J & Moore R, *Race, Community and Conflict: A Study of Sparkbrook*, Institute of Race Relations, Oxford University Press, London, 1967.

Rex J & Tomlinson S, *Colonial Migrants in a British City: A Class Analysis*, Routledge & Kegan Paul, London, 1979.

Rex J & Solomos J, *Migrant Workers in Metropolitan Cities*, European Science Foundation, Strasbourg, 1980.

Rich P B, *Prospero's Return: Historical Essays on Race, Culture and British Society*, Hansib, London, 1994.

Richmond A, *Colour Prejudice in Britain: A Study of West Indian Workers in Liverpool 1941-1951*, Routledge & Kegan Paul, London, 1954.

Richmond A H, *Migration and Race Relations in an English City: A Study of Britain*, Oxford University Press, London, 1973.

Riley J, *The Unbelonging*, The Women's Press, London, 1985.

Roediger D R, *The Wages of Whiteness: Race and the Making of the American Working Class*, Verso, London, 1990.

Rose E J B et al, *Colour and Citizenship: A report on British Race Relations*, Oxford University Press, London, 1969.

Russel, R J and McIntyre, W G, *Barbuda Reconnaissance*, Lousiana University State Press, Baton Rouge, 1966.

Safe H & du Toit B (eds), *Migration and Development, Implication for Ethnic Identity and Political Conflict*, Mounton, The Hague, 1975.

Samuel R (ed), *Patriotism: The Making and Unmaking of British National Identity*, Vol 1 and II, London & Karachi, London, 1989, page 270.

Sarup P, *Education the Ideal of Racism*, Trentham, Stoke on Trent, 1991.

Scafe, B D & S, *The Heart of the Race: Black Women's Lives in Britain*, Virago, London, 1985.

Sewcharan R, *There's No Place Like 'Back Home'? Memories and Experiences of Leicester's Black Elders*, West Indian Senior Citizens Project, Leicester, 1986.

Simmons J, *Leicester Past and Present, Vol 2, Modern City, 1860-1974*, Eyre Methuen, London, 1974.

Simon B (ed), *Margaret Grace, A Teacher for our Time*, 1980.

Sewell T, *Black Masculinities and Schooling*, Trentham, Stoke on Trent, 1977.

Sherwood M, *Many Struggles: West Indian Workers and Service Personnel in Britain (1939-1945)*, Karia Press, London, 1984.

Shyllon F, *Black Slaves in Britain*, Oxford University Press, London, 1974.

Shyllon F, *Black People in Britain 1555-1833*, Oxford University Press, London, 1977.

Shyllon F, *The Black Presence and Experience in Britain: An Analytical Overview in Essays on the History of Black in Britain*, Avebury, Aldershot, 1992.

Sivanandan A, *A Different Hunger: Writings on Black Resistance*, Pluto Press, London, 1982.

Small S, *Racialised Barriers*, Routledge, London, 1994.

Smith D J, *Racial Disadvantage in Employment*, PEP, London, 1974.

Smith Susan, *The Politics of 'Race' and Residence*, Polity Press, Cambridge, 1989.

Solomos J, *Black Youth, Racism and the State: The Politics of Ideal and Policy*, Cambridge University Press, Cambridge, 1988.

Solomos J, *Race and Racism in Contemporary Britain*, Macmillan, London,1993.

Solomos J & Wrench J (eds), *Racism and Migration in Western Europe*, Berg, London, 1993.

Solomos J and Back, L, *Race, Politics and Social Change*, Routledge, London, 1995.

Spencer I R G, *British Immigration Policy Since 1939: The Making of Multiracial Britain*, Routledge, London, 1997.

Sponza L, *Italian Immigrants in Nineteenth Century Britain: Realities and Images*, Leicester University Press, Leicester, 1988.

Stone M, *The Education of the Black Child in Britain*, Fontana, Glasgow, 1981.

Sweeney C, *Flight: West Indians Sojourning in Britain*, Eureka Press, Leicester, 1979.

Tabili L, *We Ask for British Justice: Workers Racial Difference in Late Imperial Britain*, Cornell University Press, New York, 1994.

Thomas-Hope E M, *Perspectives on Caribbean Regional Identity*, Centre for Latin American Studies, The University of Liverpool, Monograph Series II, 1984.

Thompson P, *The Voice of the Past*, (2nd ed), Oxford University Press, London, 1988.

Thompson E P, *The Making of the English Working Class*, Penguin, Hamondsworth, 1962.

Thurlow R, *Fascism in Britain: A History 1918-1985*, Basil Blackwell, Oxford, 1987.

Tierney J, *Race, Migration and Schools*, Holt, London, 1982.

Tomlinson S, *Educational Subnormality*, Routledge & Kegan Paul, London, 1981.

Townsend P, *Poverty in the United Kingdom*, Penguin, Harmondsworth, 1979.

Troyna B, *Public Awareness and the Media: A Study of Reporting on Race*, Commission for Racial Equality, London, 1981.

Troya B and Williams J, *Racism Education and the State: the Racialisation of Educational Policy*, Croom Helm, London, 1986.

Troyna B, *Racial Inequality in Education*, Tavistock, London, 1987.

Troyna B & Hatcher R, *Racism in Children's Lives*, Routledge, London, 1992.

Troyna B, *Racism in Education: Research Perspectives*, Open University Press, Buckingham, 1993.

Van Dijk T, *Racism and the Press*, Routledge, London, 1991.

Verma G & Bagley C, *Self-Concept, Achievement and Multicultural Education*, Macmillan, London, 1982.

Verma G K. & Ashworth B, *Ethnicity and Educational Achievement in British Schools*, Macmillan, London, 1991.

Visions of Bena Balunda: A Documentary History of the Black Power Movement in Leicester 1970-1972, Raddle Publications, Leicester, 1990.

Walby S, *Patriarchy at Work*, Polity Press, Cambridge, 1986.

Walvin J, *The Black Presence: A Documentary History of the Negro in England 1555-1860*, Orbach and Chambers, London, 1971.

Walvin J, *Black and White: The Negro on English Society 1555-1945*, Penguin, London, 1973.

Walvin J, *Passage to Britain: Immigration in British History and Politics*, Penguin, Harmondsworth, 1984.

Walvin J, *Black Ivory*, Harper-Collins, London, 1992.

Watson J L (ed), *Between Two Cultures: Migrants and Minorities in Britain*, Blackwell, Oxford, 1977.

West J (ed), *Work, Women and the Labour Market*, Routledge & Kegan Paul, London, 1982.

Western J, *A Passage to England: Barbadian Londoners Speak of Home*, University College Press, London, 1992.

Westwood S, *All Day, Everyday: Factory and Family in the Making of Women's Lives*, Pluto Press, London, 1984.

Who's Who, A and C Black, London, 1995.

Wickenden J, *Colour in Britain*, Oxford University Press, London, 1958.

Williams E, *Capitalism and Slavery*, Andre Deutsch, London, 1964.

Wilson A, *Finding a Voice: Asian Women in Britain*, Virago, London, 1978.

4   Chapters in Books

Besson J, 'Family Land and Caribbean Society: Toward an Ethnography of African Caribbean Peasantries', in Clarke C G, *Perspectives on Caribbean Regional Identity*, 1984.

Brown K, 'Race, Class and Culture: Towards a Theorisation of the Choice/constraint Concept', in P Jackson and S J Smith (eds), *Social Integration and Ethnic Segregation*, Academic Press, London, 1981.

Bruegel I, 'Sex and Race in the Labour Market', in Mary Evans (ed), *The Woman Question*, Sage, London, 1994.

Carby H, 'White Women Listen! Black Feminism and the Boundaries of Sisterhood', in Centre for Contemporary Cultural Studies, *The Empire Strikes Back: Race and Racism in 70s Britain*, Hutchinson, London, 1982.

Carby H, 'Schooling in Babylon', in Centre for Contemporary Cultural Studies, *The Empire Strikes Back: Race and Racism in 70s Britain*, Hutchinson, London, 1982.

Carter B, Harris C & Shirley J, 'The 1951-1955 Conservative Government and the Racialisation of Black Immigration', in Winston J & Harris C (eds), *Inside Babylon*, Verso, London, 1993.

Cesarani D, 'The Changing Character of Citizenship and Nationality in Britain', in Cesarani D & Fulbrook M (eds), *Citizenship, Nationality and Migration in Europe*, Routledge, London, 1996.

Dahya B, 'The Nature of Pakistani Ethnicity in Industrial Cities in Britain', in Cohen A (ed), *Urban Ethnicity*, Tavistock, London, 1974.

Doom A, 'Education and the Race Relations Act', in Arnot Madelain (ed), *Race and Gender Equal Opportunities Polices in Education*, Open University Press, Oxford, 1985.

Hall S, 'Racism and Reaction: A Public Talk Arranged by the British Sociological Association', in *Five Views of Multiracial Britain*, Commission for Racial Equality, London, 1978.

Harris C, 'Post War Migration and the Industrial Reserve Army', in James W and Harris C (eds), *Inside Babylon*, Verso, London, 1993.

Lawrence E, 'In abundance of Water the Fool is Thirsty: Social and Black Pathology', in Centre for Contemporary Cultural Studies, *The Empire Strikes Back: Race and Racism in 70s Britain*, Hutchinson, London, 1982.

Lawrence E, 'Just Plain Common Sense: The Roots of Racism', in Centre for Contemporary Cultural Studies, *The Empire Strikes Back: Race and Racism in 70s Britain*, Hutchinson, London, 1982.

Lewis G, 'Black Women's Employment and the British Economy', in James W & Harris C (eds), *Inside Babylon*, Verso, London, 1993.

Miles R, 'Explaining Racism in Contemporary Europe', in Rattansi A & Westwood S (eds), *Racism, Modernity and Identity*, Polity Press, Cambridge, 1994.

Morakvasik M, 'Women in Migration: Beyond the Reductionist Outlook', in Phizacklea A (ed), *One Way Ticket, Migration and Female Labour*, Routledge & Kegan Paul, London, 1983.

Mullard D, 'Multiracial Education in Britain: From Assimilation to Cultural Pluralism', in Arnot Madelaine, *Race and Gender Equal Opportunities in Education*, Oxford University Press, Oxford, 1985.

Phizacklea A, 'Migrant Women and Wage Labour: The Case of West Indian Women in Britain', in West J (ed), *Work, Women and the Labour Market*, Routledge & Kegan Paul, London, 1982.

Stone K, 'Motherhood and Waged Work: West Indian, Asian and White Mothers Compared', in Phizacklea A (ed), *One Way Ticket: Migration and Female Labour*, Routledge & Kegan Paul, London, 1983.

Sutton C & Makeisky S, 'Migration and West Indian Racial and Ethnic Consciousness', in Safa, H and du Toit, *Migration and Development, Implication for Ethnic Identity and Political Conflict*, Mounton, The Hague, 1975.

Thomas-Hope E M, 'Identity and Adaptation of Migrants from the English Speaking Caribbean in Britain and North America', in Verma G K and Bagley C, *Self-Concept, Achievement and Multi-Cultural Education*, Macmillan, London, 1982.

Walvin J, 'From the Fringes: The Emergence of British Black Historical Studies', in Gundara, J S and Duffield I, *Essays on the History of Blacks in Britain: From Roman Times to the Mid-Twentieth Century*, Avebury, Aldershot, 1992.

Index